Evaluation Practice

Professional accountability is central to both public and private sectors. In *Evaluation Practice*, DePoy and Gilson bridge the apparent gap between practice and research to present a logical, systematic model to guide all professional thinking and action within the context of everyday professional life. Their framework embraces diverse theories, action, and sets of evidence from a range of professional and disciplinary perspectives.

"DePoy and Gilson's important work represents a giant leap forward for closing the practice-research gap and integrating evaluation activities into the real world of health and human services. This book is eloquent, simple, and profound."—*Laura Gitlin, Center for Applied Research on Aging and Health, Jefferson College of Health Professions*

"I know of no other text that offers such a comprehensive perspective on evaluation, nor one that covers both qualitative and quantitative methodologies in such an even-handed fashion. When students or working professionals read this work, they will have the best possible understanding of practice evaluation."—*Stephen M. Marson, Social Work Department, University of North Carolina at Pembroke*

"Comprehensive, engaging, and powerful, Depoy and Gilson's *Evaluation Practice* provides a masterful framework that brings together theory and practice in a balanced, meaningful manner and refuses to dissect the process of evaluation from research. Copious examples, cogent chapter summaries, and well-structured exercises make this an interesting and useful book that has caused me to fundamentally rethink the role of evaluation I am certain that scholars from any discipline will find the authors' approach to the reporting and the dissemination of knowledge highly relevant and timely."—*Laura Lindenfeld, The Margaret Chase Smith Policy Center, University of Maine*

Elizabeth DePoy is Professor of Policy and International Affairs and Coordinator of Interdisciplinary Disability Studies at the University of Maine.

Stephen Gilson is Professor of Policy and International Affairs and Interdisciplinary Disability Studies at the University of Maine.

Evaluation Practice

How To Do Good Evaluation Research in Work Settings

Elizabeth DePoy and
Stephen Gilson

Routledge
Taylor & Francis Group

NEW YORK AND LONDON

First published 2008
by Routledge
270 Madison Ave, New York, NY 10016

Simultaneously published in the UK
by Routledge
2 Park Square, Milton Park, Abingdon, Oxon OX14 4RN

Routledge is an imprint of the Taylor & Francis Group, an informa business

© 2008 Taylor & Francis

Typeset in Minion and Trade Gothic by
Florence Production Ltd, Stoodleigh, Devon
Printed and bound in the United States of America on acid-free paper by
Walsworth Publishing Company, Marceline, MO

British Library Cataloguing in Publication Data
A catalogue record for this book is available from the British Library

Library of Congress Cataloging in Publication Data
DePoy, Elizabeth.
  Evaluation practice: how to do good evaluation research in work
  settings/Elizabeth DePoy and Stephen Gilson.
    p. cm.
  Includes bibliographical references and index.
  1. Social service – Evaluation. 2. Social service – Methodology.
  3. Evaluation research (Social action programs)   I. Gilson, Stephen
  French. II. Title.
  HV40.D456 2008
  361.2072 – dc22   2007027304

ISBN10: 0–8058–6299–4 (hbk)
ISBN10: 0–8058–6300–1 (pbk)
ISBN10: 1–4106–1760–2 (ebk)

ISBN13: 978–0–8058–6299–7 (hbk)
ISBN13: 978–0–8058–6300–0 (pbk)
ISBN13: 978–1–4106–1760–6 (ebk)

Contents

Preface

A number of factors prompted us to write this book. First, as we proceed into the first decade of the twenty-first century, professional accountability has become increasingly central to both public and private sectors. Governments in the U.S. and abroad have vigorously emphasized and even developed empirical models, logic modeling, and evidence-based practice in the programs that they support, and not-for-profit, for-profit, and NGO entities increasingly rely on systematic strategies such as strategic planning, marketing research, outcome measures, benchmarking, and so forth to identify niches, needs, and to determine success. The question "How do you know?" echoes throughout actual and virtual professional spaces from diverse audiences, consumers, clients, and customers, who previously accepted claims, services, and products on professional authority alone.

Second is the intellectual trend towards pluralism. What we mean by pluralism is the acceptance of multiple ways of knowing. Thus, while evidence is requested for professional decisions, actions, and entities, the nature of the evidence is diverse. Numbers are compelling but so are narrative, image, and even maps of actual and abstract geographies.

Most important, however, is our own evaluation practice. Over the years, we have repeatedly heard from our students, colleagues, and clients about the schism between "those who do" and "those who scrutinize." Yet, in our own work, we have integrated scholarship, teaching, and commitment to our substantive areas of health, equality of access to information, and social justice and have experienced these three areas not only as related but as essential in all of our professional roles.

Recently, we entered the not-for-profit world by establishing our own company. You guessed it, the company name is "Evaluation Practice."

In all of our work, whether we are entering collaborative product development, teaching, or cooperating on professional innovations we use the model that we present and illustrate in our book to guide our thinking, activity, and determination of success.

Evaluation practice is not just a framework to guide professionals in conducting evaluation research. It is not specific to a single profession or field. Rather, it is a logical, systematic model to guide all professional thinking and action within a context of purpose and what is practical in everyday professional life. Evaluation practice reminds us to begin at the beginning, at the point of identifying values about what our action or entities should change, what is needed to achieve the change that we want to see, to look critically at our own activity, no matter what the field, and to examine the extent to which, and how, our activity or entities "worked" to produce the change.

Evaluation practice bridges the practice–research separation. The framework embraces diverse theories, action, and sets of evidence from a range of professional and disciplinary perspectives.

How to Use this Book

Because we are intimately familiar with our own work, we have used it as the basis for our primary exemplars throughout the book. Each set of examples illustrates thinking and action throughout the entire evaluation practice model.

The book is divided into four sections and 15 chapters. We have purposively kept the book short and easy to read with lots of examples to illustrate the model in thinking and action. The main points are summarized at the end of each chapter with exercises to help you make this model part of your own thinking and action. We hope that you, too, find this model not only valuable but integral to your daily work life.

Beginnings

CHAPTER 1

Introduction to Evaluation Practice: A Problem Solving Approach through Informed Thinking and Action

In a recent evaluation project, we were asked to examine the process and outcomes of a grant competition. A state-wide grant-maker, which we will refer to as "Grant-maker," concerned with citizen access to health care was not only interested in knowing the outcomes of the individual projects that it supported, but also wanted to examine the collective impact of the programs on health care access. We revisit this exemplar among many others in this chapter and throughout the book. As you begin this chapter, think of the complexity of the questions posed by Grant-maker and the values that inhere in them.

What is Evaluation Practice?

In this text, we discuss and illustrate "evaluation practice." Unlike terms such as evaluation, evaluation of practice, or program evaluation, the term "evaluation practice" denotes a comprehensive approach to the integration of systematic appraisal with professional thinking and action. Because evaluation practice considers both anticipated and unanticipated results it expands beyond mere empirical examination of the process and outcome of professional work activity. Rather, we see "evaluation practice" as all of the following: (a) a framework that integrates evaluation thinking and action within professional thinking, action, and entities; (b) a means to examine and respond to articulated problems and issues; (c) a set of thinking and action strategies through which profession-specific theories and skills can be organized, examined, and verified; and (d) a systematic examination of explicit or implicit behavior change.

Let us take a closer look at each of the criteria.

(a) *Evaluation practice as a framework that integrates evaluation thinking and action within professional thinking, action, and entities.* A framework is a conceptual scaffold, so to speak, which constrains, provides direction, and structures a phenomenon (Dottin, 2001). The evaluation practice framework guides and structures a systematic process through which professionals themselves, or in concert with others, scrutinize the "why, how, what, and the results of their own activity." Our model, therefore, holds the professional, not an "external evaluator," accountable for systematic thinking and action, for careful examination of his/her practices, and for critical appraisal of the results of professional functioning. So who conducts evaluation? Educators, providers, policy makers, public health practitioners, technology experts, business specialists, and so forth: in other words, you do! That is not to say that you must conduct all systematic evaluation in isolation. Evaluation can be done by one individual, a team, in collaboration with others, or in consultation. However, in the evaluation practice model, professional thinking and action cannot be separated from systematic evaluation and, thus, it is the responsibility of all professionals to engage in evaluation practice.

By the term "entities" we refer to the programs, interventions, materials, and so forth that are part of professional activity but do not comprise it in total. In the example of Grant-maker, an entity would be a grant competition program, a grant proposal proffered by an agency, materials and programs resulting from funding, or even a website, all of which are goal oriented.

(b) *Evaluation practice as a means to examine and respond to articulated problems and issues.* Unlike many evaluation approaches that begin with need, we suggest that evaluation begins with problem identification, which then forms the basis for all subsequent professional activity. Grant-maker missed this important point and invited us into the evaluation process after all funded projects were completed. The absence of a clear problem that Grant-maker was trying to minimize or eliminate was therefore not clear and had to be reconstructed. Without this understanding Grant-maker would not be able to ascertain if the individual and collective project results addressed the implicit problem of limited access to health care. As we discuss in detail in Chapter 3, problem identification is an essential thinking strategy as it clarifies, specifies, and lays bare what conditions are desirable and undesirable and thus what outcomes need to be accomplished to reduce or eliminate undesirable circumstance.

(c) *Evaluation practice as a set of thinking and action strategies through which profession-specific theories and skills can be organized, examined, and verified.* Our third point suggests that evaluation provides the forum in which to apply and test the efficacy of theory and skill, not just programmatic outcome. Thus, evaluation practice is a dynamic model for myriad professions, not a theory or method-specific framework. Thus, in evaluation practice, we not only assess professional action, but also test knowledge and contribute to its further development. For us, as you look in on your own activity, what you learn informs others as well as the knowledge base in your own field. As we address in more detail below, this third point is contentious.

(d) *Evaluation practice as a systematic examination of explicit or implicit behavior change.* Whether or not behavior change is explicitly named as the desired outcome of professional activity, we suggest that management of human behavior, or its causes, correlates, and consequences, is the goal of professional action and thus inheres in all evaluation practice activity. Let us consider Grant-maker to illustrate. Grant-maker funded diverse projects all designed to improve access to health care for all citizens. So whether the project was focused on the creation of a product such as software to promote access to electronic health information, a policy to guide alternative funding for underinsured citizens, a study to reveal attitudinal barriers to seeking health care, or even the creation of electronic medical records, all of Grant-maker's funds in some way were designed to change human behavior. Expansion of electronic access to health information assumes that information is of value in prompting informed health behaviors. Policies mandating alternative funding for those who would otherwise not have the financial resources to seek care, ostensibly remove a cause of poor health and, thus, change professional and consumer behavior. Research investigating attitudinal barriers to seeking health care is applied to behavioral change that follows attitudinal shifts. And the creation of the entity of electronic medical records changes the behavior of health care practitioners, insurance professionals, and others involved in the health care enterprise. Moreover, inherent in Grant-maker's overarching goal of improved access to health care is a change in health behaviors, and the causes, correlates, and consequences of limited access to care.

Historically, and even currently, as we suggested above, evaluation in most fields (McDavid and Hawthorne, 2006) has been taught and treated as separate and distinct from professional activity (Unrau *et al.*, 2001). Some

(Grinnell, 1999) suggest that evaluation is an end process to examine the extent to which a desired outcome has been achieved. Others (Patton, 2001; Rossi et al., 2004) describe evaluation as ongoing for the purpose of using feedback to improve practices. Look at the range of definitions of evaluation from current scholars:

- assesses if product or program was successfully developed and implemented according to its stakeholders' needs (Lockee et al., 2001);
- professional judgment (McDavid and Hawthorne, 2005);
- systematic assessment of the worth or value of an object (Joint Committee on Standards for Educational Evaluation, 2003);
- systematic assessment of an object's worth, merit, probity, feasibility, safety, significance, or equity (Stufflebeam and Shinkfield, 2007).

As you can see, one set of approaches to evaluation combines both outcome and process evaluation (Rossi et al., 2004) while others see evaluation as a set of methods to examine "evaluation objects," in which the object is a program or person rather than an interactive set of processes and resources (Fitzpatrick et al., 2004). And finally, as the field of evaluation grows and diversifies, many evaluators have developed methods to examine parts of practice as they differentially relate to, and influence, intermediate and final outcome (Mertens, 2004). All of these models are presumed to exist apart from, and provide the empirical systematic structure for others to "look in" on, professional activity and entities (Berlin and Marsh, 1993). A consequence of the separation of evaluation and professional activity has been the mistrust and maligning of each camp by the other. On one extreme, professionals suggest that they do not need evaluation to support the efficacy of their work, and, on the other, evaluators assert that without empirical support, claims are not worthy of professional behavior (Berlin and Marsh, 1993). Yet, in the twenty-first century, trends favoring both professional expertise and accountability continue to expand. The two must find a way not only to co-exist, but also to complement one another (DePoy and Gitlin, 2005; Reed et al., 2006).

In concert with current thinking, we have written this text in proactive response to the dilemmas, challenges, and trends to integrate inquiry with practice. The chapters that follow provide the rationale, thinking, and action processes to bridge the gap between professional processes, outcomes and entities, and evaluation, and provide the skills and examples to guide both students and professionals in incorporating evaluation as an essential and omnipotent professional action. Consistent with this view, we formally name our approach evaluation practice and define it as comprising of the following elements:

- the *purposive* application of evidence-based, systematic thinking and action;
- processes and actions that define and clarify problems and identify what is needed to resolve them;
- examination of the way in which and extent to which problems have been resolved.

Does this definition remind you of any fields? Think of the words "problem," "systematic," "logic," and "evidence." These are the foundations of research and practice thinking (DePoy and Gitlin, 2005; Hickey and Zuiker, 2003). It is, therefore, curious that despite the similar descriptors and characteristics, there remains a significant debate across fields regarding the distinction between evaluation and research (Alkin, 1990; Thyer, 2001), and most recently among research, evaluation, and professional practice (MacQueen and Buehler, 2004). At one end of the spectrum, some suggest that despite their empirically-based, systematic activity, neither evaluation nor professional practice qualifies as research or parts thereof because they focus on "doing" and on the assessment of the outcomes of "doing" rather than the production of generalizable knowledge (Fitzpatrick *et al.*, 2004; Lockee *et al.*, 2001).

In looking at the distinction among research, evaluation, and professional activity, scholars such as Weiss (1997) claim that evaluation and research are not distinct fields at all. She draws our attention to the role of evaluation in systematically examining professional activity as a basis for developing knowledge. Yet, others such as Merten (2004) and Fitzpatrick *et al.* (2004) hold the criterion of "generalizability" as central to research and thus any activity that is context based cannot be considered as research without the presence of this essential characteristic. But let us think about Grant-maker. Grant-maker funds programs and research that meet the criterion of reducing disparities in access to health care. In Grant-maker's guidance, all professional activity must be solidly anchored on well-established theory and must have a clear and comprehensive evaluative component that can be shared to inform access beyond the scope of the individual project itself. So, to a large extent, the "program" and evaluation meet the criterion of generalizability. Moreover, all research proposals must be applied to Grant-maker's priority of reducing access disparities. So, for Grant-maker, the distinctions among research, evaluation, and professional activity are not clear despite their efforts to separate competitions into the two categories of research and programming.

Further obfuscating the debate are the differences among research traditions and methodologies, and, even, within the same tradition, regarding generalizability. Not all approaches to research have generalizability as their goal and, even when they do, not all methods can achieve that goal (DePoy and Gitlin, 2005). Grant-maker funded two ethnographic studies of health care access, one examining elder access to mental health care in a small rural town, and the other examining access barriers to rural health services for recent African immigrants.

We transcend the debates by asserting that evaluation practice serves both research and professional action and bridges the gap among the three. Evaluation practice is grounded in the logic structures and the systematic thinking that undergird all evidence-based thinking processes. However, unlike other definitions of research that adhere to the essential element of generalizability (Rossi *et al.*, 2004; Unrau *et al.*, 2006), the purpose in evaluation practice is explicit, may or may not include generalizability, and is a major determinant of the scope and approach chosen by the inquirer. The centrality of political purpose is the element that, we suggest, sets evaluation as a distinct subset of research. And the thinking and action processes of the evaluation practice provide a reasoned, evidenced-based structure for practice thinking as well. Consider the example in Box 1.1 which refers to our opening exemplar.

Can you see how important purpose is in evaluation and how you might design the evaluation to meet the practice, administrative, and/or funding

---

Box 1.1 Grant-maker

To address Grant-maker's questions, we first recreated the central problem statement that guided all of Grant-maker's activity during the years that the evaluation covered. Through a process which we call "problem mapping" (see Chapter 3), we located the articulated or implicit problems in each proposal and, through the literature, looked for their relationships to disparities in access to health care. For example, one project proposed to disseminate information about Medicaid support to those who were potentially eligible, suggesting that a factor in limiting access was lack of information. The extent to which information was disseminated was the desired outcome of that proposal. We took the outcome one step further to look at the associations between information dissemination, information acquisition, and changes in access to health care. Clearly, the purpose of the original proposal and the purposes of our evaluation differed although they bore an important relationship that was at the heart of successful funding. But access to health care, while a desired long-term outcome, was neither the central purpose nor proposed success criterion for the individual project.

purposes? Both the individual grantee and our approach to evaluation described in Box 1.1 would give you valuable information, one looking at long-term outcomes and one looking at immediate controllable outcomes. The choice to examine immediate outcomes resulted in success and continued funding, sustaining, and ultimately expanding the individual grantee's program.

What becomes clear here is that the purpose of evaluation will drive the evaluation practice method that the professional selects. Keep this important example in mind as we move onto an introduction of evaluation practice thinking and action processes.

Reasoning in Evaluation Practice

Inductive, deductive, and abductive reasoning form the basis for evaluation practice thinking processes. Moreover, the two major research design traditions, naturalistic and experimental-type inquiry, and their integration through mixing methods, are based on these logic structures (DePoy and Gitlin, 2005) and thus they are used to guide thinking and action and to support claims regarding the processes and outcomes of professional action. The logic structures in evaluation practice are not only defined by the questions to be answered but by the political context, nature of the practice to be evaluated, purpose, and intended use of the knowledge generated by evaluation (Chronbach, 1982; House and Howe, 1999; Rossi *et al.*, 2004).

History

Now let us turn to a brief history of evaluation to understand its development and current context. According to Shadish, Cook, and Leviton (1991), evaluation is an inherent human trait. That is to say, humans in daily living automatically assess the change potential of human action. Even more expansive is the role of evaluation in evolutionary psychology in which mutations are evaluated for their capacity to produce desired change for enhanced survival (Buss, 2007). However, while evaluation has been characterized as an inherent biological activity, we look towards the field of evaluation scholarship to inform current evaluation practice.

According to Rossi *et al.* (2004), systematic program evaluation was first addressed in the field of public health and education. Between World War I and World War II, evaluation slowly expanded, and researchers such as Lewin, Lippitt, and White (1939) became well known for their work in the application of scientific method to determining the outcome of practice efforts in several fields including public health and psychology.

The scholarly field of evaluation became well known and extensively practiced in the late 1950s and early 1960s during which evaluation theories were developed to guide practice. Due to the extensive amount of money spent on social programs by the federal government, the value of these expenditures in achieving desired outcomes was subjected to scientific scrutiny (Mertens, 2004).

Three major phenomena were responsible for the current field of evaluation research: the need for accountability as social programs grew in scope and number, the increase in the sophistication of research and statistical methods, and the explosion of computer technology (Owen, 2006). With these three factors operating, methods texts, journals, academic programs, and the professional field of evaluation have taken hold and are now commonplace in practice, education, and scholarship in social sciences, education, business, technology, public health, and many other applied fields (Stufflebeam and Shinkfield, 2007). Current evaluation is based on skepticism, the need for accountability, fiscal conservatism, and, to a large extent, a history of ineffectual social programs (Gambrill, 2001).

Most current approaches to evaluation do not merely examine desired outcomes and processes by which these outcomes were achieved, but expand to many other arenas. Included in these are viability of products, use of information, adequacy of venues, cost effectiveness and containment, differential comparisons of approaches to defining and resolving problems, and examination of the influences of contextual and change factors on program, activity and entity process, and outcome (Fitzpatrick et al., 2004; Thyer, 2001).

The Need for Evaluation Practice in Today's Climate

As we have indicated above, since the late 1950s, numerous factors have been responsible for the growth of the field of evaluation. In today's competitive, fiscally conservative, and skeptical climate, evaluation is essential if any field is not only to demonstrate its benefits, but also to survive (Gambrill, 2001). Since the late 1970s, numerous professions have asserted the importance of evaluation in all arenas of practice (Fitzpatrick et al., 2004; Thyer, 2001). It is curious, however, to note that despite the recognition that evaluation should be an essential professional activity, the separation between evaluation and activity continues.

We build on past efforts such as evidence-based practice and empirical practice (Macmillan and Shumaker, 2005; Thyer, 2001) by proposing evaluation practice as the conduct of three major thinking and action process areas: problem and need clarification, reflexive action, and outcome assessment.

Problem and Need Clarification

Because of the complexity of defining and understanding social, educational, economic, and political problems, methods to alleviate and/or address them are often unclear. As we so frequently see in professional action, as we see in the example of Grant-maker, initiators frequently do not specify a problem but jump directly to an activity that they believe is needed. Why it is needed and to what problem the activity or entity responds is, unfortunately, omitted from many professional efforts. We can look at Fischer's classic work on evaluating clinical social work practice as an example of this issue. In 1973, Joel Fischer wrote a seminal article on the failure of clinical therapeutic practice. However, what problems clinical practice was designed to address and resolve or what part of a social problem clinical practice could resolve were not clear. Was the problem mental illness and its behavioral correlates or just isolation on the part of clients? Moreover, the distinction between problem and need was not clear either. Was counseling needed and, if so, what problem was it intended to resolve? Why was clinical intervention needed over other methods of intervention? As you can see by this classic evaluation example, the clarification of the problem is critical to any professional effort. The way in which a problem is conceptualized, who owns it, who is affected by it, and what needs to be done about it are all questions that are based in political/purposive and ideological arenas. Thus, the problem forms the basis on which all subsequent evaluative activity takes place. Problem statements provide the ultimate foundation for the implementation and continuation of professional action.

In the case of clinical social work practice, if mental illness was the problem and a cure for mental illness was determined as a need, it would seem futile for clinical social work to be the selected profession to intervene. But if isolation leading to emotional pain was the problem, the need for clinical social work as an intervention becomes viable and the outcome of intervention is both "doable" and reasonable to expect. If the problem was conceptualized as isolation resulting from poor access to prevention, then public health, not social work, would be the most appropriate profession, and the desired outcomes would be significantly more expansive than individual health.

At multiple system levels, we assert that a clear and well-supported understanding of problem and need is essential to evaluation practice. Without problem and need clarification, interest groups might define problems differently and thus expect different outcomes from the same activity or entity. To illustrate, let us consider an example from our own practice. In the mid-1990s the Maternal and Child Health Bureau advanced an initiative entitled Healthy and Ready to Work (HRTW). Look at its historical description:

> The Healthy and Ready to Work initiative promotes a comprehensive system of family-centered, culturally competent, community based care for children with special health care needs who are approaching adulthood and may need assistance in making the transition from pediatric to adult health care and to postsecondary education and/or employment.
>
> (www.hrtw.org, 2006)

Implicit in this text was the problem statement that youth with special health care needs in transition from childhood to adulthood were not "healthy and ready to work," resulting in the undesirable consequences of unemployment, inadequate health care, and life-long public safety net support. In applying for funding, a statewide coalition proposed a needs assessment in which diverse groups were asked to refine the problem statement and suggest how to resolve it. As we discuss in more detail in subsequent chapters, none of the groups agreed on the exact nature of the "problem" and thus on how to alleviate it. The youth who were the target of the program identified their problem as unequal opportunity and access to typical teenage social and educational opportunity, while health providers indicted youth irresponsibility in caring for their own health as the issue to be resolved. From the parent perspective, limited independent living options for their children with special health care needs was the primary problem, and policy makers looked to scarce funding for specialized programs and support services to be implemented. As you might expect from these disparate problem statements, equally discrepant desired outcomes and methods to achieve those outcomes were proposed.

Moving further into evaluation practice, a clear understanding of need must be based on credible evidence. While we may make claims about what activity is needed to resolve problems, accountability in making informed professional decisions is dependent on the presence and organization of empirical evidence of need. Without such evidence, the basis for provider, policy, payer, and administrative decisions cannot be ascertained. In the example of HRTW, each problem statement gave rise to multiple needs. While youth irresponsibility was not empirically supported, unequal access and opportunity were clearly documented by the disproportionate underrepresentation of qualified youth with special health care needs who were gainfully employed or enrolled in higher education. Once that presentation of need was clarified, directions emerged for the establishment of goals and objectives to guide a program and define its expected outcomes.

Setting goals and objectives for professional activity derives directly from need. In Chapters 9 and 10, we explore goals and objectives in detail and we will look at the manner in which needs statements gave rise to different opinions about what goals and objectives should be achieved.

We now move to the second element in the evaluation practice model which follows the thinking processes problem and need. We have named this step reflexive action.

Reflexive Action

In research texts, particularly those that present naturalistic methods, reflexivity is an important construct. Typically, reflexivity is defined as self-examination for the purpose of ascertaining how one's perspective influences the interpretation of data (Denzin and Lincoln, 2000; DePoy and Gitlin, 2005). Here we expand the term to denote the set of thinking and action processes that we believe should be conducted throughout professional activity to constantly follow and make explicit the action processes, resources, and influences. Thus, the objective of reflexive thinking processes in our model is not limited to an individual but, rather, is applied to the sum total and scope of influences on the process and of the professional activity or entity.

Reflexive action involves three important foci: (a) monitoring process, (b) resource analysis, and (c) consideration of indirect influences on the professional action.

Monitoring process or process assessment is the element of evaluation that examines if and how the activity, program, or effort is proceeding. Dissimilar to Scriven (1991), who defines monitoring as a process whereby an individual or group oversees the expenditure of resources in relation to actions performed, we agree with Rossi *et al.* (2004) regarding the expansiveness and importance of this part of the evaluation practice process. We see monitoring as an essential evaluation practice step in which the actual implementation of an action or creation of an entity is systematically studied and characterized. Monitoring process not only examines the scope of the professional effort, but scrutinizes the action processes to determine who they affect, assess the degree to which goals and objectives are reflected in the activity, and provide feedback for revision based on empirical evidence. The primary purpose of monitoring process is to ascertain if an activity or entity occurred as planned so that attribution of outcome can be positioned properly.

Let's use the example in Box 1.2 to illustrate the link between monitoring and outcome assessment.

Box 1.2 Attributing outcomes through careful monitoring

Suppose we find at the end of a behavioral program designed to teach work skills to youth who perpetrated criminal offenses that they did not learn the necessary skills. An automatic response would suggest that the program failed and should be revised or discontinued. However, sound monitoring might lead to other conclusions. Suppose in the monitoring action process, we learn that the teaching staff worked with youth on attitudinal change rather than specific work skills. While the intervention might not have been implemented as specified, monitoring revealed that the staff, in their assessment of the youth, realized that attitude change was a necessary prerequisite to skill acquisition, and modified the program and time line to address this very important element of work ethic. Do we conclude that our program failed, or has the monitoring illuminated a necessary revision?

Can you see how monitoring enhances knowledge of what happened and why goals and objectives were or were not achieved?

Similar to monitoring, resource analysis occurs throughout the professional action and requires reflection. When we think of resource analysis, cost in dollars for services rendered is the most commonly examined resource. In our model, we expand reflexive action beyond cost factors to include the full host of human and non-human resources that are used to conduct professional activity. Box 1.3 continues the example from Box 1.2.

Consideration of Indirect Influences on Professional Action

Part of the process of reflexive action must be a consideration of factors external to the effort that affect both process and outcome. Without widening the scope of examination it is difficult to guess at why change is or is not occurring in the desired direction (see Box 1.4).

Many evaluation texts and scholars refer in part to what we are calling reflexive action as process or formative evaluation. These functions are both included in our conceptualization as we will discuss in detail later in the text. However, we selected the term "reflexive action" to denote a more expansive and complex approach to achieve what we consider to be the ultimate purpose of ongoing professional reflection and an essential obligation of every professional; that is, the generation and/or use of systematically derived evidence to scrutinize and revise professional activity. The term reflexivity is both descriptive and comprehensive and thus we have chosen it to denote a process of "looking inward" while simultaneously

Box 1.3 Scope of reflexive action

Continuing from the example above, we might look merely at the financial cost of salaries and day-to-day operations of the intervention and draw conclusions about the amount of dollars spent on each participant to effect attitude change without having achieved the end goal of youth employment. This focus might lead us to believe that the program is too costly to continue, since the goal of employment is not attained. But what if we expand our resource analysis to the cost of unemployment for these participants over a lifetime, something that may occur without the prerequisite step of attitude examination and change? The cost of not continuing the program in this scenario greatly outweighs the cost of funding a modified and possibly longer program and policy to support the alternative approach.

Box 1.4 External influences in reflexive action

What if the youth in our program discussed in Boxes 1.2 and 1.3 lived in a remote rural area in which they were uncertain of job opportunities. You have noted that they lack enthusiasm about skill acquisition. Considering the limited future potential to obtain a job regardless of skill would be a reasonable explanation to check out. This factor is an example of an external influence that needs to be considered in programmatic process and outcome.

acknowledging and addressing the influence of contextual factors on professional processes and products.

Outcome Assessment

Outcome assessment is the action process of evaluation practice that is most familiar to the majority of readers. It not only answers the question "to what extent did the desired outcomes occur?" but also examines more. Included in the scope of examination are the parts of a program, activity, or entity and the context related to outcome. Differential outcomes resulting from many influences, such as professional processes themselves, the target populations, the complexity of outcome expectations, and so forth, can also be examined. While the aim of outcome assessment seems obvious, that is, to judge the value of an effort in its achievement of goals and objectives, outcome assessment serves many other important purposes. Outcome assessment provides empirical information on which to make programmatic, policy, and resource decisions that influence and shape professional activity at multiple levels (Unrau *et al.*, 2006).

Political Context of Evaluation

We have already mentioned the political nature of evaluation. We wish to emphasize the importance of this understanding. In our experience, evaluation practice is the "politicalization" of research and professional thinking and action processes at multiple system levels. That is to say, the field of evaluation practice uses inquiry as political and purposive. But what do we mean by this statement? Evaluation practice provides the empirical "power" to guide and/or justify decisions about professional programs and entities. The decision to devote resources to a particular area of professional concern is always a matter of power in decision making and action, given the climate of fiscal scarcity (Alkin, 1990).

Consider the HRTW initiative as illustrative. Why were federal funds allocated to bolster the employment and health of a small segment of youth? Clearly, the cost in dollars as well as values on self-sufficiency and adult contribution to the economy were a political factor in focusing effort and expenditures on efforts to pre-empt life-long dependency.

As we proceed through this text, we urge you to pay close attention to the significant role of political power and resource allocation in all elements of evaluation practice. All evaluation practice is value based, as are professional actions and all levels of professional effort.

The Theoretical and Value-Based Foundation of Evaluation Practice

As we will see in the chapter on problem clarification and have briefly addressed above in our example of the HRTW initiative, all problems are statements of value. What is a problem to some is not a problem to others, or how the same problem is conceptualized may differ among groups and individuals. The application of a theoretical lens through which to view and explain a problem complicates problem definition even further (DePoy and Gilson, 2007). Thus the need to clarify the approach to a problem and the value-base of the problem is critical in the evaluation practice process and comprises the first major thinking process of our evaluation model.

What do we mean by value-base? A value is what we believe to be desirable and/or important. A value-base is a composite of individual, group, social, and cultural beliefs about what is just, correct, and desirable (Rokeach, 1973). Well, by now, you can begin to see why the clarification of value is so important in evaluation practice. Clearly, what one group values another might not. One group might believe, for example, that youth who perpetrate crimes are "bad kids" and thus would advocate for the need for punitive policies, programs, and outcome. Another group might see these youth as victims of unjust social systems and thus would value rehabilitation and large systems change as concurrent approaches. Each addresses the same problem, youth crime, but conceptualizes the problem and need differently as a function of value difference.

Moreover, we can now begin to understand theoretical lenses as critical factors in the thinking processes of evaluation practice. If we see youth crime through a behavioral theoretical lens, then our need would suggest behavioral programs as the professional action of choice with individual behavior change as the desired outcome. Yet, if we apply a social justice theory to the problem of youth crime, the need for large-scale social policy such as affirmative action might be indicated, with the outcome being equal opportunity.

How to Use this Book

In this text, we will proceed through each step of our evaluation practice model. At the beginning of each chapter, the element of the model that we are addressing is highlighted in the model graphic. Along with examples from actual evaluation practice, we will provide exemplars, mostly from our own practice, throughout the text as we look at the issues that surround each of them in relation to evaluation practice thinking and action processes.

As you will come to see, our discussion of evaluation practice is not prescriptive or mechanical. Rather, we pose a series of thinking and action processes through which professionals make and enact decisions about how to conduct, report, and put evaluation practice to use.

Finally we suggest exercises for you to complete that are designed to help you experience the thinking and action processes of evaluation practice.

Main Points

1. Evaluation practice is a comprehensive framework that integrates evaluation thinking and action within your daily professional activity.

2. Evaluation practice is a means to examine and respond to problems and issues and within which content- and skill-specific theories and practices can be organized, examined, and verified.
3. Evaluation practice is designed to bridge the gap between research and professional activity.
4. A formal definition of evaluation practice is the purposive application of evidence-based thinking to the definition and clarification of problems, to identifying what is needed to resolve them, and to the way in which and extent to which problems have been resolved.
5. Evaluation is based in inductive, deductive, and abductive logic structures.
6. Evaluation practice has emerged from a rich history of the inter-section of inquiry with economic and accountability concerns.
7. The three elements of evaluation practice are: (a) problem and need clarification, (b) reflexive action, and (c) outcome assessment.
8. All evaluation practice is value based and purposive.

CHAPTER 2

The Conceptual Framework
of Evaluation Practice

In this chapter, we present the evaluation practice model, its elements, the assumptions that underpin the model, and the logical structures that guide evaluation practice thinking and action. Figure 2.1 presents a visual of the evaluation practice model.

Figure 2.1 depicts our view of evaluation practice as multidimensional. The graphic illustrates the model as a sequential, non-linear set of thinking and action processes. Different from the linear logic model approach which focuses on the way in which the program components fit together (Frechtling, 2007), evaluation practice begins with a problem/issue statement. Logic models begin with inputs and resources, not problems or issues, and thus while valuable in visualizing relationships among the resources, process, and outputs of a professional action (Graig, 2006), they fail to examine the extent to which the structure and use of these human and non-human capital elements addressed the problems that they are intended to change and/or eliminate.

We have used the mobius graphic to depict the larger purpose of evaluation practice in professional activity as knowledge building. As reflected in the visual graphic, engaging in evaluation practice is an ongoing process of generating and applying systematically generated knowledge to the identification and resolution of problems and issues.

As you can see in Figure 2.1, the three areas of evaluation discussed in Chapter 1—(a) clarification of problem and need, (b) reflexive action, and (c) outcome—are further broken down into steps, which are sequential and ongoing.

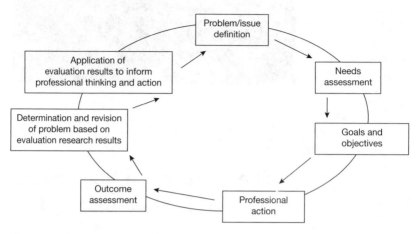

Figure 2.1 Model of evaluation practice

In the clarification stage, we specify a problem or issue to which our professional activity is directed. As we asserted in Chapter 1, the problem or issue explicitly or implicitly looks at undesirable human behavior, causes, correlates, or consequences. We then look at what is needed to satisfactorily resolve the problem or issue in part or in total, and establish goals and objectives that will guide the professional activity or entity to fulfill the need. As we implement professional efforts we engage in reflexive action, in which professional action, entities, resources, and influences are elaborated and monitored. This step helps us to clearly understand what we are doing, using, and being influenced by, and how we are proceeding to meet our goals and objectives.

As we move to outcome assessment, we base our success criteria on how well the goals and objectives were met. Our final step begins the process again, in which we use evaluation knowledge to guide and inform future professional efforts.

We now clarify the assumptions upon which this model is based. Knowing these principles will help you to understand evaluation practice not only as a sequence of steps, but as an essential professional practice action embedded within your daily ethical, value-based activity.

Principles and Assumptions

Evaluation practice is grounded on the following principles: (a) all evaluation is value based; (b) evaluation practice is political; (c) evaluation practice may have multiple and competing audiences; (d) evaluation practice may have multiple and competing purposes; (e) evaluation practice (should be) the purposive application of rigorous inquiry-based thinking and action to examination of practice need, process, and outcome; and (f) evaluation thinking and actions (should) provide a meta-framework for systematic professional thinking and actions.

Let us now explore each of these critical principles.

All Evaluation is Value Based

We briefly introduced the principle of value-based evaluation practice in Chapter 1. Now let us examine it in greater depth. What are values and what do we mean by value based? *Values* are defined as beliefs and opinions about what is good (McDonald, 2004), desirable or undesirable, important or unimportant, and correct or incorrect. Values can refer to present and future desirable beliefs, attributes, intentions, actions, processes, and outcomes (McDonald), but in professional activity they all relate to human behavior. And although there is significant debate in the literature on how, and the degree to which, values influence behavior (Bardi and Schwartz, 2003), our definition of evaluation practice, advanced in Chapter 1, suggests that all evaluation activity is value based. Thus, similar to McDonald's radical axiological theory that places values as the foundation for all subsequent thinking, the role of values in evaluation practice must be recognized as primary to the planning, execution, and use of evaluation knowledge.

Evaluation practice is value based because its primary purpose is to examine how, and the extent to which, an action resolves a problem and thus directly or indirectly changes behavior. As we will examine in depth later in this chapter, problems themselves are statements of value. What is desirable and what requires change? You might note that the word "value" is the root of the term evaluation and thus serves to remind us of the essential role that values and ethics play in evaluation (Fitzpatrick *et al.*, 2004). As we noted in Chapter 1, Grant-maker valued health care as the means to increase informed health behavior.

Moreover, the recognition that diverse groups have differing and sometimes competing values and, thus, define problems in diverse ways suggests the complexity of evaluation practice thinking and action. What problem(s) an action or entity is designed to address, how the effort is designed to address the problem, and who and what are being evaluated for what audience(s) and purpose(s) can be both confusing and complex to decipher. Sound evaluation practice takes these factors into account to assure the appropriate and purposive use of the new knowledge resulting from evaluation practice process and findings (House and Howe, 1999). Rossi *et al.* (2004) remind us that problems change over time as well.

Consider the complex and moving-target problem of "substance abuse." In some of our recent work, we are focusing on the undesirable behavior of illegal drug acquisition as an important point of prevention. Before the omnipotence of the internet, the "problem" occurred through sales or exchange in geographically situated spaces. Yet, with the advent and increasing use of the internet, illegal drugs are accessed in virtual spaces, thus changing the nature of the problem and the public health and law enforcement strategies that follow. Or think about homosexuality, which until 1973 was considered to be a problem of pathology to be cured (American Psychiatric Association, 1968 [7th printing 1974]).

Evaluation Practice is Political

As we introduced in Chapter 1, in large part, evaluation practice deals with the distribution of resources and the related behavioral correlates, causes, and consequences of resource inequality. Those resources can be human, programmatic, financial, intellectual, and so on (DePoy and Gilson, 2003). Regardless of the content, when resource distribution in the form of intervention and desired change enters into a process, stakeholders emerge, sometimes with competing perspectives (Stein, 2006). Of particular importance to the evaluation practice process is how power and position control resources and come to define the target for change, how change should occur, and how it should be recognized (Bamberger et al., 2006).

Since we define evaluation practice as the politicization of inquiry, some might err in thinking that rigor is not as important as it is in research conducted for the purpose of knowledge and theory generation and testing. Quite to the contrary, it is imperative that evaluation practice be ethically conducted and methodologically sound. In evaluation practice, political purpose informs rather than obfuscates the use of the findings. Political power, dissonance among groups, and stakeholding, whether explicit or implied, play essential roles in the conceptualization, conduct, and use of evaluation findings (Bamberger et al., 2006; House and Howe, 1999). Political considerations along with other ethical and methodological factors influence each thinking and action step in the evaluation process.

Consider, for example, how state and federal politics in the United States have made significant changes in substance abuse prevention approaches. Prior to the Republican George W. Bush administration, substance abuse prevention was aimed at lowering risk and promoting protective factors. However, the emphasis has shifted from risk and protective factors to personal responsibility and consequences. Similarly, the No Child Left Behind Act passed on January 2, 2002 by a Republican administration has elevated measurement as the accountability criterion for student achievement. These two political changes conceptualize the "problem" differently and thus the professional action and outcomes shift in response to political agendas. Understanding this phenomenon as an essential part of, rather than a weakness in, the evaluation process is important in crafting sound evaluation approaches.

Evaluation Practice May Have Multiple and Competing Audiences

As a result of the value-based and political nature of evaluation practice, audiences may be multiple. But what do we mean by audiences? *Audience* is an individual or group of individuals who have a role in some or all thinking and action processes of an evaluation including the initiation, receipt, and use of findings. Beginning with problem identification and proceeding through all steps to the use of findings, diverse groups from which multiple perspectives emerge may be involved. These audiences can change throughout a single evaluation practice process or remain stable. Let us look at an example of how the concept of audience plays out in evaluation practice.

Consider the example of the HRTW initiative. This federal program has multiple stakeholders all with competing agendas, beginning with different conceptualizations of undesirables to be changed.

Evaluation Practice May Have Multiple and Competing Purposes

This principle, although seemingly contrary to traditional understandings of systematic inquiry as *bias* free, is critical to the planning and conduct of evaluation practice and central to our definition of evaluation practice. By definition, evaluation practice is purposive because of its aim to empirically examine activity value, integrity, and/or inform change. However, let us consider this principle in more detail. While all evaluation has the same basic explicit purpose of empirical scrutiny of professional processes and/or outcome, each study is initiated for particular purposes within the context of practice assessment, and conducted and used for those purposes. Factors such as the problem that the activity addresses, the identified targets of professional efforts, audiences, and stakeholders, and the political issues associated with actions, entities, and other efforts, all impact the manner in which the basic purposes are actualized. For example, evaluating program integrity for some may mean elaborating best practices with clear evidence, while for others it may mean determining the degree to which an entity achieved a success criterion such as sales and profit. Both are purposively designed to examine the integrity of professional activity, however, each with a potentially different outcome for the practitioner, client, funder, and so forth. Think back to our example of Grant-maker in Chapter 1, which funded diverse approaches to achieve a single goal of access to health care.

Now, consider another exemplar, a project that we have been developing for five years. The project is designed to advance full access to web-based information. The effort has multiple purposes, including social justice, full access, and technological advancement. However, the project is proprietary as well, and thus as the software is developed and rolled out for commercialization, the extent to which it promotes job creation, economic development, and profit becomes an evaluative factor and purpose.

Evaluation Practice (Should be) the Purposive Application of Rigorous Inquiry-Based Thinking and Action to Examination of Professional Action, Need, Process, and Outcome

This principle is not new, but is the synthesis of the previous assumptions and the ethical foundation of evaluation practice as we see it. As we have said and will discuss throughout the text, evaluation practice is conducted for explicit and implicit purposes. Evaluation practice has a primary impact on users of professional services, program developers, policy makers, and product developers, educators, and business, but also broadly informs knowledge through incrementally adding empirical knowledge to professional scopes (Alkin, 1990; McDavid and Hawthorn, 2006; Thyer, 2001). Not in spite of, but, in our opinion, because of the complex context of evaluation practice such as stakeholding, resource distribution, political purpose, and competing values, rigor must be upheld in all thinking and action processes of evaluation practice. By rigor, we mean that regardless of evaluation design, all evaluation activity must be carefully and soundly planned and executed. All thinking and action processes should be clearly articulated, conforming to high standards of inquiry. Processes should be well justified so that the audience understands the knowledge generated and the context and process through which knowledge was derived. This principle becomes even more important when evaluation is not welcomed by those who are wary of the intended use of empirical knowledge derived therefrom.

As example, in a recent application to secure funding, we systematically examined the accessibility of public health websites as the basis to determine the need for innovative software that would provide alternatives for access to health care information. Several of the agencies whose websites were not accessible became defensive and saw the needs assessment as pejorative and critical rather than a positive step towards advancing access to health care information for all people.

Evaluation Thinking and Actions (Should) Provide a Meta-Framework for Systematic Thinking and Actions

Although inquiry and action are often conceptualized as separate, the logical thinking and action processes that are used in evaluation practice are not different from the processes that we use in all domains of professional activity (Bamberger *et al.*, 2006; Berlin and Marsh, 1993; Gambrill, 1999). One difference, however, lies in the perception of evaluation as outside and in judgment of professional efforts, programs, process, and outcome. Another difference is based on the systematic nature of evaluation practice through which each logical step is scrutinized for its knowledge foundation, process, and outcome.

Different from the current treatment of research as distinct from action, our contention is that regardless of the professional domain, inquiry-based thinking and action are essential in order to be aware of why, how, and what should emerge from what we are doing. Thus, while evaluation practice at its basic level is based on, and perceived as closest to, principles of logical inquiry, we suggest that it should inform professional action in multiple ways. First, the model of evaluation practice builds on previous systematic approaches such as empirical practice and evidence-based practice (Thyer, 2001). Second, evaluation thinking and action processes contribute to professional knowledge through incrementally adding empirically derived information to fields of professional practice. Look at Box 2.1 to illustrate.

The actual approach that you take within the meta-framework of evaluation practice will depend on the substantive theoretical and domain-specific knowledge and experience that you hold and value.

Finally we come to a discussion of thinking and action. We introduced and defined these terms in Chapter 1. Let us now examine them. As we discussed in Chapter 1, while complicated by its context, all evaluation practice is based on three distinct forms of human reasoning: deduction, induction, and abduction.

Deductive Reasoning

Deductive reasoning begins with the acceptance of a general principle or belief and then proceeds to apply that principle to explain a specific case or phenomenon. For example, if you are the CEO of a company who believes in social exchange theory, it is likely that you will approach business relationships with your employees as a negotiation of social, productive, and monetary benefits (Miller, 2005). This approach in evaluation practice involves "drawing out" or verifying what already is accepted as credible

---

Box 2.1 Incremental contribution of knowledge and action

Once again, consider the issue of limited access to electronic health information. Using evaluation practice as a framework, action and inquiry are intimately intertwined. First, the values that inhere within the problem statement are: (a) that all people should have equal access to information, and (b) that health information is valuable in framing healthy behaviors. Given these values, resolution of this problem would aim to equalize access. Based on previous inquiry conducted by Stephanidis (2000), we acquired the foundation for subsequent steps in the evaluation practice process, thereby integrating inquiry and action at the very first stages of our process. We then examined what was *not* in the literature that may be contributing to the maintenance of the "problem" of unequal access, conducted the needs assessment discussed above, and decided to proceed to tackle part of problem of limited access through software development. To ascertain further what type of software design was needed, we conducted a systematic needs assessment through clarifying the preferences and needs of diverse users of electronic health information. Combined with the needs assessment documenting the pervasive lack of access, the subsequent needs study formed the basis for our goals and objectives and shaped the design of the software entity and its expected outcome.

---

and correct. Deductive approaches to thinking lead the professional to examine outcome with pre-existing views of success. Evaluators typically use quantitative, experimental-type designs to conduct deductive inquiries (DePoy and Gitlin, 2005).

Consider social exchange theory as an exemplar. Consistent with the theoretical framework, you offer (or exchange) financial bonuses for increased worker productivity. In order to ascertain individual performance as well as collective increase in productivity, you establish quantitative benchmarks as individual employee and collective outcome measures. Thus, the amount of financial remuneration for each individual is exchanged for his/her incremental increase in measured productivity and the overall success of the social exchange strategy is measured by aggregate increase in productivity. If the strategy fails to meet its success criterion, you would look no further than to the nature of the exchange as the culprit. Perhaps you offered an insufficient bonus or the "wrong" bonus. Through the logico-deductive lens, alternative reasons for failure to raise employee productivity would not be sought.

Inductive Reasoning

This type of cognitive activity involves a process in which general rules evolve or develop from individual cases or observations of phenomena. The CEO, proceeding inductively, seeks to reveal or uncover a truth based on aggregation and analysis of the multiple perceptions of informed "knowers." This approach assumes to a greater or lesser degree that the professional does not know the "truth" but seeks it from credible involved sources (i.e., employees). Business practices, processes and methods to achieve a desired level of profit then would be developed based on aggregated and inductively derived principles.

Based on inductive thinking, you would not use exchange of benefits for work output and testing as in the example above, but would observe the work environment to see what factors emerge to stimulate both individual as well as overall productivity. Appreciative inquiry (Preskill and Catsambas, 2006) is a contemporary example. Using this framework, you would use the naturalistic tools of interview and observation to find and capitalize on the strengths and assets of your organization. Can you see the difference? In deductive thinking, the theory is established and the method for testing its application and efficacy is set prior to the inquiry. In an inductive approach, there are no previously established expectations that can be tested. Thus, observation is intended to reveal information that can be examined for emergent knowledge and principles.

Abductive Reasoning

This logic structure involves the selection of the most feasible explanation for phenomena. As you can see by this simple definition, abduction assumes that there are multiple viable explanations for a set of observations or claims, that each has a "truth value" so to speak, and that the reasoning process involves weighing the adequacy of multiple explanations against one another and arriving at the one or more that is most likely to produce a valid and useful explanation (Walton, 2004). Returning to the CEO's dilemma of insufficient productivity, multiple reasons would be invoked, verified, and then put to the evaluative test. Perhaps exchanging benefits for productivity, by itself, was insufficient to change performance but adding social recognition to human resource management strategy resulted in the desired outcome.

How Thinking Processes Guide Evaluation Action Processes

Although in any evaluation project, all three types of reasoning are used, the overall process can be characterized as following the structure of the type of reasoning used. Each type of reasoning can result in different action strategies to derive evaluation knowledge.

The professional working deductively assumes a truth before engaging in the evaluation practice process and applies that truth to the thinking and action processes. Evaluation practice based on deductive thinking would utilize experimental-type action strategies such as standardized testing and statistical analysis in needs assessment and benchmarking and the a priori selection of success indicators to guide process and outcome investigation. Problem statements would be drawn from pre-existing theory and experience characterized in the practice and scholarly literature.

In an evaluation effort proceeding inductively, the professional action and desired processes and outcomes emerge from what is learned from observations, interviews, and even artifact analysis from key audiences and entities respectively. Action strategies would rely primarily on naturalistic, qualitative traditions of inquiry and inductive systematic analysis.

Using abductive reasoning, multiple theories and approaches to guide and assess professional action might be considered. Following from this logic structure, experimental-type, naturalistic, and/or mixed methods and integrated inquiry could be used throughout the evaluation practice process, depending on feasibility and purpose.

An inductive reasoning approach in evaluation practice is used to reveal rules and processes (Patton, 1997), deductive reasoning is used to test or predict the application of theory, processes, and rules to specific areas of concern, and abductive logic provides the most feasible guidance for professional activity and evaluation practice. All three approaches can be used to describe, explain, and predict phenomena. Table 2.1 summarizes the major characteristics of each type of reasoning.

As you can see by examining Table 2.1, induction and deduction, while not opposite, take alternative approaches not only to thinking and action, but also to the view and related credibility of knowledge derived from each approach. Abductive logic provides the thinking framework to consider alternative perspectives and select one or more based on purpose, context, and viability. We suggest that deductive, inductive, and abductive thinking and related action are viable and credible approaches to evaluation practice and that they can be integrated as well, given the contextual factors of purpose, audience, and politic. However, in concert with Bamberger et al. (2006), we acknowledge the purposive aim of evaluation and thus encourage the use of abductive logic. In their discussion of integration of research methods, Creswell and Plano-Clark (2006) and Tashakkori and Teddlie (2002) identify pragmatism as the basis for method selection and thus the precedent for abduction in evaluation practice is set in a sound philosophical foundation.

Table 2.1 Characteristics of inductive, deductive, and abductive thinking

Inductive	Deductive	Abductive
No a priori acceptance of truth	A priori acceptance of truth	Explanatory viability rather than truth is the concern
Alternative conclusions can be drawn from data	One set of conclusions is accepted as true	Alternative conclusions can be drawn from data
Theory development	Theory testing	Selection of most feasible theory
Examines relationships among unrelated pieces of data	Tests relationships among discrete phenomena	Provides most feasible explanation for data
Development of concepts based on repetition of patterns	Testing of concepts based on application to discrete phenomena	Development and/or selection of existing concepts
Holistic perspective	Atomistic perspective	Teleological perspective
Multiple realities	Single separate reality	Multiple realities

Next, we illustrate how deductive, inductive, and abductive thinking underpin thinking in all domains of professional action. As we explore these logic structures below, think again about evaluation practice as an organizing meta-approach to professional thinking and action.

Applying Evaluation Practice Thinking and Actions across Professional Domains

If you carefully examine the knowledge that you use to make professional decisions, you will see that the same thinking and action steps that we suggest in our evaluation practice model characterize this reasoning and activity. Look at Table 2.2 below for more detail.

Let us use an example to illustrate. As we have noted, some of our current work focuses on substance abuse prevention in a rural state in the U.S. In professional practice, there are multiple stakeholders, each defining the problems and issues differently. Consider the perspectives of just such groups, state-level public health professionals and law enforcement officers. From the public health perspective, substance abuse is a major health threat to communities with many suggested causal explanations in the literature, including, but not limited to, learned behavior (Miller and Carroll, 2006), poverty (Daugherty and Leukefeld, 2005), and local lack of resources and readiness to implement a pervasive prevention infrastructure (Hogan et al., 2002). From the law enforcement perspective, inadequate

Table 2.2 Professional reasoning and evaluation practice

Reasoning in all domains of practice	Evaluation practice
Presenting problem or issue to be addressed.	Mapping problems through literature support and values clarification to identify and obtain a comprehensive understanding of the problem.
Obtain information about the target group, issue, entity of interest, or concern.	Empirical needs assessment.
Based on information, what approaches/ skills do I use? What needs to be done?	Specification of goals and objectives, with process and outcome assessment indicators based on empirically supported needs statement.
What about the professional activity should be changed so that the best result is achieved?	Reflexive action.
Did my activity "work"?	Outcome/summative evaluation. Was the activity, entity, or effort successful in achieving its desired outcomes?

and unenforceable laws to control availability, distribution, and use are among the major problems to be addressed (Steffen and Candelaria, 2002). Each set of problems is supported by a significant body of literature and provides a confusing and even contradictory maze of causal explanations. As we discuss in depth in Chapter 3, problem mapping is a thinking strategy that organizes literature and teases apart complex problems and relationships and creates the logical guidance for professional action.

In order to identify what is needed to resolve the problem or issue of concern, professionals typically engage in collecting information. In evaluation practice, information collection is systematic and relies on empirical data. So the evaluation practice analog of professional staff meetings to plan approaches might be the aggregation and analysis of epidemiological, consumption, consequence, and policy data as the basis to determine need. Depending on the logic structure and foundation problem statement, diverse needs statements might look very different and would give rise to varied goals and objectives. As example, through systematic policy analysis, we found that our state allows "underage drinkers" to work in restaurants and bars and to serve liquor (Hanson, 1997–2007). The role of this policy in facilitating underage alcohol consumption is suspect and of concern to law enforcement but has not been targeted by public health officials. The harmful consequences of underage drinking, such as automobile accidents, were of concern to public health officials and incidence and prevalence data supported this critical relationship. Each needs assessment shapes different, sometimes related and sometimes conflicting, goals and objectives to guide professional activity. Once enacted, the intuitive professional process of monitoring one's activity is realized as a critical, deliberate, and purposive step in evaluation practice. Finally, the professional question "Did the activity work?" in evaluation practice narrows and clarifies the professional question to the extent to which the activity or entity achieved its desired goals and objectives. Through subsequent chapters, we illustrate these points using this complex example as well as others that illuminate evaluation practice thinking and action processes.

Main Points

1. The evaluation practice model comprises a set of thinking and action processes embedded within a purposive, political context.
2. Evaluation practice is based on a set of assumptions and principles.
3. Evaluation practice comprises three distinct but integrated thinking and action phases: (a) clarification of problem and need; (b) reflective action; and (c) outcome assessment.
4. Each element of evaluation practice is founded in logical thinking and action processes, with systematically derived and organized evidence supporting each of these temporally sequenced processes.

Exercises

1. Think of an example of how you use deductive reasoning in your daily life.
2. Think of an example of how you use inductive reasoning in your daily life.
3. Think of an example of how you use abductive reasoning in your daily life.
4. Compare and contrast each example for: context, processes, outcomes, and your comfort with each.
5. Describe a professional activity and examine how it could be translated into an evaluation practice process.
6. Look at the mission statement of an agency or organization and extract the values implicit in it.

Thinking Processes
of Evaluation Practice

PROBLEM

CHAPTER 3

Identifying Problems and Issues: Mapping and Analyzing Your Territory

In this chapter, we examine the nature of professional problems and issues and illustrate specific techniques that can be used to identify, analyze, and clarify problem statements. The problem statement forms the foundation for all thinking and action processes in professional activity and its evaluation. Of particular note is the potential for the thinking techniques which we illustrate here to integrate and make complementary agendas and perspectives that might seem disparate and in opposition to one another. Therefore, careful and systematic formulation of the problem statement is critical not only in illuminating the complexity of professional problems, but also in providing the scaffold for discussion, analysis, and responses which advance tolerance and pluralism (DePoy and Gilson, 2007; Kukathas, 2003).

The Nature of Problems

Unlike many frameworks that do not differentiate problem and need, we see these two as separate and distinct in nature. As we noted in Chapter 1, a *problem* is a conceptual-value assertion of what is undesirable and in need of change while a *needs statement* is a systematically supported template of actions that are necessary to resolve all or part of the problem as it is stated.

Consider, for example, the following problem statement from Grant-maker:

Uninformed health behaviors lead to unnecessary, costly illness and may compromise health and wellness.

In this statement, what is undesirable? Rhetorically, both illness and un-informed health behaviors are implicated. Conversely, by stating what is undesirable, a problem statement directly or indirectly indicates what is valued as desirable. Let us reword our previous problem statement to illustrate:

> Informed health behaviors may prevent unnecessary, life com-promising, costly illness and contribute to health and wellness.

As you can see by this statement, the desirables are framed as informed health behaviors, prevention of illness, and promotion of health and wellness.

Although we often consider problems to exist as entities outside our-selves, consistent with contemporary thinking (Leon-Guerro, 2005) we assert that problems are contextually embedded in values. Thus, a problem statement is a social construction emerging from the values and interests of those who are naming the problem (DePoy and Gitlin, 2005).

Let us illustrate with some examples from the substance abuse preven-tion effort that we introduced previously. First, consider alcohol abuse. Public health professionals might see excessive alcohol consumption as community and individual problem due to the potential safety and illness consequences, respectively. However, the owner of the local bar or liquor store might not see alcohol consumption as a problem at all, but would point to driving under the influence of alcohol as the harm consequence and thus the undesirable. For breathalyzer manufacturers, excessive alcohol consumption creates their business and profit, and to this group of business professionals, it is likely that they, too, see the consequences of driving while intoxicated as the problem, not the actual intake of alcohol.

Now consider marijuana use. For some, any use of marijuana is a prob-lem, as it is illegal and designed to induce intoxication. Yet proponents of medical marijuana use do not see this practice as a problem at all. To the contrary, for this group it is a resolution to a problem and thus the problem is the illegal status of marijuana in 39 states (Common Sense for Drug Policy, 2000–2005).

Thus, problems are differentially defined by those in the definitional seat. So now you might be wondering how professionals locate and decide which problem statements fall within their purview and which do not. While professionals address problem statements that effect different levels of concern, from individuals through cultural phenomena, as suggested by Rossi *et al.* (2004) a problem becomes "public" and of professional concern only when it attracts political attention and is positioned within the public and professional arenas of resource allocation.

Consider obesity as example. People have been overweight and obese for eons, but only within the past several decades has the professional world focused its attention on obesity prevention and treatment. The conversations about the need for healthy dietary intake and exercise have been ramped up as the economic, employment, and to some extent personal costs of obesity are realized and documented.

Similarly, cigarette smoking has gained significant political and professional attention as a "problem" over the past 30 years, particularly in the U.S. But, as just illustrated, inherent in defining obesity and cigarette smoking as problems to be eliminated are negative consequences to those who do not agree.

Thus, a well-developed problem statement in which values are clarified is essential if professionals are to examine their domains as well as identify countervailing arguments necessary to efficaciously target professional activity to problems and issues at all system levels within their scope. Further, as we will discuss in detail in subsequent chapters, without a problem statement, the foundation for ascertaining need is absent.

Ideally, professions seek to resolve issues and problems by addressing all or part of what is needed to remediate the problem in a valued direction. And remember that we asserted the presence of behavior change sometimes explicitly identified as the desired direction and sometimes remaining tacit and only implied. However, with the action orientation that is so characteristic of contemporary professional practices, we typically move to activity that we believe "works" but do not carefully clarify the problem we are addressing. What do we mean by what "works"? While we are well meaning in our efforts to quickly remediate problems and diminish negative consequences, the omission of the thinking steps of problem clarification leaves us open to error and criticism. When others ask us to be accountable, it is not unusual for professionals to be vague about the problem they are addressing or to show evidence beyond personal opinion or group consensus supporting the problem description, need, or desired outcomes (Preskill and Catsambas, 2006).

Consider a study by LaViolette (2000) who conducted a study of the problems that clinical social workers address. She asked them to describe the problems/issues/concerns on which their practices focus and to identify how they know that their professional activities are effective in producing desired outcomes. More than 80 percent had no formal mechanism to discern intervention success, and over 90 percent could not clearly articulate even one problem/issue/concern for which their practice was initiated.

Now, consider how many public health campaigns and activities are initiated. Let us return to drug abuse prevention efforts as example. As part of a national effort to reduce drug abuse in rural America, a rural state on the east coast developed a professional credentialing program to certify public and direct health providers as "prevention specialists." Inherent in this initiative are several axiological principles: (a) substance abuse is an undesirable behavior with undesirable causes, correlates, and consequences; (b) substance abuse should be prevented; and (c) substance abuse should be prevented by health professional intervention.

Yet, between the assumed "problem" principles listed above and the action strategy of credentialing that resulted, no examination of professional activity as the "problem" was undertaken. Inferred in workforce development is the third statement only, yet the extent to which professional activity has effected, or ever can effect a change in substance abuse behavior is unclear. Skeptics in the state suggest that credentialing has little to do with alcohol, tobacco, and drug abuse prevention but, rather, is a planned effort for providers to garner economic advantage through training fees and carving out and claiming ownership of the practice of a new, reimbursable professional activity.

Thinking Processes in Articulating Professional Problems

By professional problems, we are referring to the problem statements that professionals identify and address. Although it might seem simple to specify a problem, problem clarification is an intricate task that requires careful and succinct thinking processes. Let us narrow our example of substance abuse prevention to tobacco to examine some of the common mistakes made in problem statements.

Vague problem specification. The first and most basic error is the failure to articulate a problem statement at all. By examining the myriad examples of "the problem" of substance abuse that we have discussed it is simple to see how broad, complex, and differentially bounded this phenomenon is to those individuals and groups who are concerned with it.

Just consider the diverse ways in which "tobacco abuse" is defined and seen as a problem. We just returned from a trip to Europe in which, unlike many states in the U.S., cigarette smoking remains an accepted public behavior rather than a "substance abuse" problem. Cigarette smoking is allowed and frequently observed in public spaces including restaurants, public buildings, and even some hospital areas. But we need not look internationally to illustrate the vagueness of the "tobacco use problem" since, in the U.S., the nature of tobacco abuse is differentially defined depending on context, values, and perspectives. Legally, any tobacco use by minors is considered problematic, while for those over the age of 18, tobacco use is a choice. Public health professionals might consider tobacco use of any kind as substance abuse, while owners of popular cigar bars would not. There is a large body of systematic inquiry identifying the income, age, gender, and class correlates of tobacco use laying bare the contextual nature of defining tobacco use as a problem.

Failure to state the scope and complexity of a problem. Another common mistake related to vague problem definition is failure to state the scope and complexity of a problem. For example, why would tobacco use be problematic? Who smokes, where, what are undesirable consequences, which consequences can be tolerated by whom, where, and when, and so forth. Why does the articulated problem exist?

Stating a problem in terms of a preferred solution. As illustrated above, the solution stated in problem #2, "substance abuse should be prevented," is a preference statement since it speaks to what should happen rather than what is problematic.

As we hope that you are now beginning to see, the logical and conceptual difficulties that are typical of many problem statements are vast and too numerous to cover here. We refer you to literature on cognition and logic to further explore conceptual errors that might contribute to vague and ill-defined problems (DePoy and Gitlin, 2005; Kane and Trochim, 2006; Reike *et al.*, 2004; Walton, 2005). To avoid being limited by an inadequately stated problem, we now offer problem mapping, comprising thinking strategies to conceptualize and clarify complex problems from multiple value perspectives. Problem mapping is based on the technique of concept mapping first popularized by Novack in the 1970s (Kane and Trochim, 2006; Novack, 1996). Simply put, concept mapping is the visual representation of relationships among concepts or ideas. According to Trochim and Linton (1986), concept mapping is a cognitive operation that falls under the rubric of "structured conceptualization" in which a logic sequence can be traced, documented, and visually represented. Concept mapping techniques have been used in multiple areas including, but not limited to, business (Nast, 2006), nursing (Carpenito-Moyet, 2005), education (Margulies and Maal, 2001), multi-media and digital design (Alpert and Gruenberg, 2000), communications and technical writing (Krandall *et al.*, 1996), and public policy (Trochim, 2006; Trochim and Linton, 1986). Our application of concept mapping is conceptualized as "problem mapping." This technique is a purposive thinking and visualization strategy that links disparate views together for the purpose of professional activity and its scrutiny. To briefly illustrate its potency to forge conceptual and

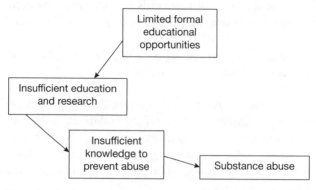

Figure 3.1 Problem map #1

human collaborations, let us revisit the prevention strategy of workforce development.

A simple problem map, as shown in Figure 3.1, would have been useful in locating workforce development within the larger rubric of substance abuse prevention. Moreover, as we will see, problem mapping is a useful tool in drawing out logical and incremental outcome assessment approaches when the initial problem statement is too vague or large to be assessed.

Our two-step method has proven very useful not only to expand the thinking process about problems but to identify values, forge a direction for subsequent thinking and action processes in evaluation practice, and, ultimately, to bring disparate conversations and perspectives together to advance understanding and tolerance that we believe are essential to improve our world in the twenty-first century.

To interpret this diagram, look at the text boxes and directional arrows. The four concepts are sequentially linked beginning with limited formal education, which is necessary for workforce development. The conceptual argument of limited research and knowledge necessary to prevent substance abuse is compelling and thus would have made sense if positioned in a problem map. Furthermore, evaluating outcome at any point in the map becomes relevant to evaluating prevention of substance abuse, even if prevention cannot be directly observed and measured (DePoy and Gitlin, 2005). So, now we turn to a detailed presentation and discussion of problem mapping.

Problem Mapping and Force Field Analysis

The framework that we present consists of two sequential thinking processes: problem mapping followed by force field analysis. Both are structured conceptualizations (Trochim and Linton, 1986) but each has a different purpose in evaluation practice. Together, they make a powerful thinking team.

Problem mapping is a thinking process through which problems, no matter how they are initially conceptualized and/or articulated, can be expanded and grounded in value, literature, and evidence. Problem mapping is a superb tool to assist professionals to identify the context in which their activity takes place, specify what part of the problem can be addressed within each professional domain, and point to what might be needed to do so.

Problem mapping is a method in which one expands a problem statement beyond its initial conceptualization by asking two questions repeatedly: "What caused the problem?" and "What are the consequences of the problem?" In the simple map in Figure 3.1, only the causal question was posed.

Let's work with this problem statement to illustrate the process:

> Cigarette smokers continue to smoke despite the evidence that smoking is harmful.

To conduct problem mapping, we first conceptualize a problem as a river. The initial problem statement that we just articulated above is analogous to stepping into the river and picking up one rock. As we map upstream, we look at cause; as we map downstream, we look at consequence. Thus, the flow of ideas from above the initial statement shapes the problem and the flow away from the initial idea is influenced by the statement. Using our example, let's look upstream at only six of many possible causes: (1) cigarette smokers might not be aware of all of the negative primary, secondary, and tertiary health and environmental consequences of smoking; (2) cigarette smokers might not believe assertions about the negative primary, secondary, and tertiary health and environmental consequences of smoking; (3) cigarette smokers do not care about the negative primary, secondary, and tertiary health and environmental consequences of smoking; (4) nicotine is extremely addictive; (5) advertising promotes smoking as "chic;" and (6) cigarettes are available and legal for purchase for adults over the age of 18.

If we map upstream again from our initial set of causal statements, we expand our causal gaze even further. Let us consider several causes of our causal statement #1 (cigarette smokers might not be aware of all of the negative primary, secondary, and tertiary health and environmental consequences of smoking) only as an example for now: (a) there is insufficient information available to the public about the negative primary, secondary, and tertiary health and environmental consequences of smoking; (b) available information to the public about the negative primary, secondary, and tertiary health and environmental consequences of smoking is not accessible to many, including those with low literacy; (c) the placement of information available to the public about the negative primary, secondary, and tertiary health and environmental consequences of smoking is not efficacious and thus does not reach a large spectrum of individuals; and (d) smokers ignore information about the negative primary, secondary, and tertiary health and environmental consequences of smoking.

Let us map upstream one more level using statement (c) (the placement of information available to the public about the negative primary, secondary, and tertiary health and environmental consequences of smoking is not efficacious and thus does not reach a large spectrum of individuals) from above. Consider these three causes: (a) provision of ubiquitous information about the negative consequences is expensive; (b) provision of information about the negative consequences is limited by tobacco companies and lobbyists; and/or (c) dissemination of information about the negative consequences of smoking is a task that requires special skills.

Remember our discussion above about the prevention of workforce development in the rural eastern seaboard state? Can you now see a logical link between this professional action strategy and the initial problem statement (Cigarette smokers continue to smoke despite the evidence that smoking is harmful)? As illustrated, in this conceptualization workforce development is linked to the broad problem articulation through a rather convoluted path, but nonetheless makes logical sense, given the structure and content of this problem map.

Now let's look downstream at consequence mapping.

We illustrate with only five of many possible consequences: (1) cigarette smoking causes lung damage; (2) cigarette smoking causes health damages to non-smokers; (3) cigarette smoking creates excessive trash; (4) cigarette smoking is expensive; and/or (5) cigarette smoking carries a negative stigma in some social groups.

Now, through asking the question again (What are the consequences?) of the first set of consequences, we can map further downstream. For illustration purposes let us look at some second-level consequences related to the initially articulated consequence: cigarette smoking causes lung damage. We only posit three of many consequences here: (a) lung damage compromises health, leading to illness and premature death; (b) lung damage interferes with daily function; and (c) lung damage is costly in lost productivity and excessive health care costs.

Figure 3.2 illustrates the full problem map that we have just created. Each box above the initial problem is a broad answer category to what caused

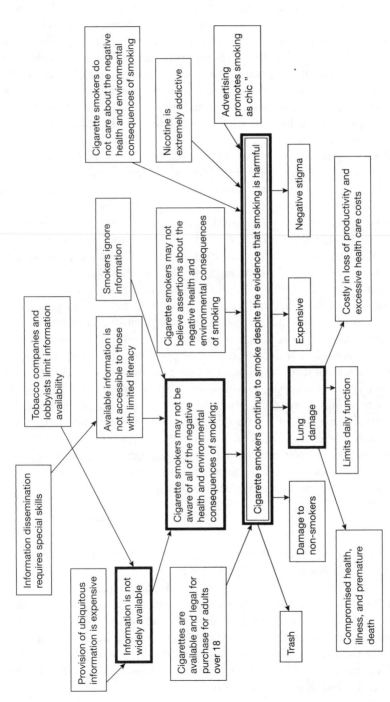

Figure 3.2 Problem map #2

the problem. As we have demonstrated above, creating the problem map is an iterative process. Once we identify first-tier causes of the problem we continue to ask the question "What caused the cause of the problem?" and so on until we reach cultural and/or social value statements. Below the initial problem statement, we repeatedly ask the question "What are the consequences?" As with the upstream map, we repeat this question about the consequences of consequences and so forth until we reach the impact of the problem on individuals. The problem map therefore expands the problem statement from cultural–social causes to personal impact and values and gives us many different places to target our professional activity, as well as topical areas for further inquiry and specification.

As you can see, there are many causes and consequences, some of which are addressed by multiple professional groups, some by one, and some by none. For example, physical health issues would be the primary province of pubic health professionals and providers, while information access would be the concern of multiple educational, health, and business professionals. Issues related to social stigma might be the purview of advertisers, interventionists, public health professionals, community organizers, and school personnel, while policy and legislative allowance for tobacco production and consumption would be the concern of legislators and lobbyists.

Using the problem mapping technique, the initial task of each professional is to identify the elements of the problem map that are within his/her professional scope, skills, and resources. However, a second and critical use of problem mapping is collaboration. By locating one's professional activity within a broad analytic context, professionals can visualize the potential activity of others outside of their own professional groups and seek potent interdisciplinary relationships that can only enhance and hasten complex problem resolution. Once the scope of the problem and the points of action are identified in the problem map, planning through force field analysis can be conducted. We turn to that topic now.

Force Field Analysis

A historical overview will help us understand the context in which force field analysis was developed. Force field analysis is a planning tool that was developed by Lewin (1951) in the 1940s. This planning approach was based on "holistic psychology," which suggests that a network of factors affects an individual's decision-making process (DePoy and MacDuffie, 2004; Hustedde and Score, 1995: 5). Lewin (1951) was interested in the contribution to the analysis of phenomena and their subsequent actions to factors such as government, the kind of work an individual did, family members, and an individual's personal ambitions.

Lewin demonstrated force field analysis techniques by using elaborate diagrams of "life space" or "psychological space" pertaining to and affecting individuals (Hustedde and Score, 1995: 5). These diagrams appeared as a series of directional vectors depicting the nature and strength of the influence of relevant factors on the object of change. Lewin (1951) viewed group use of information and influences to set and attain goals as a systematic, collaborative thinking process.

Force field analysis has been widely used in diverse professional domains including, but not limited to, business, psychology, education, economics, social science, and public health and community planning. As evidence of its value, force field analysis software and online tools have become increasingly popular over the past decade to guide the analytic process (Mind Tools, 2006; SkyMark, 2006). Across these fields, there are several basic models of force field analysis, all of which tend to share common elements (Brager and Holloway, 1992; Cohen, 1994; De Panfilis, 1996; DePoy and MacDuffie, 2004). The first commonality is the use of force field analysis for problem identification, analysis, and goal setting. A second common element is the thinking process of applying a relevant body of information to the identification of restraining and driving forces that impact goal attainment for resolving problems. Third, all models share the step of identifying which influences and resources can be targeted for action. Thus, at its basic level, force field analysis includes a clear definition and dissection of a problem, specification of goals for resolving all or part of the problem, and a systematic identification of resources available to achieve the targeted changes (Bens, 1994).

Of course, in addition to the commonalities, the scholarly literature and web resources on the use of force field analysis as a planning tool to frame and structure change reveals variations of Lewin's (1951) original model (Brager and Holloway, 1992; De Panfilis, 1996). In general, force field analysis provides a diagrammatic picture of all identified influences that maintain and/or impact a situation at a given moment. Through force field analysis processes, assessment and change can be systematically planned if the following three areas are addressed: (a) a multilevel analysis of an issue, (b) inclusion of diverse types of information and evidence from numerous variables to examine the influences that affect a situation, and (c) an analysis of the factors that serve to affect the stability and change in a situation (DePoy and MacDuffie, 2004). If these three elements are addressed, force field analysis can be used to examine the probability of reaching issue-specific change goals that have been agreed upon through a structured group process of critical, collaborative thinking.

Given the history and use of force field analysis, we have found it very useful in further clarifying and honing the scope of the problem to which professional activity is directed. Force field analysis is an excellent tool in identifying primary and secondary targets of change, resources that can enhance problem resolution, impediments to be avoided or eliminated, and stakeholders who affect or will be affected by a professional action.

Where does one begin? Review the problem map in Figure 3.1 above. Each professional would identify targets for change depending on purpose, professional scope, timing, and context. Look at the choices of causal statements below by selected diverse professional groups: (a) there is insufficient information available to the public about the negative primary, secondary, and tertiary health and environmental consequences of smoking—public health, health education—*literacy professionals, technology experts, technology corporations*; (b) the placement of information available to the public about the negative primary, secondary, and tertiary health and environmental consequences of smoking is not efficacious and thus does not reach a large spectrum of individuals—*advertising and marketing, public health, health education*; and/or (c) smokers ignore information about the negative primary, secondary, and tertiary health and environmental consequences of smoking—*public health and direct care providers, insurance industry*.

Now let us look at force field analysis for the following causal statement:

> Available information to the public about the negative primary, secondary, and tertiary health and environmental consequences of smoking is not accessible to many, including those with low literacy.

Once the statement is selected it becomes active and functions as a center point of analysis to identify what contributes to maintaining the problem, what factors could make it worse, and what factors could remediate the problem in part or in total. Although a single individual can do force field analysis, it is usually conducted as a "group think" activity (Brager and Holloway, 1992; Mind Tools, 2006). However, we suggest that collaborative work enhances the process by bringing diverse evidentiary and experiential sources to bear on the analysis. Decisions about who is involved and the specifics of the process are dependent on purpose.

Following the clarification of the problem, participants in the analysis identify the driving (positive) and restraining (negative) forces that would affect movement toward the desired goal of alleviating part or the entire problem as stated. The forces can be grounded in evidence provided to the participants in the force field analysis process or can be brainstormed. How the analytic process is staged depends once again on purpose, resources, and context. In the example below, members selected for the force field analysis group were asked to consider their own experiences and knowledge in identifying influences on the problem statement. There were many forces identified by the group, but for illustrative purposes we will work with just the six driving and restraining forces that follow:

Driving forces: (a) the potential and diversity of electronic information delivery systems; (b) reasonable costs of the internet; and (c) extensive information already exists on the negative consequences of smoking.

Restraining forces: (a) diverse methods of information consumption among the target population; (b) limitations of print material for the diverse target population; and (c) lack of skilled professionals who can make information available in multiple formats.

Once these forces have been identified, each is then rank-ordered to represent its perceived importance in maintaining the status quo or eliciting social change (Brager and Holloway, 1992; DePoy and MacDuffie, 2004). Directional problem articulation can then be targeted to a complex understanding of the problem in terms of its restraining and driving forces. Moreover, those factors that cannot be changed by the planning group can be identified and discarded as targets for action.

Looking at need and action planning based on the driving and restraining forces identified in the two lists, rank order and analysis of each would reveal that all are important and can be used and/or addressed by the appropriate professional group. Further, one or more professional groups might collaborate to develop a strategy for the creation and dissemination of accessible educational information about smoking consequences. The driving forces would be maximized and efforts to decrease or eliminate the restraining forces would be undertaken. No action would be initiated until a full systematic needs assessment was conducted to verify the accuracy of the analytic outcome.

A two-phase approach to problem identification using mapping and force field analysis is depicted in Box 3.1. See also Figure 3.3, which follows.

As you can see, a value between 1 and 10 is assigned to the initial active statement, ranging in ascending ranking from 1 denoting the problem or issue being as "bad" as it can get and 10 denoting that the problem is no longer active. The rating scale is not static or prescribed and thus can be selected based on purpose and context. We find the 1–10 range useful as it can be translated into percentages of change over time. Although Figure 3.3 is a rudimentary map, so to speak, of the thinking processes of professionals and key informants, it provides what Tufte (2006) suggests

---

Box 3.1 Two-phase force field analysis

Phase 1

Preparation—problem statement is clarified through constructing a problem map and identifying the arena for professional attention.

Phase 2

Conducting the analysis—participants identify the magnitude of the problem and place it within a grid illustrating the severity of the problem.

Based on literature, practice wisdom, personal and professional experience, or other relevant information, participants identify and visually depict driving and restraining forces.

Each force is rank-ordered as a target for intervention from most important to those that will not be addressed at all.

---

as beautiful evidence. That is to say, the visual grounds the concepts within a context and, depending on purpose and resources, force field analyses can be represented with a full range of complexity to simplicity, with various visuals integrated to communicate the point of the process. In Figure 3.3, the location of the active problem statement between 1 and 10 denotes the magnitude of the active problem and the length of the arrows denotes the contribution of each vector to the maintenance of the phenomenon. This simple diagram provides a rich visual tapestry to guide subsequent action, through identifying barriers and resources to be addressed in subsequent needs assessment, planning, and professional activity. In addition, the construction of a visual provides the basis for assessing and representing movement and change against the initial understandings of the active problem.

Main Points

1. Professional problems are statements of value.
2. What is considered to be a problem may differ among diverse professional groups and individuals.
3. Problem mapping is a thinking process to locate an initial problem statement within an expanded context of its causes and consequences. This systematic process is important to obtain an understanding of the complexity of problems and to identify potential areas for change.
4. Because problem maps are values in themselves, many problem maps can be developed to depict differential views of the causes and

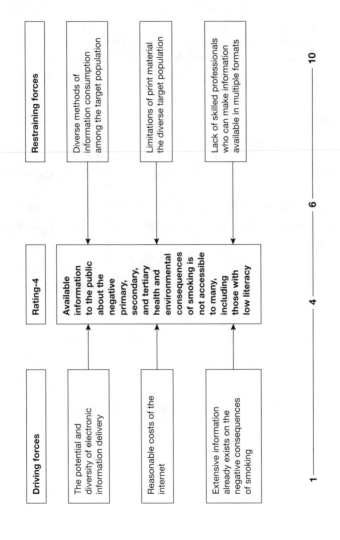

Driving forces

The potential and diversity of electronic information delivery

Reasonable costs of the internet

Extensive information already exists on the negative consequences of smoking

Rating-4

Available information to the public about the negative primary, secondary, and tertiary health and environmental consequences of smoking is not accessible to many, including those with low literacy

Restraining forces

Diverse methods of information consumption among the target population

Limitations of print material the diverse target population

Lack of skilled professionals who can make information available in multiple formats

1 ———— 4 ———— 6 ———— 10

Figure 3.3 Visual force field analysis: the visual depiction of the force field analysis

consequences of an identical problem statement, adding to complexity and pluralism of understanding and multiple avenues for professional action.

5. Force field analysis is a thinking process to further clarify the influences on problems and to identify correlates that can be acted upon.

6. Purposively including stakeholders in the process may help formulate the problem in a way that is meaningful and relevant to a wide range of those who are affected by the problem.

7. Clarifying the problem will lead you to ascertain what is needed to resolve the part of the problem that you will address.

Exercises

1. Identify a problem that you believe is within your professional domain and analyze its explicit and implicit values.

2. Create a problem map using your problem statement from Exercise 1.

3. From your problem map, select one point from causes and one from consequences for professional attention, and conduct force field analysis on each.

PROBLEM

CHAPTER 4

Obtaining and Organizing Information: How Do You Know?

In the previous chapter, we discussed and illustrated the critical concepts of "problem." We proposed a thinking process to expand and clarify problems, and differentiated "need" from problem. In this chapter we look at the purpose of information in evaluation practice, sources of information, including traditional and e-sources, and methods through which to select, retrieve, organize, critically analyze, and use information throughout the evaluation practice process. Let us first look at the nature and roles of information in evaluation practice.

The Thinking Process of Information Review

Historically, credible information in any inquiry was derived from research literature. However, over the past several decades, multiple ways of knowing have been encouraged by scholars and researchers (Bodhanya, 2002; DePoy and Gitlin, 2005). Acceptable sources of knowing can include practice wisdom, popular culture, intuition (DePoy and Gilson, 2003, 2007), art, fiction, and so forth.

Building on the work done by DePoy and Gitlin (2005) we suggest that reviewing information is a thinking process in which the professionals critically delimit relevant information and then use that body of knowledge to inform the content and process of the problem and all subsequent steps of evaluation practice. Moreover, as we indicated previously, finding out what others know and how they come to know it helps determine how each evaluation effort and element contributes to existing problem definition and resulting practice (Bamberger *et al.*, 2006).

Unfortunately, the need to review information as an essential part of evaluation practice is often misconceived and undervalued. In reviewing many evaluation texts, we noted that few direct the reader to the literature and other information as a basic step. However, similar to Bamberger *et al.* (2006), Chen (2005), and Preskill and Catsambas (2006) we suggest that evaluation and knowledge are reciprocal and thus an essential thinking and action process. We present this section on how to review literature and other sources of information to inform evaluation practice and to contribute to the body of professional knowledge.

Purpose of Information Review

Reviewing information in evaluation practice serves a slightly different purpose than a review you might have conducted for other types of activity. Nonetheless, it is equally important. One purpose of doing a review is to obtain direction and rationale for the focus of the content and strategy of an inquiry and to position one's work within an existing body of knowledge (Leeuw, 2003; Preskill, 2006). In evaluation practice, the professional combines the purposes of information review to support both systematic inquiry and professional action.

In addition to literature, numerous sources of information are important to consider. Among these are practice wisdom, political factors (Bamberger *et al.*, 2006), economic, and program-based information such as mission statements, organizational charts, agency policies and procedures, news, and anecdotes. Art, popular culture, and web-based information (Barney, 2004; Gilson and DePoy, 2005/6) have also been recognized as important sources in informing the context of professional action and evaluation practice.

Look at the following points for a summary of the "thinking" purposes of information review in evaluation practice:

1. to ascertain what knowledge has been generated previously that informed the problem, need for and gave rise to the professional action or entity;
2. to examine the social, cultural, political, economic, and theoretical context of the activity;
3. to obtain knowledge of competing approaches;
4. to identify resource issues;
5. to identify potential uses and misuses of the evaluation findings.

In addition to the thinking purposes of information review presented above, we consider practical and professional reasons for the role of information in evaluation practice. As you have seen, many evaluations are merely developed for one-time limited inquiries about a program or professional effort. These types of evaluations tend to be developed without a sound theoretical or methodological basis and, as such, might provide limited information but will not contribute to the knowledge base informing professional activity (Stufflebeam and Shinkfield, 2007). As we have said previously, in our view, evaluation practice is an organizing meta-framework for professional action in which knowledge is generated to inform multiple scopes of practice beyond the direct target of the articulated activity or entity. Thus we believe that it is critical to ground any evaluation project in sound, systematically generated and organized information.

Another point is that many evaluation designs are developed to meet the needs of a specific action or entity. Reviewing multiple sources of information helps professionals select a method based on the successes and lessons learned from previous evaluation practice (Patton, 2001).

Finally, consider how evaluation findings can add to the knowledge base for credibility and rationale for professional action. Positioning evaluation knowledge, no matter how small in scope, in contemporary peer-reviewed literature and/or resources, contributes supported practice wisdom to the body of professional knowledge.

Think about Grant-maker. Each funded project ostensibly was intended to address the same goal of increasing access to health care, but the projects all took diverse paths. Had each project conducted a sound, theory-based evaluation, the aggregate knowledge would have significantly contributed to professional literature and informed action in this domain of concern.

When to Review Information in Evaluation

Use of information can occur at any point in the evaluation practice process, following the initial identification of a problem. Keep in mind, however, that the use of information, in concert with the political nature of evaluation, is purposive.

Since the problem statement is fundamentally a value assertion, the potential exists for multiple and, sometimes, competing values to differentially shape the nature of problem statements for diverse stakeholder groups. As we have noted, what some might not consider a problem, others might see as an imminent deficit to be addressed (Pena et al., 2005). What evidence would one need in order to assert that resources ought to be directed to eliminate what we do not value and to produce what we do value? In our culture, authority and empirical evidence provide the most credible support for a position or value statement (Audi, 2002), and these sources are extracted from the corpus of information that is peer reviewed or generated by respected thinkers and experienced practitioners.

Those of you who have read and/or conducted naturalistic research may be familiar with the term *audit trail*. In the naturalistic tradition, an audit trail is the clear explication of both thinking and action processes (DePoy and Gitlin, 2005). That is to say, the naturalistic researcher provides the details of how method was conceptualized and implemented along with a clear explanation of what evidence was used, and how it was used to support and verify an inductive claim. Applying this concept to the information review element of evaluation practice means that the professional clearly identifies the nature of information reviewed, details how the information was organized, and demonstrates how knowledge was used to support a problem statement.

Consider the example of substance abuse prevention that we previously introduced. There are numerous theories defining "the problem" of substance abuse, positing its causes (Schuckit, 2006) and then identifying the appropriate prevention strategies (Arthur and Blitz, 2000). Values frame the literature support for all three. Just think of the multiple definitions of alcohol abuse. A recent article (Dorn *et al.*, 2007) suggested that women who drink one or two alcoholic drinks daily experience cardiac benefits from this practice, while the Centers for Disease Control and Prevention (2006) indicate that this amount of consumption fits within the parameters of excessive drinking. Neither perspective is correct or incorrect but each is supported with evidentiary claims. What the professional selects as the "problem" parameter, its causes, and its prevention, is value based and purposive. So if a professional defines daily alcohol abuse as problematic, and its causes residing in socialization (Berkowitz, 2003), the professional might look to the social milieu as the locus of preventive change. However, if daily alcohol intake is not considered to be problematic, but beneficial to cardiac health, the problem might be redefined to focus on cardiac illness and then the prevention approach would identify strategies to support moderate drinking for healthy hearts. The sound evaluation contains a literature-based audit trail, so to speak, in which the support for definitions, theories, claims, and approaches is transparent, cited, and clear.

In the needs assessment phase, information can be used fully, partially, or not at all to substantiate what is needed to resolve a problem. Moreover, the literature can provide model evaluation methods for needs assessment and subsequent thinking and action evaluation processes.

Consider the problem stated above. What is needed to resolve each problem could emerge from multiple sources including research literature, practice wisdom, marketing, and so forth. Just consider the power of marketing to support moderate daily consumption of alcohol.

Proceeding to goals and objectives, information can provide the guidance and rationale on why particular goals to structure activity were specified and others not addressed. In our example, without the recent support for moderate alcohol consumption (Dorn *et al.*, 2007) one might wonder why a substance abuse prevention effort was not aimed at reducing daily alcohol intake.

Professional activity can be fully, partially, or not informed by existing knowledge. In the presence of knowledge that is sound and describes successful professional activities that have resolved articulated problems, replication of the activity might be indicated. Consider social marketing as an example (Andreasen, 2006). It has been a well-supported prevention approach that has met with sufficient success to be encouraged for widespread use by the U.S. Substance Abuse and Mental Health Services Administration (n.d.).

In disagreement with, or in the absence of, formal knowledge supporting the value of specific professional approaches, the gap in knowledge calls for innovation. In such cases, reflexive action and assessing outcome would follow more exploratory strategies. For example, in our recent substance abuse prevention activity in a rural border area, urban prevention models to limit the availability of illegal drugs might not necessarily fit, given the large geographic distances and the proximity of the Canadian border. We, therefore, turned to a context-based exploration of how illegal drugs become available as well as accessible, and used this new knowledge as the basis for an innovative set of public health prevention strategies.

When implementing a previously tested strategy, professional experience and literature can identify what outcomes the professional can expect from which parts of an activity. Moreover, one's assessment inquiry might move beyond previously tested process and outcome to incrementally add to the professional knowledge. As example, consider the use of social marketing for prevention. Many of the outcomes of social marketing have been identified as productive in achieving substance abuse prevention goals (Underage Drinking Prevention and Social Marketing Project. West Virginia Prevention Resource Center, n.d.) and thus could be selected and tested using existing outcome inquiry approaches. However, new knowledge generated through further evaluation practice could potentially expand the use of social marketing in unexamined contexts.

Publication of evaluation assessment results examining why social marketing approaches did or did not accomplish stated goals would be important additions to the literature and could inform other professionals who are seeking to use social marketing in their practices.

Box 4.1 Steps in reviewing knowledge in evaluation practice

Step 1: Determine the purpose of the review

Step 2: Delimit the scope of the search

Step 3: Access databases, websites, and other comprehensive lists of relevant information

Step 4: Obtain relevant information

Step 5: Organize the information

Step 6: Critically evaluate the information

Step 7: Prepare a report of the information review

Mechanics of Information Review

With the explosion of information, approaching the multiple bodies of information can be a daunting action process. However, there are tricks of the trade, so to speak, to facilitate a systematic and comprehensive review process that is purposive, manageable, and even enjoyable. We begin with strategies to identify, delimit, critically examine, and use sources of knowledge in the evaluation practice process.

Box 4.1 presents the steps that can lead you through a well-executed and useful review of information.

Step 1: Determine the Purpose

As we have discussed above, attention to purpose and clear acknowledgment of the influence of purpose on the evaluation design, conduct, and use is a hallmark of evaluation practice. Thus, the purpose or purposes must be clearly identified to guide the professional in searching for and using sources of knowledge. Consider the potential purposes of the following example. Suppose you are concerned with reducing and eliminating the barriers to electronic obesity prevention information experienced by individuals with limited English literacy. Once the purpose is clarified, you will be able to delimit the search to guide when and how to approach the vast amount of literature and other important sources of information.

Step 2: Delimit the Scope of the Search

Once you have made a decision about the purpose and timing of the review, your next step involves setting parameters on what is relevant to search. After all, it is not feasible or reasonable to review every single topic that is somewhat related to your problem statement. Delimiting or setting boundaries to the search is an important yet difficult step. The boundaries you set must assure a purposive and rigorous review but one that is practical and not overwhelming (Bamberger *et al.*, 2006).

Delimiting the search begins with knowing what sources are available and what each source of knowledge is likely to provide. Consideration of time, use, and audience must be factors in determining what sources to search and ultimately use in one's thinking processes.

Of course, the library is the most traditional location of sources. The library at our university lists the search options and resources presented in Figure 4.1.

As you can see, libraries have moved from simple repositories of text-based material to global collections in multiple formats. They are no longer

Fogler Library – Resources

Find Books & more
URSUS (Books, CDs, Videos, Government Publications, etc,) -- MaineCat & Other Library Catalogs -- Unique Fogler Collections -- UMaine Authors -- New Materials -- Quick Reference

Find Articles & Journals
Articles on your topic: Indexes and Databases
Journals and newspapers by title: URSUS -- ejournals@umaine

Services and Forms
Renew Materials -- E-Reserves -- Interlibrary Loan -- Library Services -- Library Forms -- Faculty Services

Research Advice
Ask A Librarian -- Introduction to Library Research -- Subject Guides -- Course Guides -- Subject Specialists

About the Library
Hours -- Library Contacts -- Library Maps -- Library News -- More...

What's New

Figure 4.1 Library exemplar

Box 4.2 Our favorite web-browsers

- Explore the Internet—from the Library of Congress
- Google—uses text-matching techniques to find pages that are both important and relevant to your search
- Google Scholar—focuses its search engines on scholarly material
- Health Abstracts Online
- Study Web—comprehensive searchable categorized index with reviews of over 17,000 educational and reference websites
- Yahoo!—category-based web directory
- Opera—www.opera.com web browser and more

---

restricted to the resources that they own but have joined networks that allow users to obtain materials from any library in the physical or virtual world.

If you are not acquainted yet with the multiple browsers and search engines on the internet, refer to Box 4.2 above for those that we find most useful and comprehensive.

Box 4.3 identifies specific websites that we have used frequently in our own evaluation practice. They are general sites that are of interest to professionals and each has links to many other sites.

To limit your search to a reasonable time frame, you might want to use a search engine or browser that not only provides content direction but also rates sites for their quality on the parameters that you find important to your search. The lists in Boxes 4.2 and 4.3 only begin to scratch the surface of databases that you might find of general use.

We also want to call your attention to Dissertation Abstracts, a compendium of annotations of dissertations, as an excellent resource in uncovering comprehensive treatment of topics. Because the dissertation process requires a substantive coverage of knowledge, the author of the dissertation has already done much of the work that you would have to do to find such a comprehensive selection of sources.

Step 3: Access Databases and Websites

While so much information is currently available online, don't forget that the majority of scholarly and professional information is still found in peer-reviewed online and print journals and scholarly books from text and university presses. Our students often omit these sources since the internet

---

Box 4.3 Websites we use frequently

- State Health Statistics by Sex and Race
- U.S. Census Bureau
- CRISP (Computer Retrieval of Information on Scientific Projects)— searchable database of NIH grant opportunities, funded projects, and archived projects
- www.Business.com—search engine for business and marketing entities)
- www.acf/dhhs.gov—Department of Health and Human Services
- www.whitehouse.gov—accesses information on federal activities, legislation, and so forth
- www.Questia.com—online access to diverse scholarly journals, books, and articles

---

is readily available. For us, the joy of being in the library is an important determinant in our use of library sources. However, as we indicated above, in the twenty-first century the library expands way beyond the walls of a building, presenting sometimes too many options for reviewing information. To avoid or lessen confusion, three factors that can guide your selection of search tools are trial and error, personal preference for style and presentation, and content. Availability, of course, is the most important factor with time limitations also driving the choice that you make for search venues. We find it helpful and informative to take some time and browse the web browsers and other types of databases. Hands-on experience can help you learn efficiency techniques as well as identify your preferred search venues.

Step 4: Obtain Relevant Information

This step seems self-evident. However, we include it to remind you that there are numerous ways to obtain information, each with differing time and access requirements. Many professionals identify specific sources in the search process and then find that they are difficult to obtain in a timely fashion. For example, if your library or electronic book site does not have the book that you want to review, obtaining your resource through interlibrary loan can take up to two weeks or ordering a book available in electronic format can be very costly. The most readily available information exists on the internet. Increasingly, universities and websites such as Google are uploading and making full texts available. These instantaneous sources can be accessed and examined, downloaded to a computer, and/or printed. Whatever way you choose, do not forget to record the full citation immediately. We have had too many experiences of losing a citation in total or in part and then spending hours searching for it.

For a speedy perusal of relevant information in scholarly journals, abstracts and reviews of the literature can often give you a good overview. Of course, you cannot derive specific and detailed knowledge for critical review from either of these sources, but each can provide the lay of the land, so to speak. Accessing articles from print or online journals may require the use of a web browser such as Google Scholar or an on-site library visit, but you can often access the same journals online through general sites such as Questia or discipline-specific sites. Increasingly, many journal publishers are providing e-subscriptions with no print copy at all. For example, Common Ground Publishers (http://commongroundpublishing. com) produces international scholarship in electronic journals only. One can subscribe or purchase individual articles in their fields including, but not limited to, diversity, learning, humanities, and the arts.

Art, literature, journals, and so forth can be accessed on the web, in the library, or in numerous other arenas such as museums and stores.

Practice wisdom is another story. How to access professional experience, record what you have learned, and then use this knowledge in an organized fashion can take many forms. A few examples include consulting with colleagues, attending regular meetings and supervision, joining a web-based discussion group or listserve, reading blogs, and interviewing professionals who have the knowledge that you are seeking. As example, in evaluating the Healthy and Ready to Work National Center, we are obtaining rich and complex information about project activity and outcome through regular calls to project staff. Again, carefully and completely record the source of information, no matter how you obtain it.

Step 5: Organize the Information

There are an infinite number of "correct" ways to organize information for use. Common to all, however, are five basic elements of a review that provide guidelines: content, structure, author, venue, and date.

Content is the topical substance of the literature. In organizing literature to inform substance abuse prevention theory, we included literature on the topical areas of social norms, behavioral theory, community readiness, social marketing, law enforcement, and environmental approaches.

Structure refers to the way in which the content is approached and addressed. Typical forms include research articles, theory papers, relevant narrative, professional position papers, program and entity descriptions, legislative briefs, and other government documents. For example, looking at substance abuse prevention, we might compare geospatial maps of illegal drug use with statistical analysis to illustrate use patterns that are geographically located (Gilson and DePoy, 2007).

Author refers to who created and presented the knowledge. Typically, authors are researchers, academics, theoreticians, and professionals. However, once again, as evaluation grows and expands its scope, authors might be consumers, artists, etc., particularly as models of participatory evaluation are encouraged and espoused.

Venue refers to the vehicle through which the knowledge is made available to the public. As we noted above, these include scholarly journals and government documents, the internet, personal communication, presentations at local and national conferences, newsletters, newspapers, etc. Structure is limited only by creativity and purpose.

Date includes not only the time when the source was made public, but also when the source was developed and finalized, and, for internet sources, when the site was accessed. It is important to consider that most articles appear in scholarly journals two years following their submission. Thus the work that is presented in these journals is retrospective. E-journals provide more timely publication often only taking eight months to a year from submission to publication.

As we said, there are an infinite number of ways to approach information. Here we suggest charting as one strategy that we have found to be useful for many students, professionals, and researchers. In this approach, you select pertinent information from each source you review and record it in an organized fashion. You first need to determine which element (content, structure, venue, or date) is your primary organizer. Once you have done that task, you can begin the action process of organizing your information for use. The approach you choose should reflect the nature and purposes of your evaluation practice project. Charting knowledge will allow you to reflect on your sources as a whole and critically evaluate and identify the important points that support your purpose, evaluation design, and use.

Figure 4.2 illustrates a template chart in which topic is the primary organizer. Important concepts and constructs are identified and labeled across the top column. What each source then has to say about each of the important topical areas, how each is organized, date, venue, author, and critical comments are then recorded under each column. A concept/construct matrix, therefore, organizes information you have reviewed and evaluated by key concept/construct. Figure 4.2 displays an example of a

	Prevention theories	Prevention approaches	Current evaluative strategies	Evaluation findings
Date				
Venue				
Author/s				
Critical comments				

Figure 4.2 Topical template

concept matrix template for an information review which would be used by us to support substance abuse prevention social constructs to be evaluated.

This structure can be used for one or more sources and modified for personal preference. It is also possible to keep information organized in this or a similar fashion in a computer word processing program or electronic database.

Step 6: Critically Evaluating Information

Here we propose guiding questions to assist you in critically approaching and using knowledge. The questions in Box 4.4 are intended to guide your reading and comprehension of evaluation and research literature, theoretical literature, and professional resources. The questions in Box 4.5 are designed to prompt your evaluation of non-research literature. Using these questions to guide your thinking processes will provide an analytic structure through which to approach and judge the credibility and efficacy of diverse sources of knowledge.

As you can see, there are many questions to answer in order to critically review and use information and resources. While this element of evaluation practice might seem overwhelming for novices, and especially for those whose primary function is not inquiry, you will see that with experience and practice, critical review becomes natural and indispensable for all aspects of your professional activity.

Step 7: Preparing a Report of the Information Review

You have now searched, obtained, read, and organized your sources of knowledge. Finally, it is time to prepare a report. Again, what is reported

Box 4.4 Guidelines for analysis of research and evaluation sources

1. What is the nature of the problem statement? Is it clearly stated? Can it be addressed? Is the problem stated too narrowly to be remediated? Is the problem statement feasible, credible? What are the ethical dilemmas presented by the problem statement? Who owns the problem?

2. Does the needs statement address the problem? Is there sufficient and credible evidence to support the needs statement? Is the evidence systematically ascertained and revealed? Is the need one that specified professionals should address? Can address? Who is in need? What is the scope of the need?

3. Are the professional activity goal statements clear and well defined? Do they address the need and the problem? Fully, partially? Are they feasible? Are the goals consistent with the values of the profession? Can the accomplishment of the goals be evaluated? How?

4. Is reflexive implementation presented? How detailed? To what extent are formative data used to improve the professional activity?

5. Criticize the outcome assessment plan. Is the method appropriate to the assessment questions? Are the procedures ethical? What purpose for assessment does the method imply? Is the plan systematic and grounded in sound investigative procedures? What are the limitations of the method? How might these methodological limitations influence the findings? Has confidentiality been protected? Is the data collection plan valid? Trustworthy? Is there any evidence that instrumentation or assessment procedures are discriminatory?

6. Criticize findings. Are the author's conclusions believable? Who do they benefit? Was the problem addressed? If a needs assessment was conducted, was it sufficient to define need and to form the basis for the stipulated program goals? Were the goals met? Are there alternative explanations for the findings? What purpose can the findings serve?

Box 4.5 Questions to guide analysis of non-research resources

1. What types of claims or principles are being made, implied, and represented? How do these claims or principles inform, emerge from professional knowledge and activity? Who made the claims or proffered the principles and in what context?

2. What support is advanced for the claims and principles? To what extent is the support credible?

3. How do these resources inform problem and need? What are their limitations? What degree of reflexive action is presented and to what extent can it inform your thinking and action?

4. How are desired outcomes examined/asserted?

5. How current is the resource?

6. Who benefits by this information, representation? Who does not benefit?

7. What ethical dilemmas are elicited? What values? How consistent is this work with professional values and ethics?

---

and how the report is structured is dependent on the purposes of the evaluation and audiences with whom evaluation will be shared. For example, if an evaluation is designed to examine the outcome of public health prevention strategies relying on individual behavior change on specified health variables such as obesity, sources that illuminate individual behavior would be examined, particularly if the attribution of changes was identified as the professional action, and reporting might be prepared in multiple formats for funding sources, academics, students, and for health providers. However, if you are considering obesity prevention efforts to change marketing and nutrition signage through financial incentives, the resource review would look at the following:

1. extent to which and why business practices were changed;
2. the desired outcome of individual weight maintenance and nutrition.

Reporting would most likely be targeted to the policy and business arenas, with a clear discussion of the economic benefits and costs of the successful strategies.

So, as you seek, critically review, and apply information to your own professional thinking and action, attend to purpose, values, elements of the problems to be addressed, relevance to your aims, credibility, and feasibility for your purposes.

Main Points

1. While professional and research literature has been the primary credible information used to support evaluation, the use of multiple sources of knowledge has been increasingly discussed and recommended by educators, researchers, business professionals and technology experts, policy makers, and other professionals.
2. Review of information and sources are purposive.
3. Review of information and sources can occur at any time during evaluation practice.
4. Review of information and sources can occur through many different approaches, depending on purpose, timing, and available information resources.
5. Delimiting the scope of information and sources is a critical step as these resources continue to expand.
6. There are specific strategies and tools for conducting an information and resource search, and methods for organizing sources and preparing a report for multiple purposes and audiences.

Exercises

1. Using an example from your own professional activity, identify where a review of the literature and other relevant resources would be most useful in the evaluation practice model. Why?
2. Select a professional scenario and determine when and how literature, images, and other resources should be used to inform the activity.
3. From the information in #2, determine the nature and timing of, and delimiting factors for, literature and resource review. Why have you selected these?
4. Select a topic and conduct a literature and resource review, beginning with a clarification of your professional purpose through reporting to diverse interest groups.

NEED

Ascertaining Need: What Is Needed to Resolve All or Part of the Problem or Issue?

In this step of evaluation practice, one must clarify what is needed to resolve the problem, or part of the problem, that has been identified. Before exploring need in detail, let us revisit the distinction between problem and need. As we discussed in Chapter 4, a problem is a value statement about what is undesirable or in need of change. For a problem to be relevant to a professional group it must be within the boundaries and theoretical domains of each profession. For example, even though we would need to be conversant and knowledgeable about the recently posited genetic causes of substance abuse, diagnosing a medical condition would not fit within the professional knowledge base of public health, business, educational, and policy professionals. Thus, if presented with a medical "problem," these professionals would refer that "problem" to a biogenetic professional.

What is a Needs Statement?

Related to but different from a problem statement, a needs statement is a systematic, evidenced-based claim, linked to all or part of a problem, which specifies what conditions and actions are necessary to resolve the part of the problem to be addressed. Thus, the identification of need involves collecting and analyzing information such as assessment data, interview, images and artifacts, and so forth to ascertain what is necessary to resolve a problem.

Let us consider what could happen if need is not clarified and the professional moves from a problem immediately to an action. As professionals, we might assume that we know the needs of a population, group, or individual. Consider the following example from one of our research classes.

A study was initiated by two students to examine how adults with developmental disabilities wanted to be included in community recreation. The students had already worked with the local YMCA to develop fully inclusive events and programs. The students developed an interview schedule in which each respondent was presented with the community recreation options and was asked to rate the degree of interest and likelihood of attendance. Not even one of the respondents was interested in the inclusive programming. What should have happened here? Perhaps before assuming that adults with developmental disabilities would naturally want to be included in community events, the researchers should have asked. The two students immediately realized that they had made an assumption about need that was not accurate for the respondents. They, therefore, redesigned their study by initiating a focus group series, at which time they found that to their respondents, inclusion was frightening and unsafe. The respondents, therefore, developed activities to which they invited community members. They wanted to say who could and could not be included in their planned recreation (Ippoliti *et al.*, 1994).

In our recent work on substance abuse prevention infrastructure, one of the aims is the development of a credentialed prevention workforce. Yet, as we noted previously, the extent to which certified professionals have been, and could be, effective in reducing substance abuse has never been examined or systematically tested, shedding doubt on this strategy as one that is needed to reduce substance abuse.

At this stage of the evaluation practice sequence, one might already have information on which to formulate need or one may collect data in a systematic fashion to clearly delimit and identify need. A needs statement should specify who is (are) the target(s) of the problem, what changes are desired, what targets will change, the degree of change, and how one will recognize that the change has occurred. In evaluation practice, need must be based on systematically derived data that already are contained in the literature, in documentation, or in what is revealed in needs assessment inquiry. But why do we need empirical data in order to ascertain and support need? Can't we just ask without all the effort necessary to meet empirical standards? Not exactly. Besides the error of assuming without verifying one's hunches, as discussed above, it is important to acknowledge another issue.

Once again, we face the considerable disagreement in evaluation efforts regarding the extent to which empirical inquiry is or is not value neutral. Looking back to the diversity of evaluation theory presented in Chapter 1, you may remember the *fact–value* debate that not only underpins all research thinking, but poses dilemmas when multiple perspectives and stakeholders differ in their opinion of need. We do not purport to solve the philosophical dilemmas of the field. Rather, we suggest that empirical inquiry, no matter what position one takes in the fact–value argument, clarifies both the nature of evidence on which a claim or effort is based and the logical thinking trail, so to speak, of how evidence was used to support or determine a claim. Evidence and its interpretation are thus public. Given the clarity and capacity in empirical inquiry to follow knowledge derivation and use, can you see that an empirical needs statement holds within it the evidence base for what it claims or proffers? Thus from where the need emerged, who perceives it as a need, and who does not, are points that are clarified and on which informed action decisions can then be made.

Knowing why, how, who, what, and when about a need will help you determine if you think the evidence is compelling, convincing, and important enough to warrant a specific action. If you do believe that the need must be met, the empirical approach provides a structure through which you can develop goals and objectives that point to how you will know that the need has been successfully filled. Systematic inquiry may also reveal if planned action is what is needed to resolve the problem as stated.

Think about workforce development and what evidence might be compelling enough to direct fiscal resources to support this strategy as needed to prevent substance abuse. One set of evidence that might be used to support the need for training and credentialing is information on professional curricula requirements and the rationale for content. In writing a grant proposal to the National Institute on Alcohol Abuse and Alcoholism (NIAAA), we found that because they see so much substance abuse in their own practices, nursing accreditation standards require substance abuse and addictions prevention content (The National Organization of Nurse Practitioner Faculties, 2007).

In any needs assessment, formal inquiry strategies or previously and well-conducted studies comprise the knowledge base upon which professionals, scholars, researchers, policy makers, and funders can communicate about, and come to a well-documented consensus of, need. That is not to say that empirical understanding is the only way to determine need. Rather, as we asserted above, inquiry-based need provides the rigor, and through well-described, clear, logical steps shows how a claim or effort was derived and on what evidence the initiative is anchored. The use of research thinking and action therefore allows funding, policy, and professional decisions not only to be made on values (as would be the case if the problem statement solely were used for allocation decisions), but adds a set of evidence and thinking strategies to support the values as well as define a clear and rational direction for practice and expected outcome.

Consider the following example. How would Grant-maker be able to make funding decisions without empirical support for need? Grant-maker identified the problem to which each applicant responded. But, in order to convince Grant-maker that each proposed strategy was critically needed over other strategies, the task of the applicants was to provide a compelling rationale. Would you accept belief as a sound rationale? Or would you prefer a strong, organized, systematic evidentiary basis that presented the logic structure for a proposed need? For Grant-maker, empirical evidence was the common comparative denominator. The proposals that provided the most direct and rigorous support for need were those that were selected. Moreover, as we mentioned above, once need is empirically supported, it provides the foundation for magnitude of needed change and the guidance for approaches to ascertain if and how this degree of change has been accomplished.

Needs Assessment Thinking and Action

Now that we have discussed our conceptual approach to empirical needs statement, let us turn to needs assessment thinking and action. How do we develop and use empirically based need in evaluation practice? If you were a public health professional, you might look to epidemiological data to identify high substance consumption and consequences. However, two trends in data for geographically situated public health prevention actions are operative. First, given the huge amount of information, how do you decide how to identify and delimit the evidence you are going to collect to examine or determine need? And second, what if the data sets do not provide the information that you need? In our work, we have seen both. The State Epidemiological Work Group in our state has been grappling with the multiple data sets that exist coupled with the dearth of data that are local enough to provide needs data for rural geographies that are both sufficient and confidential.

So how do you decide how to proceed? First, you would consider the context in which you plan to conduct your professional activity. While we were looking for needs data to inform statewide substance abuse prevention, we were only able to access a rigorous data set that was generated on school-age youth. Because these data were local and generated through sound methodological processes that allowed comparisons, we made the decision to use these data as proxies, or approximations, of comparative local substance abuse magnitude. Given the standard nature of the data, we were able to import the numbers into geostatistical mapping software (GIS—Geographic Information Systems) for visual comparisons of alcohol consumption rates. If, however, you were in law enforcement, you might want to look at the alcohol and illegal drug outlets as the context for need and thus you would seek other data. You might also examine crime and individual harm consequences of substance abuse reflected in hospital admissions and car crash data.

So your professional context and function would help you delimit what evidence to amass. Consider the factor of time as well. If you had only three weeks in which to obtain and analyze data, you would certainly not obtain the same magnitude of information that you would seek if you had unlimited time. Thus, both the public health professional and law enforcement professional would seek existing data sets rather than creating new ones or approaching existing data with time-consuming analytic strategies such as GIS mapping.

Third, the purpose of your intervention would certainly be a factor in your choice of evidence. If your purpose was informing efforts to limit access to illegal substances, you would most likely generate data to identify outlets and opportunities to obtain drugs and alcohol. In our work, we looked beyond geographically located access to virtual opportunities for drug and alcohol seekers.

As we have asserted, evaluation practice thinking and action provide the logical meta-framework for professional decision making. Using this framework, we suggest that there are three important questions to answer in choosing needs assessment action strategies:

1. What is known about a need?
2. What else needs to be known and how?
3. What limitations are imposed on needs assessment by resources and time?

The answer to each of these questions requires specific attention and will lead the professional to sound decisions about how to design and conduct needs assessment.

Let us examine how to respond to each question.

What is Known About a Need?

To ascertain what is already known about need, a comprehensive information review is indicated. As we discussed in Chapter 4, reviewing information is a large task that must be approached both practically and systematically. Different from other forms of information review, this task in the needs assessment action step must be purposive and delimited to the scope of the problem that has been identified in the thinking step of problem definition. Not only does the professional need to consider the general knowledge about need, but, in this step, must look at the existing nature of knowledge about the specified need (including the level of theory development, explicit and implicit value base, and the methods used to generate the knowledge), the degree to which this knowledge is relevant to the purpose of the needs assessment, and the extent to which the knowledge is applicable to the target(s) of change. Let us examine each of these components in detail now.

A major consideration in the nature of knowledge is the level of theory development explicated in literature. Consistent with the research literature (Anastas and MacDonald, 1994; Rubin and Babbie, 2004), we identify three primary levels of empirical knowledge: (a) descriptive, (b) relational, and (c) causal/predictive. These levels are anchored on research thinking and action in both naturalistic and experimental-type inquiry (DePoy and Gitlin, 2005) and on a set of value-driven thinking and action processes. We have discussed values in detail in Chapters 1 and 2. At this point, however, we also highlight that values not only guide knowledge content, but also influence the methods that a professional selects to assess and generate knowledge. As we discuss the action processes of needs assessment, be on the lookout for values that are implicit in each methodological approach. Now, we turn to levels of theory development to clarify their relevance to needs assessment.

The descriptive level of knowledge provides an understanding, illumination, and detailing of a phenomenon (Mertens, 2005). The essential characteristics, examples, non-examples, and borderline cases of the phenomenon emerge from a descriptive process. From empirical description, what the phenomenon "is" and what it "is not" should be clear (Wilson, 2006). What is and what is not needed, therefore, can be clarified and understood. As we will discuss in detail later in the chapter, descriptive knowledge can be produced by naturalistic and experimental-type inquiry or by a combination of both.

Consider some of the issues with evidence-based substance abuse practice. The primary and valued methods in evidence-based approaches rely on nomothetic (group) analyses that use deductive logic structures. We recently attended a presentation that detailed the How to Cope Program, an educational intervention to teach families of alcohol abusers to eliminate the disruptive effects of alcohol abuse on their own lives (Evans *et al.*, 2007). This evidence-based intervention was developed in an urban area and involves regular meetings of family members in a specific location. And while it is viable for urban settings, convening sufficient numbers of family members in rural areas was not successful. To ascertain how to implement the principles of this program in diverse geographies, and to learn more about the nuances of the program, the provider/evaluators decided to integrate naturalistic interview methods with experimental-type needs assessment.

What naturalistic-type inquiry will give us that experimental-type inquiry may not is a sense of the unique needs of individuals, groups, and communities. So, in the case of rural environments, desirable meeting venues were identified as web-based because of the difficulty in regularly commuting long distances to attend the program.

Once a phenomenon is described, its relational context can be ascertained. This type of knowledge is called relational knowledge. What factors are present and/or change as the phenomenon appears and changes? How strongly are two or more factors associated? What is the direction of the association? What is the web of association? This level of knowledge begins the process of expanding understanding beyond knowing "what" something is to knowing "how" something relates to, or is embedded in, something else. Thus, an understanding of need moves beyond a unitary lens to begin to construct how need is distributed, related to other needs, embedded in contextual factors, and ranked in priority. Moreover, understanding how phenomena relate to one another might shed light on how each will change as specific needs are met and addressed.

For example, in efforts to decrease disparities to obesity prevention resources and entities, we explored the factors that were related to limited access. This inquiry was extremely valuable in that we found that the digital divide (or disparities in computer ownership) was not an issue in our area, but rather digital inequality (disparities in access to, and comprehension of, web-based information), a more complex set of barriers, was associated with access barriers. Had we assumed that disparities in computer ownership needed to be eliminated, we would have missed the key need, reducing digital inequality.

Typically, experimental-type research has been used to examine relationships, based on the notion that in order to relate something to something else, both "somethings" must be clearly understood. However, as naturalistic traditions become more widely valued in evaluation research, these methods too can reveal important and complex relationships that may be overlooked with deductive approaches. Of particular note is the value of naturalistic inquiry in explicating the natural setting, as is often the case in evaluation practice. One caution about relational knowledge is in order. "Association is not causation" is a phrase that we have often heard and too frequently do not heed. When we ascertain association and context, we cannot determine predictive or causal inferences without appropriate methodological action processes. We will examine the causal/predictive level of knowledge and strategies to elicit it more fully later in the text.

In our example of digital inequality, we were able not only to identify digital inequality as the key trend that needed to be reduced, but we used multiple experimental and naturalistic methods to further elucidate the nature of the inequality and associate it with possible remedial options.

Causal/predictive knowledge answers the question of "why?" Once we accept that phenomena are related, we then might want to look at explanations for cause as a basis for further understanding need and positing goals that address the "why" rather than the "what" or "how" of a need. If we look at the body of knowledge through which causal relationships are examined, we note that true experimental design is the most widely accepted and valued method of supporting causal claims (DePoy and Gitlin, 2005). However, as we will see later in the text, naturalistic strategies can also be used to induce understandings of cause within natural settings (Patton, 2001). Consider the example above. Because of their conceptual distance from one another, it is not likely that an experimental design itself would be able to support a direct causal relationship between digital inequality and maintenance of substance abuse levels. However, through naturalistic inquiry, we were able to develop a contextual understanding of the following causal relationships: (a) access to prevention knowledge contributes to healthy decision making; (b) limited access to information does not provide individuals with information on which to make informed substance use decisions; and (c) limited access to information in our rural state is caused by limited English literacy and inability to comprehend electronic information (Gilson and DePoy, 2007).

Equally important as content is the relevance of knowledge to the specific part of the problem that you have delimited. Does the existing knowledge describe your domain of concern, apply to the population who owns, identifies, or is concerned with the problem, address policy, resource, and issues that you are addressing? The thinking strategy of identifying the boundaries of your evaluation, and the extent to which existing knowledge informs need within those boundaries, is a critical step in needs assessment. Let us look at an example to clarify this important point through the HRTW program that we have previously discussed.

The federal government identified the difficulty of transition to adulthood for adolescents with special health care needs as a problem warranting attention (Institute for Child Health Policy, n.d.). Specifically, the problem was narrowed to the disproportionate numbers of adolescents who leave secondary education unprepared to maintain their health and/or to earn a sufficient living. From a comprehensive review of the literature, it was clear that the existing knowledge about adolescent transition, their experiences, and their service needs, was generated primarily from the perspective of providers and educators. Given that the existing supports and services were developed on that knowledge base and were deemed to be fragmented and in need of significant revision, it became obvious that using the current body of literature would not be useful in informing systems change efforts, with the exception of providing a non-example of what should be done. Thus, while a large body of knowledge existed on adolescent transition, it was not relevant to the scope of the change effort. A comprehensive, mixed-method needs assessment was therefore undertaken with particular emphasis on giving voice to adolescents. The findings of the needs assessment were so far afield from the needs identified in the professional literature that the dilemma on how to resolve the disparity continues to be debated (DePoy and Gilmer, 2000).

The example given above not only demonstrates the principle of relevance, but also addresses the issue of who is the target population. If the target is the adolescent, then the existing literature had no use in informing adolescent need. However, the literature did inform us about provider perspective and could have been a useful rationale for provider-centered systems change. However, given that the problem as identified related to adolescent capability and preparation for transition, suggesting that current services and supports were not achieving desirable outcomes, it made sense to ask adolescents themselves to articulate their needs as a basis for systemic revision (Hartman *et al.*, 2000).

This point leads us to the second thinking strategy guiding needs assessment, that of what else in addition to the literature needs to be known and how?

What Else Needs to be Known and How?

As illustrated in our example above, the literature does not always provide the empirical foundation on which to assess need. Based on what the literature does not tell us, we then formulate a strategy to determine what we must know and how we can come to know it.

The following guiding questions, when answered, will equip the professional with the necessary information to move on to the next step in our evaluation practice model, setting goals and objectives:

1. What about the existing literature is inadequate to inform need?
2. What level of information is needed?
3. What source(s) of information should be consulted?
4. How should these sources be approached?

Let us look at an example to illustrate how answering each of these questions thoughtfully and systematically defines the direction and scope of the needs assessment.

Let us revisit the HRTW example. Clearly, the perspectives of the youth and their families were missing from the literature. In order to create "buy-in" from those who would be affected by a professional programmatic entity it became clear to us that the opinions and experiences of the youth and their families were critically needed. So the level of information that was needed was complex. Descriptive information was insufficient to make desired changes. We had to know what caused the current level and maintenance of the "problem" of youth dependence on public support. The sources that were consulted were the youth and families, and they were approached not only to answer questions posed by professionals but to work in a participatory evaluation model to guide and conduct the needs assessment.

What Limitations are Imposed on Needs Assessment by Resources and Time?

As you might be thinking, the type of needs assessment that we outlined does seem time consuming and, perhaps, expensive. A professional might even be wondering about the costs not only of conducting the needs assessment but of then implementing what is identified as need. So what does one do when it is apparent that comprehensive needs assessment will be cost efficient in the long run to reduce the likelihood of intervention failure, but immediate resources are limited? You might want to think about the types of inquiry that are least resource consuming but most productive. Several examples from the HRTW initiative included survey, key informant interview, and group interview. We will examine these strategies later in the text.

Main Points

1. There is a distinction between problem and need that is critical to acknowledge in evaluation practice.
2. Since inquiry-based need shows how a claim was derived and on what evidence the claim is anchored, this approach to asserting need supports value-based development of professional efforts, while defining a clear and rational direction for practice and expected outcome.
3. The three critical questions to answer in order to examine need are: (a) What is known about a need? (b) What else needs to be known and how? and (c) What limitations are imposed on needs assessment by resources and time?

Exercises

1. From the literature, select a "problem" which is clear and delimited as relevant to your field. Pose three different needs statements and identify which part of your problem they address.

2. For each needs statement, examine the literature and determine if there is sufficient empirical evidence to support the need as you have stated it.

3. Select two needs assessment articles from scholarly literature and resources; one conducted through experimental-type design and one through naturalistic inquiry. Compare and contrast the articles on the following: (a) What scope of need is supported? (b) Who defines the need? (c) Who is the target? and (d) What needs to be changed and how?

NEED

Examining Need with Previously Supported Approaches: Designing Experimental-Type Inquiry

Now that we have conceptually analyzed the distinction between problem and need and have examined the thinking processes related to the nature of knowledge, planning, conducting, and reporting of need, let us turn our attention to the action processes for conducting a needs assessment. Selection of evaluation design, as we have discussed, is based on purpose, scope, and current knowledge related to the problem or domain of professional concern. As we discussed in the previous chapter, if existing and sound evidence does not provide the empirical foundation on which to develop a clear and comprehensive statement of need, professionals need to engage in the action process of data collection and analysis. At the other end of the spectrum, if sufficient theory and practice literature are available and relevant to the problem statement, then the professionals might choose action strategies that are founded on the viability of previously supported efforts and measurement. Each condition provides the rationale for methodological selection. Situations that fall in between the two extremes direct our attention to needs assessment action processes that might make use of multiple research traditions. These are based on abductive logic structures, such as those that include both a naturalistic and experimental-type component.

When to Use Experimental-Type Design in Needs Assessment

When sufficient literature exists to provide a theoretical direction for professional action, the professional has several action choices. From the literature, goals and objectives for initiatives and entities can be developed directly without any active data collection and analysis. This action strategy is particularly useful when time and resources are limited and the literature provides a sound and comprehensive foundation for development.

Consider an example from an entity created to reduce youth tobacco use. Biglan *et al.* (2007) extrapolated a strategy from marketing literature to shape the entity and evaluation of an anti-tobacco approach. They reasoned that the branding literature demonstrating the success in influencing people to purchase certain cigarette brands over others was compelling and thus could be used to shape anti-smoking behavior as well. Based on this approach, they identified the "needed" anti-smoking brand entities with which youth would identify.

Thus, as illustrated by Biglan *et al.* (2007), if an action has been successful in achieving its outcome in similar populations or domains, but the professional needs additional evidence to ascertain the degree to which the current knowledge fully informs the scope of a specific problem, needs assessment research strategies relying on deductive, experimental-type traditions are indicated. These designs, also called nomothetic and quantitative approaches (Babbie, 2001), reveal characteristics of groups, not uniqueness of individuals. These strategies are deductive in that they begin with existing theory and seek, through measurement, to verify or falsify the theory.

Let us now turn to a discussion of experimental-type design in the needs assessment phase of evaluation practice. Because of its wide acceptance and ease in illustrating the structure of deductive approaches to research, we use the notation system developed by Campbell and Stanley (1963).

Campbell and Stanley used the following symbols to diagram design: X for independent variable, O for dependent variable, and R for random sample selection. We also find it very helpful to use the symbol r to refer to random group assignment. We will address "r" later in the book when we discuss outcome studies, since needs assessment most frequently does not involve random assignment. This is the case because needs assessment is primarily conducted at one interval with one or more groups selected for their inherent characteristics such as gender, ethnicity, geographic location, ability, diagnosis, marketing segment, or other characteristics which distinguish groups from one another. For example, the anti-smoking branding entity distinguished youth by age groupings.

Random sample selection, denoted by uppercase R, is used in needs assessment research primarily when a population is too large to be fully included in inquiry. As example, random sampling is often used to inform large social marketing efforts to change health behavior (Andreasen, 2006).

In order to fully understand the logic of frequently used quantitative needs assessment approaches, we first need to look at true experimental design as the gold standard, so to speak, of experimental-type inquiry. This type of design is most desired in evidence-based approaches that are promoted by federal agencies in the U.S. and even worldwide agencies such as the World Bank (2007), which recently identified evidence-based approaches as the most desirable support for global alcohol abuse prevention.

As we indicated above, true experimentation does not serve needs assessment purposes, but quantitative designs which answer needs questions are founded on the rigor criteria of true experimental design. More likely, true experimental designs are used in outcome assessment, so when we discuss that phase of evaluation practice, we will illustrate the application of true experimental design in our evaluation model. Below, we describe and discuss the logic of true experimentation as a basis for our subsequent discussion of needs assessment designs relying on the logic of experimental-type methods. For detail on these designs there are many excellent research methods texts in diverse fields of study (Babbie, 2007; Cozby, 2006; DePoy and Gitlin, 2005; Schindler and Cooper, 2005).

True Experimental Design

R   O   X   O
R   O   O

The true experimental design is, perhaps, the design best known by beginning researchers and laypersons. True experimental design refers to the classic two-group design in which subjects are randomly selected and randomly assigned (R) to either an experimental or control group condition. The experimental condition (also called the independent variable) is manipulated by the investigator, usually by being present or absent. (Refer to glossary for definitions of variable, independent variable, and dependent variable). The control condition is defined as the absence of the independent variable. Before the experimental condition, all subjects are pre-tested or observed on a measure of the dependent variable (O). A dependent variable is the phenomenon that is expected to change in response to the independent variable. In the experimental group, the independent variable or experimental condition is imposed (X), and it is withheld in the control group. Subjects are then post-tested or observed on the dependent variable (O) after the experimental condition.

In this design, the investigator expects that all subjects will perform in an equivalent manner on the pre-test and thus no difference between the experimental and control groups on the dependent measure should be seen at the time of pre-test. The rationale for this expectation lies in the reasoning of probability sampling and assignment in which subjects are chosen randomly from a larger pool of potential subjects and then assigned to a group on a chance-determined basis. Random in this sense does not mean haphazard. Rather, randomization means that all individuals in the population studied (or other units of analysis) have an equivalent chance of being selected for a study sample. It is also expected that the control group, on post-test, will perform similarly to both pre-test groups since nothing has been done to change the group. However, the experimental group is expected to change on post-test because of the influence of the experimental condition.

As a result of random assignment, control, and manipulation, ostensibly the only possible cause of the change in the experimental group is the experimental condition (X). Bias (unplanned influence that confounds the outcome of a study) is therefore theoretically reduced and/or eliminated to the extent possible with true experimentation.

Note this important assumption. Because probability theory is the basis for many statistical procedures, the violation of probability through non-random sampling (that is so characteristic of evaluation inquiry) is one of the criticisms of evaluation research.

Let us look in more detail at the foundations of true experimentation and why this design is held as the ideal within experimental-type approaches to inquiry as well as within the domain of evidence-based practices (Aikenhead, 2005).

There are three major characteristics of the "true experiment": (a) randomization, (b) control, and (c) manipulation. All are designed to reduce bias.

Randomization

As we indicated, randomization is the process of selecting and/or assigning units of analysis based exclusively on chance. Theoretically, each unit of analysis not only has an equal chance of being selected in the case of random selection, and assigned in the case of random group assignment, but also has an equal chance of being exposed to all influences affecting all other units of analysis. An observed change in the experimental group at post-test time, then, can be attributed with a reasonable degree of certainty to the experimental condition.

If random sample selection is accomplished, the design notation appears as it was presented earlier (R). If randomization occurs only at the group assignment phase, the notation looks like:

```
r    O    X    O
r    O         O
```

As we indicated above, design using random assignment only does not allow for generalization of the results to a population from which a sample was selected, but it is very common in the outcome assessment of evaluation practice to reveal causal relationships within the sample itself.

Randomization is a powerful technique that is intended to increase control and eliminate bias by neutralizing the effects of extraneous influences on the outcome of a study. Without random assignment of subjects, you would not have a true experimental design and thus could not make a causal claim between the independent and dependent variable.

Consider this example. You have been given the task of determining strategies to meet the growing need for public health professionals in the field of gerontology. You establish an innovative educational program to recruit high school students into the profession of public health. To assure that this strategy will produce recruits, you randomly select high schools in two groups, one that would serve as the experimental group of schools and one as the control. Over the next six months you recruit more than 10 percent of your experimental group, but only 3 percent of the students in the control group decide to enroll in public health education. You conclude that your innovative recruitment program is a success. Without random assignment, there is no way to ascertain if the experimental and control groups are equivalent and are theoretically exposed to identical conditions, such that the only cause for change could be the independent variable. Because the two groups were assigned randomly to the innovative recruitment and control condition, the potential for sampling bias (a confounding influence resulting from characteristics of the sample that are not controlled) is eliminated.

Control

Control is a set of processes to eliminate sampling or experimental bias. In true experimentation, the investigator, therefore, uses a control group, one that has not been subjected to the experimental condition, to see what the sample would be like without the influence of the experimental condition or independent variable. A control group is expected to theoretically test the same throughout the experiment since it has not had the chance of being exposed to the experimental condition. Therefore, the control group represents the characteristics of the experimental group before being changed by participation in the experimental condition.

Manipulation

In the true experimental design, the independent variable is manipulated by either having it present (in the experimental group) or absent (in the control group). It is the ability to provide and withhold the independent variable that is unique to the true experiment.

As we indicated, we have discussed true experimentation so that you can understand the foundation thinking processes of all experimental-type inquiry. We remind you, however, that true experimental design is rarely appropriate for use in needs assessment inquiry. Let us now look at designs based on experimental-type logic structures that serve needs assessment questions.

In most needs assessment, the professional is interested in answering the following important questions: (a) What is needed to resolve the scope of the problem? (b) According to whom? and (c) What is expected to occur as a result of needs being met?

The professional using experimental-type design is, therefore, looking for descriptive through predictive value-based information that empirically points to specific actions and their desired outcomes. Moreover, the professional might expect that the responses to needs assessment questioning could differ according to who provides the empirical information.

But why use experimental-type design here rather than open-ended questioning? Indications for using experimental-type needs assessment inquiry are presented in Box 6.1.

Let us take a closer look at the reasons to employ experimental-type needs assessment listed in Box 6.1. As we have indicated, experimental-

---

Box 6.1 When to use experimental-type design in needs assessment

Use experimental-type needs assessment when:

1. You already are comfortable with knowing the universe of need

2. You are limited to professional actions and entities which fulfill delimited, predefined needs

3. You are looking for selection preferences to guide your activity and its outcomes

4. You are attempting to provide the most compelling evidence of need in order to garner resources

5. You have sufficient theory to predict the likelihood of success with given approaches

type designs are based on the philosophical foundation of monism, or the existence of a single truth, and the assertion that pre-existing knowledge and theory developed and verified through these experimental-type methods test, falsify, or verify that truth. If you already feel that you know the full scope of successful approaches for problem resolution, then needs assessment actually becomes a selection process. That is to say, of the scope of known options, using experimental-type strategies illuminates the most preferred or supported approach and its expected or predicted results. Using experimental-type needs assessment, therefore, assumes that the professional already knows the nature of need but is looking for verification, clarity, delimitation, and expected outcomes from the universe of activities, programs, and/or entities that have already been theoretically and empirically verified in other situations.

Experimental-type needs assessment is also used in situations where, even if the need might expand beyond the options given, these approaches could not be provided. Moreover, the use of quantitative verification of need and outcome is well accepted as evidence and can be compelling in obtaining resources to implement actions.

Finally, experimental-type needs assessment clearly creates an empirical path to the development, possible prediction, and ultimate measurement of expected outcomes.

To illustrate, let us consider obesity. Given the obesity epidemic in the U.S., there has been an increase in efforts to identify behavioral programs to reduce overweight and obesity (Flegal *et al.*, 2004). To examine the need for tailoring programs to residents of diverse geographic locations, experimental-type needs assessment research has been conducted (Ford *et al.*, 2005). We have used the epidemiological findings that revealed disproportionately high rates of overweight and obesity in rural areas, and GIS maps illustrating the limited opportunities for walking, as the partial basis for a grant application to support a rural obesity and overweight public health approach in our state.

In most cases, experimental-type needs assessment designs fall into Campbell and Stanley's (1963) category of non-experimental designs. The survey discussed above would be an example of a non-experimental survey design. Let us look at some non-experimental designs that are frequently used in needs assessment.

Non-Experimental Designs

These designs, based on the logic of probability, are those in which the criteria for true experimental design (random selection, control, and manipulation) cannot be met. Non-experimental approaches can range in use from exploration to prediction and are most useful when measuring a concept, construct, or relationship among constructs. For the most part, non-experimental designs examine naturally occurring phenomena and describe or examine relationships. Any manipulation of variables is done post hoc (after the occurrence of the phenomenon) through statistical analysis (see Appendix for a review of data analytic techniques).

The designs that are most frequently used in needs assessment are:

1. surveys;
2. passive observation;
3. ex post facto designs.

Survey

Survey designs are used primarily to measure characteristics of a population (Friis and Sellers, 2003), including their knowledge, opinions, and attitudes (Buckingham and Saunders, 2004; Sapsford, 2006). Through survey design it is possible not only to describe population parameters but to predict relationships among those characteristics as well. Questions are posed through mailed questionnaires, online surveys, or telephone or face-to-face interviews. The obesity research conducted by Ford *et al.* (2005) is an example. In their work, they compared obesity and overweight rates in diverse geographic areas.

Passive Observation

Passive observation designs are used to examine phenomena as they naturally occur and to discern the relationship between two or more variables. Often referred to as "correlational designs," passive observation can be as simple as examining the relationship between two variables, for example, height and weight, or can be as complex as predicting scores on one or more variables from knowledge of scores on other variables. As in the case of the survey, variables are not manipulated but are measured and then examined for relationships and patterns of prediction.

In the past decade, mapping has become increasingly popular in research. Although not typically categorized as a passive observation approach, we locate mapping through geographic information systems (GIS) software under this rubric in that it can capture, depict, and relate multiple characteristics of a defined space (Steinberg and Steinberg, 2005). GIS methods utilize specialized software for "capturing, managing, analyzing, and displaying all forms of geographically referenced information" (ESRI, 2007). We have used GIS for what we refer to as concrete and abstract elements of a space. By concrete we mean the observable characteristics, such as population density, locations of community resources, and so forth.

Abstracts that can be mapped include such constructs as policies that shape marketing, public health approaches, distribution of resources, and even spatially situated attitudes (Gilson and DePoy, 2007).

Ex Post Facto Designs

Ex post facto designs are considered to be one type of passive observation design. However, in ex post facto design (literally translated as after the fact), the phenomena of interest have already occurred and cannot be manipulated in any way. Ex post facto designs are frequently used to examine relationships between naturally occurring population parameters and specific variables. Within this group of designs are needs assessment action processes relying on secondary data analysis. Let us look at examples to illustrate.

Revisiting the obesity project, obesity and overweight rates that are measured have already occurred. While the goal is to change these variables, what was assessed by Ford et al. (2005) is a "slice-in-time" retrospective look at the weight of residents in geographic areas. Moreover, policies and walking opportunities were mapped as they existed to inform areas for targeted desired change.

Thinking Process of Experimental-Type Design Selection in Needs Assessment

As you can see, needs assessment findings generated from experimental-type designs provide the numeric data not only on which to describe a need, but to compare perceived needs among diverse populations and to provide a clear empirical foundation for expected and/or predicted outcomes of an action.

Now that you are aware of experimental-type design structures and techniques typically used in needs assessment, you still might wonder how to select a design to fit your particular purpose and questions. Begin by asking yourself the following important guiding questions presented in Box 6.2.

If you are able to answer each of the questions in Box 6.2 comprehensively and thoughtfully, you can begin to have confidence in your needs assessment approach and its capacity to meet its purpose. However, one critical question remains: does the design answer the needs assessment question(s)and meet the purpose?

This question gets to the heart of rigor in inquiry. Within experimental-type design, validity and reliability are the two criteria on which the soundness of your design can be judged.

Box 6.2 Guiding questions in the selection of experimental-type needs assessment design

- What purpose does the needs assessment serve? Why am I doing it? What is (are) my question(s)?
- Is the design consistent with the limitations of the professional arena?
- Does the design yield information sufficient for articulating goals, objectives, and expected outcomes of an action or entity?
- What are some of the ethical and field limitations that influence the design?

Validity refers, in general, to the extent to which the action processes of an inquiry are consistent with the conceptual thinking processes. In other words, does the design answer the needs assessment question? In order for you to be able to judge validity, you must have clear questions in which you specify the concepts to be investigated and the scope of the investigation.

Consider this example. The public health professional working with obesity and overweight programming is examining what nutrition information and opportunities for physical activity within one's daily activities need to be developed. The following needs assessment questions are posed in scenario #1:

a. What barriers to nutrition information need to be reduced or removed?
b. What barriers to physical activity within daily activities need to be removed or reduced?

As stated, these needs assessment questions are vague. What is the scope of the environment, nature of barriers, and barriers for whom? The public health professional develops a needs assessment relying on online survey and distributes it to health providers in a rural county. In the survey, s/he lists a series of barriers that emerge from the literature and that might be present in rural areas. Does this approach answer the needs assessment question? It is impossible to know because the questions are too broad.

Now consider the wording of the questions below in scenario #2:

a. What do public health personnel currently employed in the local health department articulate as barriers to nutrition information?

b. According to adults who are employed in full- and part-time remunerative jobs in the specified rural location, what barriers to physical activity during one's day exist?

In the revised questions, you see two important changes from the questions in scenario #1: the clarification of exactly what knowledge is being sought and who is providing it. Thus, two validity concerns are resolved: internal and external validity.

Internal validity assesses the extent to which the planned approach to collecting and analyzing information answers the needs assessment question. In these scenarios, one would look at the instrumentation to see if it measures the construct of "articulated barriers to nutrition and physical activity" stated in the question. Moreover, how the information was sought and what might interfere with accurate responses would be considered. For example, suppose there is a new building being constructed and the construction site is temporarily interfering with the walking opportunities for those who work at a particular factory in town? Administering the survey under these conditions would certainly create a challenge to the long-term validity of the responses.

External validity, as suggested by the term, is concerned with the extent to which the findings of an inquiry are relevant beyond the inquiry itself. Specifically, the relationship between the population and the sample is addressed. By population, we mean the group of people (or other units of analysis) that are delimited by the investigator. A sample refers to a smaller number of people or units of analysis selected from those in the population named by the inquirer.

To ascertain external validity or extent to which what has been found in the sample is accurate for the population from which the sample was selected, the population must be specified in the question. In scenario #1 above, there was no population specified and thus external validity cannot be judged. However, in scenario #2, the populations were named and the extent to which the sample represented the populations could be ascertained.

The second criterion for rigor is reliability. Reliability is defined as the stability of an inquiry approach. Clearly developing, following, and articulating procedures for the inquiry enhance reliability, along with using measures that provide stable and consistent data. If you read a study that you can easily replicate, the likelihood is that the investigators were concerned with reliability. To improve the reliability of the needs assessment conducted in scenarios # 1 and 2, carefully detailed procedures in the administration of the surveys would be indicated with a survey that was well constructed. We address survey construction in the next chapter.

Validity and reliability are essential in needs assessment. Many evaluations have been severely criticized for lack of attention to these criteria. In our opinion, attention to rigor is not only important but is the only way to conduct ethical inquiry. If we don't attend to excellence in revealing need for professional effort, professionals might implement activities that do not remediate the problems with which we are concerned.

Main Points

1. Experimental-type design is indicated for needs assessment when looking at the needs of a group, rather than the needs of an individual.
2. Deductive logic underpins all experimental-type inquiry.
3. Experimental-type designs are based on probability theory.
4. True experimental design, while not appropriate for needs assessment, is the standard of excellence for experimental-type design and therefore must be understood if other experimental-type approaches are to be rigorously implemented.
5. Measurement is the foundation of experimental-type tradition.
6. Validity and reliability are the two primary criteria on which to judge the rigor of experimental-type inquiry.

Exercises

Select an experimental-type needs assessment journal article and answer the following questions about it:

1. What type of needs assessment questions are being answered; descriptive, relational, causal/predictive?
2. To what extent does the literature support the use of experimental-type design? Give evidence for your answer.
3. Discuss the rigor of the design approach (validity and reliability).
4. You are a public health professional in a rural community in which obesity is disproportionately high. Consider how you would go about designing an experimental-type needs assessment to inform your approach. Who would you include in your population and why? How would you design your inquiry and why?

NEED

CHAPTER 7

Obtaining Information in Experimental-Type Needs Assessment

As we indicated in Chapter 6, the primary method of obtaining information in experimental-type design is measurement. Here we define measurement as the translation of observations into numbers. This action process creates variables from lexical concepts (operationalization) that then are ordered and examined. Through measurement, concepts (defined as abstractions of observed or experienced phenomena) can be reduced into their basic elements or indicators and benchmarks, quantified, and empirically examined. Thus, measurement involves both conceptual and operational or empirical considerations.

These considerations fall into two basic categories: content and structure.

Content

By content, we mean the lexical definitions, the limits of concepts to be measured, and the relationships to be examined. By this time, we are sure that you know that the purpose and practical constraints are important determinants of the content of instrumentation in evaluation. The thinking process of delimiting content involves a careful and clear analysis of the concept(s) to be measured and what one wants to know about the concept. The questions in Box 7.1, extracted from philosophical language analysis techniques (Wilson, 1963), should be answered in order to accomplish this initial process.

We illustrate with the following example. In our own work that focuses on expanding access to electronic information, the term access is defined differently by different groups. For software designers, access refers to the

---

Box 7.1 Questions to guide the thinking processes of delimiting content

1. What theoretical frame of reference provides the foundation for the concept(s)?
2. How shall I define the concept(s) in words?
3. What are the essential characteristics of the concept(s), without which it would not be the same concept(s)?
4. What characteristics are non-examples of the concept(s)?
5. What do I want to know about the concept(s)?

---

availability and navigability of a website or software program, while for disability activists, access to information means that a site can be read by a screen reader and conforms to design standards that have been specified for individuals with visual impairments. Yet, for literacy instructors, access refers to the consistency of the literacy level with the reading ability of the user. So when we use the term access, we speak the same word but not the same meaning. In order to determine the scope and full content of one's construct, a clear lexical definition has to be formulated. In our work, electronic access is defined as a civil right for all people, which then behooves us to consider the full range of information consumers before a website is even designed. If we look at the distinction among the diverse definitions of access, we note that ours subsumes the others, at least indirectly. Each of the others is population specific and defines access as actionable, whereas our definition does not. Lack of access for us would be a rights violation that required design rethinking, while lack of access in the other two definitions would call for expertise and redesign on the basis of functionality (Gilson and DePoy, 2007).

Structure

Structure addresses the question of "How can we know the extent to which the concept exists, relates to, and/or predicts another concept?" The two elements of structure are: the nature of the instrument and the level of measurement.

Nature of the Instrument

Nature of the instrument refers to the way in which data are obtained. There are many types of methods used in inquiry, from complex surveys to structured observation. For the most part, experimental-type needs assessment in evaluation practice relies on questionnaires, interviews, and observations. We will look in more detail at these approaches later in the chapter. In the example above, we used numerous measures to test web access as we defined it: (a) HiSoftware (2003–2007) to test accessibility for text reader, (b) Flesh Kincaid Readability Test to test readability of the text (Juicy Studio, 2000–2007), and (c) user preference and functionality to ascertain access for all (DePoy and Gilson, 2006).

Level of Measurement

The second element of structure is the level of measurement. By level of measurement we mean the properties and meaning of the numbers assigned to an observation and the type of mathematical manipulations that can be performed with those numbers. Determining how a variable is measured directly shapes the type of statistical analysis that can be performed and is an important part of the structure of instrumentation.

Variables can be formatted as discrete or continuous. Discrete variables have a finite number of values, each of which is mutually exclusive. These values comprise all of the potential observations of the concept. For example, if we conceptualize gender as male and female, then the total concept of gender has two possible options. Each is denoted with a number (e.g., 1 = male and 2 = female). There is no in-between category.

Continuous variables have an infinite number of values. Age measured in years and height measured in inches are good examples. Now we turn to the four categories of numbers that are assigned to discrete and continuous variables.

The simplest level of measurement is nominal, which involves classifying observations into mutually exclusive categories. The word nominal means name and, therefore, nominal numbers provide numeric names for attributes of a variable. These numbers cannot be subjected to mathematical manipulation. Examples are your telephone number, the number on a soccer jersey, or your driver's license number. If you possess one of these numbers, you are a person who has a telephone, is a soccer player, or is a driver, respectively. No one else has your number and thus you are a mutually exclusive member of the variable with a unique numerical name. Nominal numbers are used primarily to code (assignment of a number) variables with discrete categories.

For example, we might classify individuals according to their political or religious affiliation, gender, or ethnicity. In each of these examples, membership in one category excludes membership in another. Another example of mutually exclusive categories is: visually impaired (1) not visually impaired (2).

The assignment of numbers is purely arbitrary, and no mathematical functions or assumptions of magnitude or ranking are implied or can be performed.

Ordinal numbers give "order" to a set of numbers and thus provide ranking. Take, for example, the following ranking:

Suppose you ranked individuals according to their degree of visual impairment: 1 = not able to see, 2 = somewhat able to see, 3 = no visual impairment.

We can say that middle condition is ranked higher than lower condition, but we can say nothing about the extent to which the conditions differ. The assignment of a numeric value is arbitrary as in the case of nominal variables because the distance or spacing between each category is not numerically equivalent. However, the numbers do imply magnitude, that is, one is greater than the other. Because there are no equal intervals between ordinal numbers, mathematical functions such as adding, subtracting, dividing, and multiplying cannot be performed.

Interval/ratio numbers are both continuous and available for mathematical calculation because there are equal intervals between them. Height in inches is an example. If you are 51 inches tall and I am 53 inches tall, I am exactly two inches taller than you. If we were measured ordinally, I would only know that I was taller than you, but not by how much. The difference between ratio and interval numbers is that ratio numbers have an absolute zero which allows you to compute a true ratio between numbers.

In professional literature we often see considerable debate about whether attitude scales represent interval levels of measurement. Such scales typically have a Likert-type response format in which a study participant responds to one of five or seven categories such as strongly agree, agree, uncertain, disagree, or strongly disagree. Some assign interval-level numbers to each response asserting that the distance between strongly agree and agree is equivalent to the distance between disagree and strongly disagree. However, because there is no empirical justification for making this assumption others suggest that ordinal numbers are the appropriate level of measurement.

We suggest that based on purpose, you determine what level of data to assign. With interval-level data more statistical options are available so first determine what type of analysis you require and then make your decision about what level of data to assign.

As we indicated above, answering the guiding questions for instrument selection led us to administer numerous instruments to assess electronic access as a right for all. Thus, we chose to observe the construct through four indicators: testing the selected websites themselves for compliance to text reader accessibility standards, testing for readability, testing functionality, and testing for design preference. These instruments create a complex instrumentation approach in which several instruments were included. Because they are all scored differently, we had to make decisions about both the content and structure of instrumentation plan. A time-efficient structure, and one which was considered by the literature to be accurate in content, was therefore chosen. We assigned interval-level scores to each of the measures and summed them to get a total access score.

Instrumentation Structures that are Useful in Experimental-Type Needs Assessment

Now we turn to a discussion of instrumentation structures that are typically used in experimental-type needs assessment. As we discussed in the previous chapter, these include survey, structured observation, and interview.

Surveys are questionnaires that are administered through paper and pencil, electronic oral, on-site or virtual face-to-face, and/or telephone formats. Because need is a characteristic, surveys are often used to obtain information to define need.

Dissimilar to surveys in which the rater is a member of the group you are investigating (raters are referred to as a subject or respondent), structured observations are scored by the investigator who looks at a phenomenon such as ease of computer use, then rates it according to a specific scheme. For example, in rating the functionality and ease of use of selected websites, we video-recorded diverse individuals as they conducted specific navigation web activities and then observed and rated the videos on an ascending interval-level scale of ease of use. We responded to specific items including timing, key strokes, and so forth to guide and standardize our observations.

As we noted above, another increasingly popular form of observation is looking at the attributes of a space through GIS mapping. For example, you might look at computer ownership and other computer resources such as availability of computers in libraries and schools in a defined community to ascertain computer saturation. The magnitude and patterns of distribution of computer saturation could then be depicted on a visual map. We have mapped prevention-supportive and prevention-inhibitive policy to identify needed policy changes that would support substance abuse prevention in local rural communities.

Structured interviews are similar to surveys. The professional uses a scripted list of questions with codes for the answers already developed to obtain data from an informant either on-site, virtually, face-to-face, or on the telephone. The interviewer usually completes the rating depending on the responses that he/she obtains in the interview. Below we highlight survey methodology to illustrate instrumentation thinking and action processes. All of the principles that we discuss related to survey apply to these other frequently used needs assessment instrument structures as well.

Surveys

Three types of questions can be included in surveys: closed ended, semi-structured, and open ended.

Closed-ended questions pose a limited range of responses from which the respondent chooses, all of which are posited by the professional. As example, we refer to our needs assessment work to inform our HRTW approach. The questions that were answered in the needs assessment were: (a) How do diverse stakeholder groups define independence for youth with special health care needs as they transition into adulthood? (b) What unmet needs do youth encounter in achieving independence? and (c) What differences in preferences and outcomes exist among diverse interest groups?

Some possible items to illustrate are presented in Box 7.2. In this example, we were interested in knowing about the knowledge and opinions held by three populations: youth, agency educators, and state-level policy makers. We only present part of the survey for illustration.

As you can see, responses to the first question on the survey are nominal. Responses denote group belonging. The remainder of the questions could have ordinal or interval-level responses and each response has a numeric code to depict its value.

Adding an open-response category to a closed-ended item creates a semi-structured item. For example, suppose we included an "other" category in items #2 and #3 presented in Box 7.2 below. What rationale would support the addition of this open-ended response?

Open-ended questions are those in which the respondent is asked to offer his/her comment on a topic without being directed to specific answers. These types of items are included when you are interested in obtaining responses that you might not have considered or known. It is possible that respondents in our example might suggest a different approach than those mentioned, such as special incentives and higher education programs, telecommuting, housing for young adults, and so forth. If you make a choice to include open-ended responses on a needs survey, you must be at least willing to consider them as options. Otherwise, you are wasting your time and misleading the respondents.

Box 7.2 Questions to guide the thining processes of delimiting content

1. Are you a (please check all that apply to you):
   i. Youth (1)
   ii. Educator (2)
   iii. Policy maker (3)

2. On the list below, please rate each outcome to indicate the degree to which you believe each represents independence for youth with special health care needs in transition to adulthood. Indicate your rating by circling the *ONE* response that best depicts your opinion:

   a. Remunerative employment immediately after leaving high school
      Must occur (3) Should occur (2) Not necessary to occur (1)

   b. Enrollment in higher education after leaving high school
      Must occur (3) Should occur (2) Not necessary to occur (1)

   c. Support from public welfare funds
      Must occur (3) Should occur (2) Should not occur (1)

   d. Health insurance apart from parents' policy upon leaving high school
      Must have this (3) Should have this (2) Not necessary to have this (1)

3. Now please rate each option below for the degree to which you believe it will meet your defined outcomes for independence for youth with special health care needs in transition to adulthood.

   a. Education about health insurance
      Very likely (3) Somewhat likely (2) Not likely (1)

   b. Policy to support public health insurance for this group
      Very likely (3) Somewhat likely (2) Not likely (1)

   c. State-supported employment training for this population
      Very likely (3) Somewhat likely (2) Not likely (1)

   d. Tax incentives for employers to hire this group
      Very likely (3) Somewhat likely (2) Not likely (1)

Table 7.1 Frequency table

Type of respondent	Frequency	Percentage
Youth	23	23
Educator	30	30
Policy maker	47	47

Analysis of the closed-ended responses would first occur as descriptive. For illustration purposes, we have provided responses from 100 respondents. Counting the number of people who checked each category created the frequency and percentage chart in Table 7.1. A frequency is a count of how many times a value was checked. In this instance the frequency could have exceeded the number of respondents if anyone had checked more than one category. However, we found that each respondent checked only one. The percentage refers to the percent of total responses to the question for each category.

As you can see, the largest group is policy makers. This information is important when we consider how the responses and opinions differ according to groups.

To analyze the responses to questions 2 and 3, we decided to compute mean scores for each option. A mean is an average. Table 7.2 presents the mean responses for item #2. Table 7.3 presents the preferred approaches to achieve the goal of independence as defined by the respondents.

Table 7.2 Mean responses for survey item #2

Item	Remunerative employment	Enrollment in higher education	Support for public welfare funds	Health insurance
Mean	2.7	1.8	1.6	2.5

Table 7.3 Mean scores for survey responses to item #3

Item	Loans for higher education	Policy support for public health insurance	State-supported safety net for this population	Employer tax incentives
Mean	1.5	2.8	1.2	2.3

What do these mean scores tell you? On item #2, the mean scores are highest for health insurance and remunerative employment. Now look at the mean scores for the approaches. Clearly, the approaches are consistent with the elements that define independence. These statistics can tell you the average, but do not be fooled. What if a score of 2.5 was an average of very high and very low scores rather than an agreement among the respondents? The standard deviation, another statistic, can be computed. The standard deviation tells you how widely dispersed scores are from the mean score so you can look at the distribution of all scores and know more about the actual opinions of the group. (See Appendix about these basic statistics, called measures of central tendency.) Note that we decided to treat the scores as interval in order to compute these scores. Remember that ordinal and nominal numbers cannot be mathematically manipulated.

To know how each group differed from the others, we then computed a statistic that reveals the extent to which the differences in scores were likely to be significant (not caused by chance). Because the dependent variable data are interval and there are three groups in the independent variable, a one-way Analysis of Variance (ANOVA) was the statistic selected. This statistical test examines the extent to which differences within and between groups did (not significant) or did not (significant) occur by chance. Significant differences were noted indicating that the groups differed in their perspectives on both items #2 and #3. Because the ANOVA can only identify the extent to which group differences exist, but does not tell you which group or groups differed, we computed a post-hoc test (Field, 2005). There are several of these and each is selected based on the characteristics of your sample and data. To read more about post-hoc tests we refer you to Field's (2005) text.

To analyze open-ended responses within the experimental-type approach, you would first read all of the responses, list each of the open-ended answers, and then decide how to code each response. You would then record this analytic scheme in a codebook, a list of directions denoting how you have assigned labels and/or numbers to the survey responses. We suggest that you assign numbers to each response, although some investigators choose to assign names in text. Suppose on item #3, we asked for other strategies, and of our 100 individuals 57 wrote the following responses as depicted in Table 7.4.

There are three distinct suggestions to which you would assign categorical numbers to name them. The assignment of numbers allows you to enter numeric data into your statistical software package and to conduct statistical analysis. Although the assignment of categorical numbers is arbitrary, pick a numbering scheme that makes sense. In Table 7.4, we selected the numeric codes of 1–3. The frequencies above can tell you quite a bit about the

Table 7.4 Open-ended responses

Suggestion	Numbers of respondents who made the suggestion (frequency)
1. Policy supporting time limited, benchmarked safety net support	21
2. Housing vouchers	19
3. Employer training	17

Table 7.5 Categorical approaches

Category	Frequency
1. Public support	40
2. Training	17

opinions of your respondents. You can ascertain the strength of a suggestion by looking at how many individuals took the time to write it.

To simplify your findings and put the data to use, you also might want to reduce the categories into public support (1) and training (2). These categories were arrived at inductively by examining the commonalities that emerged. It might not always be possible to reduce responses into broader categories. If patterns do not emerge, do not impose them.

In our example, you would code "policy supporting time-limited, benchmarked safety net support" and "housing vouchers" as (1) and "employer training" as (2) (see Table 7.5).

You would report the frequency of each response. How you code depends, as you might have guessed, on the purpose of the open-ended items and how feasible they are to implement. If you were most interested in the breadth of responses, you would leave the responses as expansive as possible. However, if you were interested in supporting a particular suggestion, such as public support, you might reduce the categories to demonstrate the frequency with which respondents suggested this genre of action. From this simple survey, we learned quite a bit about the nature of independence and the ways in which respondents suggested that it be achieved for this group.

Perhaps the most well-known survey is the U.S. Census, in which the government administers mailed surveys and conducts selected face-to-face interviews to develop a descriptive picture of the characteristics of the population of the United States. You might want to look at this survey structure for a model of sound survey construction (U.S. Department of Commerce, 2007).

The advantages of survey design are that the investigator can reach a large number of respondents with relatively minimal expenditure, numerous variables can be measured by a single instrument, and statistical manipulation during the data analytic phase can permit multiple uses of the data set (Sapsford, 2007).

Disadvantages might include the limitations of each design action process. For example, the use of mailed questionnaires, while cost effective, might yield a low response rate and thus not provide a broad enough understanding of need (Sapsford, 2007). Face-to-face interviews, while substantive, are time consuming and might differ according to how the interviewer and respondent interact (Holstein and Gubrium, 2003). Mailed or online surveys might also exclude respondents who cannot access the instruments because of sensory, cognitive, physical, or other barriers (DePoy and Gilson, 2006).

When deciding on survey design, being adept at survey construction or having the resources for consultation are necessary advantages. Developing a survey instrument is not as easy as it may seem. Many people develop and send out surveys that yield equivocal and confusing results, not because of the respondents but because of the difficulty of developing a clear and statistically sound instrument. Survey development is beyond the scope of this text and there are many excellent texts that can guide you (Brace, 2004; Buckingham and Saunders, 2004; Fink, 1995; Sapsford, 2007). However, we mention three important considerations in measurement that must be considered in survey development and/or selection: (a) validity, (b) reliability, and (c) accessible design.

In general, as we said previously, validity assesses the relationship between concept and evidence. Instrument validity addresses the relationship between a concept and its measurement. It answers the question "to what extent does the instrument measure what it is supposed to measure?" Put another way, instrument validity is concerned with the link between a lexical definition and an operational definition (DePoy and Gitlin, 2005). Remember that a lexical definition is one in which concepts are explained in words (other concepts) and an operational definition is the translation of the lexical definition into a method of measurement.

Look back at the list in Box 7.1 to remind yourself of the questions that you answer to select instrumentation. These questions are, in essence, "validity guidelines." They assure that your thinking processes consider the concept and its operationalization in your choice of measurement strategy.

Consider the construct of electronic accessibility that we discussed previously. How one would measure this complex construct would be dependent on its conceptual definition. As we noted, electronic access defined as ability for a test reader to functionally read the content of a website would be measured by the HiSoftware instrumentation (2003–2007), while access defined as general literacy level would be measured by a readability index such as the Flesh Kinkaid Readability Test score (Juicy Studio, 2000–2007).

As you can see, instrument validity is a very important concern. Too many times, vagueness and/or misinterpretations of what is being measured lead to serious dilemmas. A classic example is the measurement of intelligence. In his classic book, Gould (1974) gives an historical account of the definition and measure of intelligence. Throughout his book, he illuminates how measurement of intelligence, selected by dominant cultural groups, discriminates against and oppresses marginal populations. Hernstein and Murray (1996) have been severely criticized for their assertion of difference in innate intelligence based on race. Instrument validity is being called into question in these examples.

There are many types of instrument validity, such as those that examine comprehensiveness and accuracy. The techniques to examine and assert validity are equally varied and numerous. It is beyond the scope of this text to examine validity in detail. However, many methodology textbooks provide an excellent and comprehensive discussion of validity (Babbie, 2006; DePoy and Gitlin, 2005; Lewis-Beck *et al.*, 2004; Rubin and Babbie, 2007; Thyer, 2001). In evaluation practice, because instrumentation is often developed to ascertain need in unique contexts, and because of time constraints, extensive validation of measures is often prohibitive (Hall and Hall, 2004). If a professional cannot use an already validated measure or cannot validate a measure, it is important for him/her to follow rigorous instrument construction steps. Following these steps, presented in Box 7.1, will increase the likelihood that your instrument will obtain the information that you want.

Reliability is the other primary criterion for rigor in experimental-type inquiry. Reliability refers to the extent to which you can "rely" on the accuracy and stability of results obtained from a study (DePoy and Gitlin, 2005). Instrument reliability focuses on the stability of instruments used in the study. That is, if you were to measure the same variable in a similar or identical situation would your result be the same (DePoy and Gitlin)? The reliability of an instrument, proxy, or indicator is important to assess in order to be assured that variations in the variable under study represent observable differences and not those resulting from the measurement process itself. If your survey yielded different scores each time it was administered, you would not get a sound and stable picture of need.

Suppose you ask the following question in your needs assessment survey:

From the list below, what topic is most needed in continuing public health education?

_____ prevention science

_____ ethics

_____ fundraising

What are the reliability problems with this item? Because of its vague wording, lack of instructions regarding how to respond, and lack of context, an individual might answer differently from one administration to another. Ambiguity increases the likelihood of misinterpretation and thus of error. Suppose during the two weeks between sending and receiving the survey, a public health initiative was eliminated because of lack of funding. Those who answered prior to elimination might want prevention science skills in continuing education, but the same individuals responding after the program elimination might prefer fundraising. Thus, clarity and careful instructions and construction of items about who would participate in continuing education, when it should be offered, and why would enhance the reliability, in that you would be measuring what you knew to be a context-embedded phenomenon rather than a static preference as implied in the original wording of the item.

The longer the test or more information collected to represent the underlying concept (i.e., service preference), the more reliable the instrument is likely to become (Sullivan, 2001). Don't forget however, that there is always some error in measurement. Take, for example, a tape measure that is not held precisely at the same place for each measure. This random error might vary with each measurement and thus the investigator must account for error in all measurement action processes.

To assert reliability, experimental-type researchers frequently conduct statistical tests. These tests of reliability focus on two elements: stability and equivalence (Sullivan, 2001). Stability refers to the longitudinal accuracy of a measure. That is, if repeated under similar circumstances, will the findings be the same? If I stand on my scale today, tomorrow, and the next day, at the same time of day, without varying my eating habits, a stable scale will give me a consistent weight.

Equivalence refers to the extent to which all of the indicators on an instrument aggregate to measure the construct to be tested. Suppose you are measuring convenience store owners' attitudes towards selling cigarettes to minors, defined as their belief in the ethics of the practice, and their moral expectations for themselves and others regarding cigarette sales to minors. Each item on your instrument should measure one element of the attitudinal construct and all should aggregate to yield a single score. Moreover, positive attitudes should yield scores that are consistent across all items and, similarly, negative attitudes should yield consistent findings. If consistency does not occur, then it is possible that the instrument is measuring a construct other than attitudes. As you have defined it.

The choice of instrumentation depends on the nature and intended purpose of the instrument. In evaluation practice, instruments are often developed for single administrations and unique situations under time-limited conditions. Establishing reliability through statistical analysis, therefore, is not always an option in needs assessment (Hall and Hall, 2004). In any case, action processes such as consistent conditions in administering instrumentation and training interviewers to ask questions in the same way, among many other strategies, should be implemented to increase the reliability of measurement.

In designing and/or selecting instrumentation, the professional should insure that the respondents can competently complete the measure. Such factors as level of education, socioeconomic background, verbal ability, access to American Sign Language, accessibility of online instrumentation or language of origin interpreters, sensory status, cognitive status, socio-emotional environment of the administration of the instrument, and participant receptivity influence the selection and design of a data collection method. Consider, for example, some online survey templates that are widely used by evaluators. Many of these templates are not accessible to screen readers or language translations (DePoy and Gilson, 2006). Thus, large segments of potential respondents are frequently excluded from participation in online measurements and thus your data might not be accurate for your intended sample. In needs assessment, accessibility is critical in order to obtain a full and accurate understanding of need from the perspective of diverse groups who are involved in a problem. So, assuring inclusive participation is essential.

The development of new instrumentation is, in itself, a specialty within the experimental-type research world. We have introduced you to the basic components of measurements and have given you some principles for ensuring that your items are reliable. However, constructing an instrument and its components is a major research task, and it is best to seek consultation.

Main Points

1. Measurement involves consideration of the content and the structure of instrumentation.
2. Content refers to the lexical definitions, the limits of concepts to be measured, and the relationships to be examined.
3. Structure refers to the nature of the instrumentation and the scoring.
4. Most frequently, experimental-type needs assessment in evaluation practice relies on questionnaires, interviews, and on-site and virtual observations.
5. Variables can be discrete or continuous.
6. Questions can be asked in varied formats, including closed-ended, semi-structured, and open-ended.
7. In experimental-type needs assessment, analysis of data is statistical even with open-ended questions.
8. The criteria for rigor in experimental-type needs assessment are instrument validity and reliability.
9. Inclusive instrumentation is essential for evaluation accuracy.
10. Constructing instrumentation is a difficult skill that requires much practice.

Exercises

1. Read a needs assessment article and select the important concepts that are being measured. List them and then try to find lexical definitions of each.
2. From the article, critically evaluate the fit between the lexical definition and the instrument that measures the concept.
3. Describe the content and structure of the instruments in the article.
4. Critically discuss the instruments for rigor. To what extent are they reliable and valid? Inclusive?
5. Look at the statistical analysis. What types of numbers (nominal, ordinal, interval/ratio) are used and how?
6. Think of a concept that you want to measure. Define it by answering the questions in Box 7.1. Now try to develop a simple survey, interview, or observation to measure your concept.
7. Have a peer critically examine your instrument for rigor.

CHAPTER 8

Ascertaining Need in Unexamined or Partially Understood Contexts: Designing Inductive Inquiry

Underlying Tenets of Naturalistic Inquiry

We now turn to the action processes that professionals can use when empirical evidence does not seem to fit, in part or in total, the problem, or when insufficient empirical study of need has been conducted to inform professional action. In these instances, we suggest that naturalistic strategies are indicated either on their own or in concert with experimental-type needs assessment. However, for the most part, as we will see, what many refer to as naturalistic or qualitative methods are, in essence, mixed-methods approaches. That is to say, even if naturalistic methods are used for obtaining information and conducting analysis, the needs assessment relies on mixed methods both in its philosophical foundation as well as its action strategies. Look back to our discussion of philosophy and the clear fit of pragmatism with both evaluation practice and mixed-methods research as the basis for this claim. As we have reiterated, because of its purposive foundation, all evaluation is, in some way, anchored on pragmatism. Moreover, because evaluation practice is designed to look at context-specific problems and their solutions, the "target" or population and, at least, its undesirable characteristics to be changed by the professional action, are already known. Pure naturalistic inquiry is based on induction in which the knowledge seeker is theoretically unaware of the boundaries or characteristics of the domain of concern. Therefore, purely inductive or naturalistic thinking and action cannot typically be used in the needs assessment phase of evaluation practice, as this phase is designed to identify what is needed to resolve an identified phenomenon. For instructional purposes, we discuss naturalistic tenets so that you will know what they are and how to integrate them into pragmatic mixed-methods needs assessments.

Naturalistic inquiry is a category of research that relies on multiple epistemological perspectives (Creswell, 2006; Denzin and Lincoln, 2003; DePoy and Gitlin, 2005). All, however, share to a greater or lesser extent the construct of pluralism, the limited knowledge that the investigator has about the phenomenon of interest, and an inductive approach to revealing principles. Yet, because of the multiple philosophical frameworks on which naturalistic thinking and action processes are based, there is no agreement in the literature on the exact nature and criteria for rigor in this research tradition. Several authors have attempted to define the commonalities of naturalistic designs. Among them, DePoy and Gitlin (2005) have suggested that there are nine attributes of naturalistic inquiry:

1. *Range of Purpose*: naturalistic strategies vary in purpose from developing descriptive knowledge to revealing complex theoretical frameworks.
2. *Context Specificity*: all naturalistic inquiry is conducted in the context in which the object or subject of inquiry occurs. Naturalistic action processes are, therefore, context specific.
3. *Complexity and Pluralistic Perspective of Reality*: because of its underlying epistemology and its inductive approach to knowing, naturalistic research assumes a pluralistic perspective of "reality" that seeks to articulate rather than reduce complexity.
4. *Transferability of Findings*: because naturalistic inquiry is context specific, the aim of generalizability is not relevant to this form of study. Rather, principles and theory derived from naturalistic study can be considered for their relevance and further tested in alternative contexts.
5. *Flexibility*: unlike experimental-type inquiry in which initial and careful planning of the design determines all subsequent action processes, naturalistic designs are flexible and changeable in response to incremental learning that occurs within the time frame of the inquiry. It is not only acceptable but expected that procedures, the nature of the research query, the scope of the study, and the manner by which information is obtained, are constantly reformulated and realigned to fit the emerging "truths" as they are ascertained.
6. *Centrality of Language*: language is central to naturalistic inquiry. That is, a major shared concern in naturalistic inquiry is understanding the language and its meanings for diverse people. Through

language, symbols, and ways of expression, the investigator comes to understand and derive meaning within each context.

7. *The Importance of Perspective*: naturalistic designs vary in their "emic" or "etic" orientation. An "emic" perspective refers to the "insider's" or informant's way of understanding and interpreting experience. An "etic" orientation refers to an outsider's perspective where the investigator brings understandings and processes external to the domain of concern to bear on the investigation.

8. *Shift in Knowing Power*: because the investigator enters an inquiry with the aim of openness to new and unfamiliar ideas, the naturalistic researcher defers to the informant or "experiencer" as the knower. This abrogation of power by the "investigator" to the "investigated" is characteristic, to a greater or lesser degree, of all naturalistic designs.

9. *Interspersion of Gathering Information and Analysis*: finally, analysis in naturalistic designs relies heavily on qualitative data and is an ongoing process that is interspersed throughout data-gathering activities. Data gathering and analysis are interdependent, simultaneous and/or interactive processes.

As you can see, naturalistic inquiry differs from experimental-type designs not only in method but in philosophical foundations, and thus provides another important set of thinking and action processes through which to understand need. In the naturalistic tradition, there are many approaches to inquiry. We discuss those that best fit evaluation practice in this chapter.

Underlying Tenets of Mixed-Method Approaches

As we noted, we support mixed methods as the most comprehensive systematic thinking and action processes in evaluation practice. Historically, because of the philosophical differences between experimental-type and naturalistic traditions, there was great skepticism about integrating the two approaches. However, given the pragmatic philosophical underpinning (Tashakkori and Teddlie, 2002) and the acceptance of abductive logic structures in the systematic world, acceptance and support have grown for mixed methods as a viable way to integrate the strengths and account for the limitations of deductive and inductive traditions used by themselves (Creswell and Plano-Clark, 2007; Tashakkori and Teddlie, 2002).

An integrated needs assessment approach involves selecting and combining thinking and action strategies from both traditions so that one

Table 8.1 Characteristics of the research traditions

	Experimental-type	Naturalistic	Mixed methods
Epistemology	Logical positivism	Humanistic or holistic	Pragmatic
Approach to reasoning	Deductive	Inductive	Abductive
Theoretical aim	To reduce complexity; test theory	To reveal complexity; develop theory	All
Context	Structured a priori by inquirer	Natural context	Multiple
Practical purpose	Need to control and delimit scope of inquiry	Reveal new understandings	Multiple purposes
Preferred way of knowing	Monistic	Pluralistic	Multiple
Level of knowledge development	Well-developed theory	Limited knowledge; challenge to current theory	Both

complements the other to benefit or contribute to a purposive understanding of the problem and what is needed to resolve it. Many investigators have implicitly used one or more forms of mixed methods without specifying that they were using mixed-methods approaches (DePoy and Gitlin, 2005), for example, using simple descriptive statistics, such as frequencies and means in ethnographic research, or the use of open-ended items in experimental-type surveys. Look at Table 8.1 (Creswell and Plano-Clark, 2007; DePoy and Gitlin, 2005; Tashakkori and Teddlie, 2002), for a comparison of the characteristics of experimental-type, naturalistic, and mixed-methods approaches.

In evaluation practice, mixed-method approaches can therefore integrate the thinking and action processes of each inquiry tradition according to context and purpose, and in concert with practical constraints of the needs assessment. Now, we turn to specific strategies of naturalistic needs assessment.

Naturalistic Approaches

Because of the vast field of naturalistic inquiry, we have selected the strategies in Box 8.1. They are used most frequently and, for us, serve the universe of purposes that professionals would encounter in conducting needs assessments.

Box 8.1 Naturalistic strategies in needs assessment

- Interview
  - Individual or key-informant
  - Focus group

- Life history

- Open-ended survey

- Ethnography

- Inductive secondary data analysis

Interview is a method in which the investigator obtains information through direct interchange with an individual or a group that is known or expected to possess knowledge. Interview technique varies in structure and degree of control over the interview process maintained by the professional. And although, as addressed in the previous discussion of experimental-type needs assessment, interview can be fully controlled and coded deductively, in naturalistic approaches, interview serves an inductive purpose and is frequently the primary naturalistic method used in needs assessment. There are numerous types of naturalistic interview, including, but not limited to, long interview (McCracken, 1988), key-informant interview, small-unit interview (that is, family interview), and focus group (Denzin and Lincoln, 2000; Patton, 2001). For the most part, investigators conducting needs assessment rely on key-informant interview and focus group.

In individual or key-informant interview, the key informants are individuals who are expected to possess a body of knowledge and a perspective that are needed to purposively inform the development of an action or entity and specification of desired outcomes. Key informants are identified and asked to meet with the professional to discuss the topic for the needs assessment inquiry. It is not unusual for key informants who represent diverse and competing points of view to be asked to participate in the interview process, especially when the problem being addressed by professional action is complex and requires the commitment of resources. It is critical to remember that informants are, therefore, chosen both for knowledge and for political purpose. We urge you to be inclusive and expansive in informant selection so that informants with a range of perspectives, from those who are seen as "having the problem" to those who have the resources to commit to problem resolution, can have voice in shaping the activity and desired outcomes.

To illustrate, we look at the HRTW needs assessment. As discussed by Hartman *et al.* (2000), three key informants were purposively recruited for life history interviews (Caughey, 2006) as the basis for enriching an understanding of the ways in which professionals, service systems, and diverse youth with chronic illnesses in transition to adulthood interacted. The informants were chosen for their diversity of diagnostic conditions, their willingness to be interviewed, and prior knowledge that these individuals and families had disparate and illuminating histories that would be relevant in informing professional action. Analysis of key-informant interviews revealed that the timing and nature of diagnosis was paramount in determining the extent to which youth receive any professional services at all and, for those who do, the nature of those services as well as their outcomes.

A focus group is a group interview in which the moderator or moderators pose topics and/or questions for group discussion. Recordings of the focus group discussions and/or interactions comprise the data set (Krueger and Casey, 2005). Although originated for marketing purposes, focus group inquiry has become one of the most frequently used methods for naturalistic needs assessment. In focus groups, professionals can choose the degree of control and direction that they introduce into the process. Box 8.2 lists the advantages and disadvantages of focus group methodology.

Although there are many variations, focus groups generally contain the following essential elements and action processes.

The first step in any inquiry is the clarification of the question or query. What should be known in order to understand need? A question or series of questions requiring knowledge that is not sufficiently developed in current literature or practice wisdom will often provide the rationale for

---

Box 8.2 Focus group methodology

Advantages

1. Qualitative data
2. Group process → group think
3. Time efficient
4. Directive

Disadvantages

1. Possibility of group pressure limiting individual responses
2. Time consuming to organize

focus group. However, why conduct a group interview instead of individual interviews?

Focus groups rely on the principle of group process. You would choose a focus group when looking for group cohesion or dissent, seeking data that capture interaction in the discourse among several individuals who are knowledgeable, attempting to obtain consensus with shades of difference, exploring and understanding a complex whole, and working with resources that limit the time that can be devoted to interview. For example, in the HRTW needs assessment, we conducted focus groups with several stakeholder groups. In all, but especially in the youth focus groups, the extent to which informants participated and built on one another's knowledge and experience was apparent.

The second step is the selection of focus group design. In this stage, you determine the degree of control you will have over the process, the specificity of the questions to be posed to group participants, the role of facilitators and participants in the process, and the method of data collection, analysis, and reporting. The questions presented in Box 8.3 will help you plan a design to meet your purpose.

Returning to our example, in each group we began with a general question about the meaning of independence to youth with special health

---

Box 8.3 Focus group guidelines

1. Begin with your questions, and delimit the scope of the focus group in informing those questions.

2. Based on what you want to know from the focus group, determine the participation and facilitation structure. How many moderators will you have? How directive should facilitators be?

3. Select an interview format. Especially with new focus group participants, try to use topic or question guides. Visual props (in accessible formats) help focus discussion.

4. Questions and topics must be clear and mutually exclusive.

5. Questions and topics must be internally consistent and sequential.

6. Begin with general questions, and then make more specific queries if answers to your queries are not embedded within the general answers.

7. Begin with positive questions, and then proceed to negative and/or sensitive ones.

Box 8.4 Sequence guide for focus groups

- Assemble room, including props and equipment.
- Decide on roles for co-facilitators.
- Welcome participants and thank them.
- Introduce participants to one another.
- State purpose and rules.
- Ask the opening question.
- Moderate discussion (moderate, but don't participate!).
- Give a summary and member-check periodically.
- End with overall summary, next steps, and use of data.

---

care needs in transition to adulthood. We did not raise questions about the barriers until late in the session. Thus, we were able to elicit positive definitions and meanings before informants raised skepticism about how that independence could be achieved in the current service and fiscal context.

In Box 8.4 we suggest a sequence to structure and organize focus groups that best fits your questions and purposes.

We have also found that several structural and process elements, such as the following, can be helpful in guiding the focus group: (a) vignettes to provoke thinking and discourse; (b) debate about specific issues; (c) closed-ended questioning (for example, lists, ratings, or fill in the blanks) to obtain targeted information (note here that this technique is a mixed method approach); and (d) role-playing activity to reveal attitudes and cultural role expectations.

There are numerous additional strategies to catalyze a focus group and introduce ideas for reflection, analysis, and discussion. Focus group provides the opportunity for imagination as long as rigor criteria are upheld throughout the process.

Focus group data most frequently are recorded transcripts of the discussion. Analysis of the data is qualitative, inductive, and, in mixed methods, can be deductive. In naturalistic inquiry, analysis is designed to reveal themes and perspectives of group members that were not necessarily known to the professional.

In the youth focus groups, we learned that youth with special health care needs defined their independence as equality of opportunity to experience what other adolescents experienced. That definition never entered our minds prior to hearing the perspectives of the youth themselves (DePoy and Gilmer, 2000).

Life history is a method whereby the investigator focuses an inquiry on individual lives in the context of the social environment (Caughey, 2006). This design can answer important needs assessment questions related both to the present and to the history that led to the current needs as articulated by individuals.

In conducting the action processes of life history methodology, the sequence of life events and the meaning of those events to the unfolding of a life are examined from the perspective of the informant and his or her significant others. Specific events, termed marker events or turnings (Denzin and Lincoln, 2003), are used as the anchor points on which a narrative life history is built. To elicit life history data, professionals frequently conduct unstructured interview, which might begin with statements such as "Tell me about your life." Once the narrative of historical events is obtained, an interviewer might look for the meaning of specific events in shaping the lives of the individual informants. Informants are asked to reconstruct their lives and to reflect on meaning to inform the purpose of the needs assessment. Among the additional data sources to construct a life history are personal artifacts, photographs, and personal records. Life history can also be obtained longitudinally. That is to say, a life history can be constructed by following an individual over time. However, because longitudinal studies can be costly and extremely time consuming, they are often beyond the resources of the professional who is examining need using this approach.

Consider the example from HRTW (Hartman *et al.*, 2000). Interviewing the three individuals required at least three hours just to elicit data. Since it is unlikely that individuals will desire to speak for such a long time, the life history interviews typically are conducted over several sessions.

Similar to interview, open-ended survey poses broad questions to informants for their responses. The survey can be structured in several ways, but the majority are administered through electronic media, snail mail, or telephone (Gubrium and Holstein, 2001).

Although there is some overlap in survey and interview, survey is designed primarily to examine multiple and delimited phenomena through the advancement of topical, targeted questions to a respondent (DePoy and Gitlin, 2005). Moreover, different from interview, discussion or written responses beyond the scope of the specified items are not desirable in survey. In naturalistic open-ended survey designs, data are primarily narrative and analyzed using inductive strategies (Gubrium and Holstein, 2001).

The life histories discussed above were just one example of open-ended interview. These interview approaches can be used for multiple purposes.

For example, in conducting a needs assessment regarding community substance abuse prevention infrastructure, we telephoned key informants in each county in the state and posed two questions:

1. What are the substance abuse resources in your county?
2. What are your unmet substance abuse prevention needs?

We then followed up with probe questions to assure that our purposes were met and that we obtained information on the prevention domains that we had previously defined. Note that previous specification of domains combined with open-ended interview is a mixed-methods approach in that we had already delimited our interview, in part, to specific content.

Ethnography is the primary inquiry method in anthropology, but it also plays an important role in needs assessment. It is a naturalistic design that reveals and characterizes the underlying patterns of behavior and meaning of a culture. Synthesizing numerous definitions, we define culture as the set of explicit and tacit rules, symbols, and rituals that guide patterns of human behavior within a group (DePoy and Gilson, 2007). While in classical ethnography a single study was often carried out over years, during which the investigator would immerse him/herself in a culture to discover its nature, tacit rules, and customs (Fetterman, 2007), given the time and practical limitations of needs assessment, ethnography used for needs assessment is typically very different from that used for anthropological and sociological research. Box 8.5 presents the elements of thinking and action processes of ethnography as we suggest they apply to needs assessment inquiry. These elements will then be further discussed below.

Most typically in needs assessment, ethnographic techniques rather than a complete ethnographic study are used to understand the experience and needs of an unfamiliar group. The professional might be etic (an outsider to the cultural group) or emic (a member of the group) and is aiming to obtain perception of needs from the "insider" perspective (Creswell, 2007).

Box 8.5 Thinking and action processes of ethnography

- Naturalistic
- Etic perspective
- Cultures of interest are those that have common problems
- Slice in time approach
- Time constraints

The notion of "subjects," in which those being observed do not participate in the methods of inquiry or analysis, is turned around in ethnography. Subjects do not exist but, rather, the members of the group or groups affected by professional action are considered to be informants or participants in the inquiry process. This ideological shift locates the "knowing power" within the group that is the subject of the needs assessment and gives an important voice to individuals and groups who are silent in more traditional approaches (Denzin and Lincoln, 2003).

As we noted above, classical ethnography relies heavily on extended observation, immersion, and participation in the culture where data are collected through several primary methods: (a) interview and observation of those who are willing to inform the inquirer about behavioral norms and their meanings, (b) the investigator's participation in the culture, and (c) examination of meaning of cultural objects and symbols (Atkinson *et al.*, 2001). As we noted, insiders who willingly engage with the investigator are called "informants" and "participants" (DePoy and Gitlin, 2005). Informants are distinguished from participants by their more integral role in the inquiry.

In needs assessment inquiry, ethnographic strategies must be selected based on purpose, resources, and the way data will be applied to informing professional activity. The cultures that professionals seek to identify and characterize are not exotic peoples but groups who are identified as having a "problem in common." Thus, principles from ethnography frame the inquiry, but classical techniques, such as full and prolonged immersion, are often truncated and modified to fit the needs assessment context.

Any inquiry relying on ethnographic principles begins with gaining access to a culture. The professional then explores the context in which the culture operates by observing the environment. Equipped with an understanding of the cultural context, the professional uses participant observation, informant interview, and/or examination of materials or artifact review to obtain data. Although materials and artifacts can be in any form, professionals frequently use existing records, narratives, policies, advertisements, blogs, websites, and so forth as important and illuminative data sources. Professionals using a "slice in time approach" might enter the culture at random times throughout the day, week, or month to obtain a comprehensive picture of the culture at different times and intervals and aggregate these data to form a chronicle of need. Thus, in needs assessment, targeted use of ethnographic techniques in a purposive manner is a reasonable and cost-effective action process to obtain a sense of cultural or group need.

Ethnographic techniques can lead the professional from a broad understanding of a culture to the specific roles, rituals, language, and patterns of the members and subgroups who belong to the culture. Notes, audio, and video recordings can provide a rich set of data through which themes emerge inductively as the professional analyzes the findings. Member checking, a technique in which an investigator checks for the accuracy of his or her interpretation of the data, is a hallmark of rigor in ethnography (Agar, 1996) and provides the vehicle for the professional to verify impressions with members of a culture.

Analysis of ethnographic data proceeds inductively and is an iterative process that co-occurs with data collection. Corrections in interpretation are made as new data reveal new and revised understandings. The end point of the ethnography occurs when saturation has been reached, the point at which new data do not provide any new insights (DePoy and Gitlin, 2005). Time constraints, however, might prevent saturation as an end point in needs assessment. If so, the professional should keep in mind that a full picture of need as experienced by cultural members might not have been obtained.

Box 8.6 suggests a sequence of ethnographic techniques in needs assessment. Of course, because naturalistic inquiry is characteristically dynamic and changing, the sequence is not prescriptive. Thus, we only provide guidelines for the professional who is thinking of using these techniques for needs assessment.

In our substance abuse prevention needs assessment, we used ethnographic techniques to conduct four community assessments. Before using this technique, we conducted GIS mapping and statistical analysis to ascertain the association between prevention infrastructure and substance abuse. To our surprise, we found no association at all. Without a theoretical

---

Box 8.6 Sequence of ethnographic techniques in needs assessment

- Gain entrance into the culture.
- Identify several key informants.
- Conduct slice in time broad observations (recording observations).
- Analyze data for initial themes.
- Interview informants for additional data, and member-check initial impressions.
- Continue to collect and analyze data until needs assessment questions are answered (saturation or time limit is reached).

explanation of our findings, we turned to inductive strategies and selected rural communities that fit into one of four categories: those with high substance abuse rates and extensive prevention infrastructure, those with high substance abuse rates and very limited prevention infrastructure, those with low substance abuse rates and extensive prevention infrastructure, and those with low substance abuse rates and very limited prevention infrastructure. For comparison, and to inform our prevention activity, we were hoping to reveal cultural elements that were unknown to us about low-consumption communities. We gained access to each community through physically going to the center of town, typically simple to identify in rural communities. We then observed roads and traffic patterns, movement, resources, human movement, store placement, signs in grocery stores, street signs, postings on public bulletin boards, and so forth as the basis for data collection. We are still in the process of collecting and analyzing data. One preliminary recurrent theme is the importance of recreation and community resources as mediators of substance abuse, but further needs assessment will be conducted to determine if this theme continues to reveal itself.

Inductive analysis of existing data sets is a frequently used strategy in naturalistic needs assessment. There are many data sources that are illuminating and lend themselves to inductive analysis. Typically, professionals use materials such as social histories, agency records, policy and legislative documents, agency mission statements and bylaws, existing narratives generated through previous naturalistic studies, and analysis of media products (for example, newspapers, TV shows, and advertising). These secondary sources are approached with specific needs assessment questions, and analysis is inductive. In our work, we have been examining written agency and health department policy to determine prevention-supportive and prevention-inhibitive policy approaches.

Selecting a Design in Naturalistic Needs Assessment

Design and methodological elements of naturalistic inquiry have been discussed but, given the complexity of this tradition, how can you select a design to answer your queries? Remember that naturalistic design is flexible and dynamic. Unlike in experimental-type design, once you begin your naturalistic inquiry, it is expected that initial methods will change as the process of the study unfolds.

The following questions in Box 8.7 will guide your selection of initial inquiry. However, as you proceed, be prepared to change and shift methods to respond to your inductive findings.

Box 8.7 Questions to guide choice of a design

- What purpose does the needs assessment serve?
- Why am I doing it?
- How informed am I about my domain of concern?
- Who best can inform me of need?
- Where will I conduct the inquiry?
- What degree of participation will I seek from my informant(s)?
- What resource and time constraints must I consider?
- Is the design consistent with the limitations of the practice arena?
- Can the design lead to the discovery of information sufficient for articulating goals, objectives, and expected outcomes of an intervention?
- What are some of the ethical and field limitations that influence the design?

Mixed-Method Designs

We have discussed a broad range of material related to needs assessment design. We have covered both experimental-type and naturalistic inquiry, examining the basic foundation of each, typical designs used in each approach to needs assessment, basic design techniques, and guidelines for selecting a needs assessment approach. As you can see, each tradition offers a range of diverse options for design structure. As we have noted, we strongly support mixing naturalistic and experimental-type design in needs assessment as a powerful strategy for examining pre-existing principles and unearthing changes in need over time. There are infinite ways to mix methods from using inductive information gathering with sampling logic, to integrating open- and closed-ended questions in surveys and interviews. In some mixed-method approaches, inductive strategies to develop theory are then followed with deductive theory testing needs assessment. Mixing methods in needs assessment is dependent on one's ontology (view of the nature of "reality"), purpose in conducting the study, potential for comprehensive coverage of complex problems, and limitations in resources to conduct the inquiry.

The following example illustrates the use of mixed methods in needs assessment. Attend to how the use of these diverse strategies leads to the generation of multiple perspectives that yield diverse and, sometimes, competing expectations for successful outcome.

We return to our HRTW example. To answer the questions "What is the meaning of independence to youth with special health care needs in transition to adulthood, and how can this transition be facilitated?" a complex mixed-methods needs assessment relying on focus group, key-informant interview, and survey design was conducted. We have already discussed elements of this needs assessment to illustrate principles and techniques. As you have read, multiple perspectives and findings were revealed in this needs assessment. From the focus groups, we found that youth, parents, educators, health providers, and policy makers all had disparate views of the meaning of independence and how to achieve it. Youth wanted equal opportunity, parents saw independence for youth as their children living in homes of their own, teachers and providers viewed independence as youth acceptance of responsibility for their own health, and policy makers were concerned with fiscal support for work and higher education for this group of youth. The key-informant interviews resulted in understanding the diagnostic basis of service acquisition and a state-wide survey that asked respondents to rank priorities for defining and meeting need resulted in diverse perspectives as well. So professional roles were defined as collaborative, and the goals and objectives for professional activity were aimed at bringing groups together for negotiation, planning, and implementation of systems change strategies to meet common ground. We will return to those goals and objectives in subsequent chapters.

Main Points

1. The basic elements and philosophical foundations of naturalistic inquiry include pluralism, dynamic process, and inductive analysis.
2. Interview, life history, open-ended survey, ethnography, and inductive secondary data analysis are frequently used designs in naturalistic needs assessment.
3. Interviews can be conducted with individuals or with groups.
4. Multiple, creative approaches to individual and group interview can be implemented providing that systematic and rigorous methods are followed.
5. Life history is a method that provides a retrospective understanding of need.
6. Within the naturalistic tradition, open-ended needs assessment surveys are delimited by topic and analyzed inductively.
7. Ethnographic techniques provide a flexible, dynamic, and complex approach to need through examination of social and cultural settings.
8. Inductive analyses of secondary data sets are an efficient method of revealing patterns of need.

9. Mixed-method designs are powerful and most supported by us for identifying and describing complex need.

Exercises

1. Locate an area in your neighborhood where adults engage in recreation (tennis court, park, movie theater, and so on). Observe the patterns of behavior among the individuals with specific attention to who is included and who is not. Through systematic observation, develop impressions about the factors that influence access to recreation.
2. Interview one or more key informants about who has access and how policy decisions are made about who can and who cannot participate. Ask each about what, if anything, is needed to expand recreation to those who are not included.
3. Based on data, suggest policy, business, and public health needs to address change in recreational access.

GOALS AND
OBJECTIVES

CHAPTER 9

Setting Goals and Objectives

Once you have a clear and well-documented statement of need, the action process of setting goals and objectives can be initiated. In this chapter we begin by defining and then examining how needs are translated into goals and objectives. Goals and objectives provide the structure for professional action and posit desired outcomes at one or more time intervals. The action process of goal and objective formulation is critical in our evaluation practice model because it is the first step in which specific accountability criteria are set.

Goals

Goals are broad statements about the ideal or "hoped for" (Coley and Scheinberg, 2001). They look forward in time to general "desirables." In evaluation practice, goals emerge directly from the needs statement and thus reflect the value set of the problem statement regarding what should be accomplished and changed through professional action. Because evaluation practice is purposive throughout its entire thinking and action processes, goals are purposive as well. Expected goal attainment can range from immediate to the long-term and can be simple or complex.

Let us look at some goals and their relationship to both need and problem statements to examine these important links and time expectations for goal achievement. We begin with an example from the HRTW project.

Let us consider one of the problem statements to which the project was directed: "Adolescents with special health care needs frequently move into adulthood without the vocational skills to be competitive on the job market." Now recall the part of the needs assessment that we discussed in previous chapters in which the adolescents clearly identified their need for equal opportunity and full inclusion. In large part, they were addressing their exclusion from, and desire to engage in, the same vocational preparation opportunities available for youth without special health care needs. Further inquiry verified that these youth were systematically excluded from vocational experience and training opportunities in large part due to negative attitudes held by teachers and employers regarding the cost of accommodation and skepticism about the capacity of these youth to compete adequately in the job market (DePoy and Gilmer, 2000). Based on this understanding of need, a number of goals were developed including the overall intermediate goal of educating teachers and employers about typical accommodation costs and about the capacity of youth with special health care needs to work. Education was an intermediate goal leading to the long-term goals of attitudinal change and an increase in vocational preparation of youth with special health care needs.

In the example above, the direct relationship between need and goal is seen in the intermediate goal of education of teachers and employers. The long-term goals of enhancing favorable attitudes of teachers and employers and increasing vocational preparation of youth with special health care needs are linked directly to the part of the problem statement that addresses underemployment of these youth. Note that increasing employment of adolescents with special health care needs is not a goal. We return to this important point later in this chapter.

Because goals are broad statements of what is desired, how the goal will be attained and how you will know that it is has been attained must be articulated. These two elements are the purposes of objectives and frame the nomenclature for two types of objectives: process and outcome. Objectives are, therefore, operationalized goal statements. If you apply the concept of operationalization, or specifying a definition in terms of how a concept or construct can be put into action, observed, ascertained, and/or measured (DePoy and Gitlin, 2005), to goals and objectives, you can see how we arrived at this definition. Goals are abstractions of what is desirable. Objectives provide the action steps on how, when, and who will do what to achieve goals, and how you will know that you have achieved them. One of the challenges in establishing objectives is to make sure that the goal will be achieved when the objectives are met. Objectives that specify actions are process objectives, and those that specify outcomes are outcome objectives.

So if you only provided education to teachers about the capacity of youth with special health care needs to work, you would not be addressing the entire goal of educating teachers and employers about typical accommodation costs and about the capacity of youth with special health care needs to work.

Objectives

Process (also called formative or monitoring) objectives state what will be done, how, when, and by whom, while outcome (also termed summative) objectives delineate how you will know that you were successful in producing a desired result from what was done. Both types of objectives are derived from goals statements.

Using the example of preparation for employment by adolescents with special health care needs, let us see what objectives we might frame from the goal statements. Review the adolescent needs assessment previously discussed so you can see the foundation for the following intermediate goal:

> Intermediate Goal Statement:
> "Educate teachers and employers about typical accommodation costs and about the capacity of youth with special health care needs to work."

The objectives that were established to achieve the goal include:

1. Assemble youth who will participate.
2. Train youth in curriculum planning.
3. Work with youth to specify content and structure of training curriculum.
4. Complete materials and formal curriculum.
5. Work with youth to develop adult education skills.
6. Conduct mock-training with an audience.
7. As assessed by the audience, youth will demonstrate excellence in training skills.
8. Revise and complete necessary youth training according to feedback from mock-training evaluation.
9. Assist youth in scheduling education and training sessions with teachers and employers.
10. Conduct two education and training sessions for educators and two sessions for employers.
11. As a result of attending training sessions, employers and teachers will obtain knowledge of typical accommodation costs and about the capacity of youth with special health care needs to work.
12. As a result of attending training sessions, employers and teachers will specify uses of their knowledge to enhance the employment opportunities for youth with special health care needs.
13. Obtain feedback from educators and employers suggesting improvements to the curriculum structure and content.

14. Revise curriculum content and structure, based on session feedback and assessments.
15. Develop and implement long-term plan for education and training of teachers and employers.

There are several important points to note in these objectives. First, they are time sequenced. Second, some are process objectives and some are summative objectives. Can you select which objectives fit into each category? Third, each objective can be assessed according to the degree of its completion. We will return to these points and to objectives related to the long-term goals later in this chapter.

If you selected objectives 7, 11, and 12 as outcome and the remainder as process, you are correct. The process objectives specify what will be done and how. They structure the sequence of professional activity and provide the mechanism to specify the source of evidence to be used to assess objective completion. Similarly, outcome or summative objectives delineate what is expected if the activity is successful and provide the foundation for determining what evidence will be used to assess success criteria.

Process objectives are those that will be used to guide monitoring and formative evaluation or, in our model, the comprehensive process of Reflexive Action. Outcome objectives are used to determine summative value of professional action. The objectives as stated in this example are not "measurable" until the source of evidence and the way the evidence will be used to assess objective completion are articulated.

Some definitions of objectives specify that they must be measurable as stated (Coley and Scheinberg, 2001), however, we do not agree. First, not all objectives will be measured. All will be assessed, but some might be assessed in ways that do not use measurement. Second, in our model, objectives provide a structure for reflexive action. Until we examine these points in more detail, suffice it to say that objectives are critical statements of action processes that provide the foundation for reflexive action and outcome assessment. If you look at the objectives above closely, you will see that they present a structure for the action processes and outcomes necessary to attain the intermediate goal of educating teachers and employers about typical accommodation costs and about the capacity of youth with special health care needs to work. But how are these objectives "ascertainable?" As stated, you can't know. However, look at Table 9.1 to show you how each objective is conceptualized and translated into a format so that attainment can be assessed.

As you can see by examining the table, linking each objective to a success criterion, evidence on which to assess the criterion, and a time line, the structure is set. The structure includes the action, the determination of

Table 9.1 Intermediate goal statement: "Educate teachers and employers about typical accommodation costs and about the capacity of youth with special health care needs to work"

Objectives	Time line	Assessment strategy
1. Project staff will assemble youth who will participate.	Month 1	Full complement of 6 youth are named and agree to participate.
2. Project staff will train youth in curriculum planning.	Months 1–6	Completion of training. All youth pass test in curriculum planning.
3. Project staff will work with youth to specify content and structure of training curriculum.	Months 1–6	Identified project staff conduct weekly sessions with youth over 6 months.
4. Youth under the guidance of the project director will complete materials and formal curriculum.	Month 7	All materials and curriculum are completed and documented.
5. Education staff will work with youth to develop adult education skills.	Months 1–6	Weekly sessions conducted with youth over 6 months. Youth pass test in adult education skills.
6. Under the guidance of the project staff, youth will conduct mock-training with an audience.	Month 8	Completion of one mock session with total curriculum.
7. As assessed by the audience, youth will demonstrate excellence in training skills.	Month 8	Mean scores from audience members for each youth will meet criterion score for excellence.
8. Project staff and youth will revise and complete necessary youth training according to feedback from mock-training evaluation.	Months 9–11	Documented revisions cross-checked in response to written audience feedback.

#	Activity	Timeframe	Indicator
9.	Project staff will assist youth in scheduling education and training sessions with teachers and employers.	Month 11	Scheduled trainings documented.
10.	With guidance from the project staff, youth will conduct two education and training sessions for educators and two sessions for employers.	Months 12–14	Documented and completed trainings.
11.	As a result of attending training sessions, employers and teachers will obtain knowledge of typical accommodation costs and about the capacity of youth with special health care needs to work.	Months 12–14	Passing knowledge scores and audience member reported attribution of learning to the training sessions.
12.	As a result of attending training sessions, employers and teachers will specify uses of their knowledge to enhance the employment opportunities for youth with special health care needs.	Months 18–20	Follow-up survey at 6 months following training to document uses of knowledge.
13.	Youth will obtain feedback from educators and employers suggesting improvements to the curriculum structure and content.	Months 18–20	Documented suggestions from educators and employers who attended the training.
14.	Project staff and youth will revise curriculum content and structure, based on session feedback and assessments.	Months 21–22	Documented revisions cross-checked in response to written audience feedback.
15.	Project staff and youth will develop and implement long-term plan for education and training of teachers and employers.	Month 23 and beyond	Documented plan.

which action process addresses each objective, and the determination of when, and the extent to which, objectives are successfully achieved. The thinking process of specifying objectives begins to illustrate how distinct parts of professional activity can be monitored and linked to outcome.

The specification of process objectives thus provides the structure to reflect on professional action. Our term reflexive action was, therefore, coined to denote our ideal approach to professional activity as one in which careful and informed scrutiny is not only possible but inherent in all professional activities and entities.

Let us now return to the HRTW project to illustrate the thinking process of establishing objectives to accomplish a long-term goal. Derived from the needs assessment, a long-term goal was specified: "Employers and teachers will demonstrate increasingly favorable attitudes about the capacity for and value of youth with special health care needs to be prepared for competitive employment."

The objectives for achieving this goal are:

1. Employers and teachers participating in training will improve on attitudinal assessments at yearly time intervals.
2. Employers and teachers will behaviorally demonstrate increasingly favorable attitudes by participating in efforts to improve employment preparation for adolescents with special health care needs.

Can you select the outcome and process objectives? If you said that both are outcome objectives, you are correct. Common sense tells us that rather than monitoring our professional processes, as time passes we become increasingly focused on outcome rather than process. Be aware that as you move from short- to long-term activity, the objectives will reflect an increasing concern with outcome and a decreasing focus on process.

So far, we have discussed the thinking process of relating goals and objectives. However, many different goals and objectives can be formulated to achieve the same need. We now move to the action processes of translating needs into goals and objectives.

Deriving Goals from Needs Statements

As has been illustrated, even though a needs statement is clear, many goals can be gleaned from the same needs statement. Consider the following example.

Let's revisit the adolescent HRTW example. Remember that this problem statement was initially posed: "Adolescents with special health care needs frequently move into adulthood without the vocational skills to be competitive on the job market." To remind you, part of the needs assessment revealed that adolescents clearly identified their need for equal opportunity and full inclusion in the same vocational opportunities available for youth without special health care needs and, further, that those with special health care needs were systematically excluded from vocational experience and training opportunities, in large part due to negative attitudes held by teachers and employers regarding the cost of accommodation and skepticism about the capacity of these youth to compete adequately in the job market. Based on this understanding of need, we presented several goals above. But were they the only goals that could have been derived from that needs statement? What if the goals did not address attitudes and training but, rather, directed professional action to policy reform mandating full inclusion of youth with special health care needs in vocational preparation? Such an approach is an affirmative action response, which would be a large social change effort, not specifically aimed at education and attitudinal change. Perhaps the goal would provide economic incentives for employers to provide work opportunities and on-the-job training for youth with special health care needs. This type of approach was used in the Targeted Jobs Tax Credit Incentive (Office of Disability Employment Policy, U.S. Department of Labor, 2007) to encourage small businesses to employ individuals with disabilities.

Each of the approaches addresses the same needs statement but from differing perspectives. Each approach has its advantages and limitations, and none is the "correct" or "incorrect" way to structure the aim of a professional entity.

How do you translate needs statements into goals? There is no simple answer or formula, but there are action processes and principles that can guide you.

First, it is important to identify who will be formulating goals for professional action. Will a collaborative model be used? If so, who is involved? How will decisions be made?

Second, what are your values and the values of collaborators if you are working with others? In which direction would they take you for goal setting? Using the previous example, would you work directly with educators to elicit attitude change, or would you go to the policy level to mandate cooperation? This decision would depend on your own values, the willingness of the educators or legislators to collaborate, and the scope of your professional domain.

Third, the literature or previous professional experience might provide clues to guide your direction. If you are engaging in a need that has been addressed previously, what was the process and outcome? How consistent were process and outcome with your vision of meeting the stated need?

Fourth, what limitations and advantages are provided by your resources? In the example of adolescents with special health care needs, if you did not have access to train adolescents to speak on their own behalf, you could not set the education and training goals discussed. On the other hand, if you did not have knowledge of, or access to, policy change, you would not be able to set goals to move in that direction.

How long can you concern yourself with the need? What fiscal resources do you have? Who is funding you, and what are the values of the funder?

Finally, purpose must be the overriding factor in translating needs into goals. This is a critical point to remember. The action processes of goal and objective setting are thus embedded within purpose and are, in essence, a delimitation of time, interaction, audience, and approach.

Action Process of Writing Process Objectives

To develop sound process objectives, the program goals should be clear, and the financial, time, material, and human resources must be known. Objectives and their success criteria are then specified to guide the intervention and illuminate how you will know if the objective has been accomplished in a timely fashion. Box 9.1 provides guidelines for the action process of writing process objectives.

Box 9.1 Action process guidelines for writing process objectives

1. Each objective must be derived directly from one or more goals.
2. Process objectives must be time sequenced.
3. Only one activity per objective should be described.
4. The objective should answer the questions what, who, when, and how?
5. Statements must be unambiguous.
6. Process objectives must be written such that the expected time of completion can be specified in assessment of the objective.
7. Process objectives are purposive.
8. Process objectives must consider resource limitations.
9. Process objective completion must be assessable by collection and analysis of empirical evidence without looking at outcome.
10. Accountability (who does what) is specified by process objectives.

Action Process of Writing Outcome Objectives

Outcome or summative objectives specify successful outcome criteria and structure how success will be conceptualized and ascertained. Similar to process objectives, outcome objectives are clear, with each addressing a single desired outcome of an intervention. Outcome objectives also provide the structure for timing of outcomes. That is, outcome objectives indicate when an outcome should occur and at what level. As you can see, the outcome objectives depicted in the example can refer to one or multiple targets and issues. Thus, in writing outcomes, you must be sure that what you expect is reasonable, is not impossible due to factors outside your control, meets the purposes of the intervention, and is within the value set of your problem statement. Revisit the outcome objectives in the HRTW example. Can you see that they specify who will do what or what will happen as a result of a professional action? Note that outcome objectives do not specify how the activity will be organized but, rather, what will occur from professional action and for whom. In our evaluation practice model, we reiterate that objective statements do not need to contain the specific measurement and success criteria but must provide the structure for that information to be articulated. In our discussion of outcome assessment later in the book we will examine how objectives structure outcome assessment and analysis.

There are some important considerations in writing outcome objectives. Box 9.2 presents action process guidelines for writing outcome objectives.

Box 9.2 Action process guidelines for writing outcome objectives

1. Articulate the desired results of your project and translate into objectives that detail each result.

2. Link outcome objectives to one or more goals.

3. Clarify the desired impact by including as appropriate, what, who, when, and where in your objective statement.

4. Delimit both the scope and the nature of the impact so that it is assessable with empirical evidence.

5. Write your objective so that it provides the structure and rationale for the selection of data and analytic techniques that can best let you know the degree of desired impact that has occurred.

As we will see later in the text, attribution of outcome to your activity is not easy to assess. The causal links between professional action and outcome are challenging to investigate due to the limitations of evaluation designs with which we work. Keep this point in mind when writing outcome objectives so that you do not create a set of expectations that are unattainable or unable to be assessed. Remember that in our HRTW project we did not select the outcome of increasing youth employment. Now you see why. Sound outcome objectives are those that make sense for the professional entity, are within the scope of what you can do, are purposive, and provide the structure to examine the links between project and outcome.

Main Points

1. The action process of goal and objective formulation is critical in our evaluation practice model because it is the first step in which specific accountability criteria are set.
2. Goals and objectives provide the structure for professional action and posit desired outcomes at one or more time intervals.
3. Goals are broad statements about the ideal or "hoped for."
4. How the goal will be attained and how you will know that it has been attained are the purposes of objectives and frame the nomenclature for two types of objectives: process and outcome.
5. Process (also called formative or monitoring) objectives state what will be done when and by whom.
6. Outcome (also termed summative) objectives delineate how you will know that you were successful in producing a desired result from what was done.
7. There is a set of action process guidelines for extracting goals from needs statements and for writing objectives to address goals. In doing this task, one must consider purpose, resources, constraints, and values.

Exercises

Based on the HRTW problem and needs statements above, establish one intermediate goal that has not been advanced in the text.

1. Link your goal to the needs statement, and state why you selected this goal.
2. Establish process and outcome objectives for your goal, and develop a table indicating the success criteria, evidence, and time line for the accomplishment of each.

Reflexive Action

REFLEXIVE
ACTION—
IMPLEMENTATION

CHAPTER 10

Reflexive Action: What Is It?

What Is Reflexive Action?

As we indicated in Chapters 1 and 2, reflexive action is the set of processes that we believe should characterize all professional activity. Reflexivity is a term used in naturalistic method to indicate the thinking process in which investigators identify the influences that they bring to an inquiry and to the interpretive process that shapes the knowledge derived therefrom (Steier, 1991). We extrapolate the meaning of the term and apply it to evaluation practice to describe professional action in which professionals individually and collectively are engaged in a systematic examination of their work, resources, and use of self, and other influences that impact professional process and outcome. Moreover, because Mollering (2006) has associated reflexivity with trust, we further assert the critical importance of reflexivity in all professional domains in order to engender trust and confidence from within and outside of one's professional group.

During the implementation of professional action, systematic thinking does not cease. A hallmark of professional practice ostensibly is systematic decision making based on empirical evidence (Freidson, 2001). Reflexive action not only guides professionals to use systemic decision making but directs the professional to seek to obtain feedback from the actual professional activity itself, as well as from examination of use of self in, and other influences on, one's professional activity. Thus, unlike the professional whose practice is skill based and intuitive, the professional who applies the principles of reflexive action carefully scrutinizes the implementation of goals and objectives through systematically monitoring all phases of action. That is not to say that practice wisdom and intuition do not occur. They do, but in evaluation practice the professional makes it a point to be well aware of the evidentiary basis from which he or she is making decisions. Then he/she carefully looks at all activity to obtain clarity about what was done and what feedback resulted from engaging in practice action processes. Knowing what was done provides important information that contributes not only to the immediate situation but also to future professional knowledge. Let us look at an example.

Think back to Grant-maker. Over the years, Grant-maker had engaged in intuitive, value-based funding aimed at expanding access to health care. And while each funded project was required to evaluate its own activity and provide a report, Grant-maker was not able to look at the extent to which its primary goal was being met by its overall funding entity. After conducting the summative evaluation of one year of funding decisions, it has decided to engage in regular future reflexive action. Grant-maker will record its decision-making processes and how those processes are informed by evidence, intuition, values, economics, policy, and other relevant influences. In order to formalize reflexive action, Grant-maker has devised a web-based monitoring system to record all of its own activity (funding, meeting minutes, negotiations, investments, and so forth). This site will cross-reference individual project activity with Grant-maker's expenditures to assess goal attainment and return on investments.

Each year in our evaluation classes, we send our students out to interview professionals about how they evaluate themselves and their activity. The students ask a series of questions that follows the sequence of our model, beginning with the problem addressed, through asking about how professionals assess outcome. It is not unusual for professionals to pause before answering the questions and to express uncertainty about the actual problems that they address or how they systematically examine outcome. Most discuss what they do but not why. The majority of professionals, however, do articulate their understanding of the need for empirical support for their activity in this fiscally oriented climate.

In concert with the trends for professional accountability (Freidson, 2001) professionals need to expand empirical methods to structure their activity. Reflexive action provides the guiding steps for translating systematic evidence from the previous evaluation practice thinking and action processes into well-conceptualized, goal-oriented activity that can be monitored and assessed for the extent to which the action addressed the initial problem statement.

Selection of an Approach—Translating Goals and Objectives into Professional Action

This point in the evaluation practice model is a clear illustration of the intersection of the evaluation practice meta-framework and substantive professional reasoning, given that we assert that no profession has a single "correct" approach to problem definition or resolution. The steps of problem definition, needs statement, and setting goals and objectives all inform the direction of professional action. These preliminary but critical steps identify the constraints, resources, and purposes that bear on professional decisions and choices. By the time a professional has reached the action phase of evaluation practice, it is likely that he or she will have a good idea of what action processes should occur. Most important, the theoretical approach and skills basis for action that are held by each professional group will guide the action process.

However, as we find each year from the assignment that we discussed above, it is not uncommon for professionals to move to action without articulating a systematically thought-out rationale. We believe that if professionals carefully examine their practice, they will see the implicit assumptions about problem and need that are being addressed. In our model, we assert that implicit assumptions are problematic in that they do not provide the clarity necessary to ascertain and demonstrate efficacy. Rather, action should be openly and explicitly anchored on the thinking and action processes of problem identification, needs assessment, and establishment of goals and objectives, and should clearly indicate how substantive professional theory, knowledge, value, and skill fit within this framework.

Look again at the discussion of force field analysis presented in Chapter 3. This thinking tool provides an excellent strategy through which to further clarify and specify actions that will accomplish objectives and attain goals. We looked at the application of force field analysis to clarifying intervention points to resolve identified problems. The initial step involved stating a problem, estimating its severity, and then looking at the forces (driving (positive) or restraining (negative)) that influence the extent to which a problem remains the same, increases, or decreases in severity (DePoy and MacDuffie, 2004).

At this point in the evaluation practice model, force field analysis serves another function: identifying specific actions to achieve goals and objectives. To use force field analysis to plan specific strategies, the thinking processes presented in Chapter 3 are applied to a specific objective rather than a broad problem statement. Even if you do not use force field analysis, we suggest that you engage in a similar systematic thinking process that helps you be specific and clear in why you are selecting actions and what you expect each to elicit in terms of process and outcome. By using a systematic approach to action planning, the link between objectives and action processes becomes clarified and allows for process and outcome assessment to examine specific parts of your activity. As we will see in the chapters on outcome assessment, it is not an easy task to attribute outcome to professional activity in total or in part. Therefore, the more clarity and specificity in how actions are conceptualized to actualize goals and objectives, the easier and more useful your outcome assessment will become. Let us look at an example.

Consistent with our own passions for equality of access to information, we have been teaching an undergraduate course sequence focusing on social change through universal access. Because we see teaching as part of our professional activity and responsibility, we apply the evaluation practice model to our teaching activity. Our initial problem statement is: "Unequal access to information and community resources and spaces is discriminatory." From a complex problem map, a cause that we identified and documented through systematic needs assessment was the lack of awareness of access barriers and the limited knowledge and skill to identify and remove these barriers (DePoy, 2004; DePoy and Gilson, 2005/6). Through force field analysis, a driving force that was present for us was the teaching environment at the university, a progressive disability studies unit, and our university's commitment to accessibility in certain domains such as electronic access (The University of Maine, Web Office, n.d.).

However, restraining forces were the narrow definition of access, the location of universal access efforts in a disability unit rather than in a unit that studies social justice, and thus limited attention to the broader social justice issue of equality of access. To meet the goal of increasing knowledge and skill to promote a progressive agenda of universal access, we developed an interdisciplinary academic concentration focused on universal access history, theory, and skill development. Each semester, we institute extensive reflexive action that includes regular faculty meetings to reflect on curriculum, assignments and pedagogy, classroom observations of process, student process assessments, and careful monitoring of expenditures and resources. From this internal examination we have been seeking explanations for less than desired outcomes in our students' achievement of course objectives. From the learning that we have derived from our own reflexive action, we have changed our assignments and readings yearly and now are partnering with the innovation center on campus, whose goal is to advance student and faculty innovation in products and services. Without this reflexive action, we would not necessarily have ascertained that the coursework, not student failure, was responsible for limiting student achievement.

Let us now turn to systematic, sequential guidelines for selecting your approach to professional action (see Box 10.1). Note that we always begin with the problem.

Box 10.1 Sequential guidelines for selecting your approach to professional action

1   Be clear on the problem statement. To whom does the problem belong, whose values are represented in the statement, which part of the problem is to be addressed, and which stakeholder groups are concerned with the problem?
2   Consult and keep the needs assessment in mind as you are planning your action. What is needed by whom and why, what is the scope of need, what disagreements exist among stakeholder groups about what is needed, and who can fill the need as articulated?
3   Be sure that goals and objectives clearly emerge from and respond to the full scope of need.
4   Use a systematic thinking process to plan action strategies, based on a sound, empirically and theoretically informed rationale that will be conducted to achieve goals and objectives.
      Consider the purposive, organizational, and resources context of the activity.
5   Clearly articulate the action processes of the activity, being sure to detail the temporal sequence, distinct action processes, and outcomes expected from each aspect of intervention.
6   Clearly link each action process to one or more objectives that it is designed to accomplish.

Returning to our example of our course sequence, look at Box 10.2. The syllabus in this box documents the sequence presented in Box 10.1 above.

Note that the problems in Box 10.2 are clearly identified, as well as the need, goals, objectives, and methods that students and faculty will use to meet them. Given this systematic approach, you now might be asking yourself why the action process failed to meet its mark. Read on and we address this question below.

The detail with which you address the guidelines in Box 10.1 will be an important determinant in the degree to which you can ultimately attribute changes in outcome to your activity. We will examine this point in greater detail later in the text. Now let us turn to reflexive action processes.

Reflexive Action Processes

Reflexive action consists of three important evaluative processes: monitoring, cost analysis, and analysis of external influences on professional process and outcome.

Monitoring

Monitoring is the set of actions used by professionals to regularly examine their actions and record information about the strategies that will be used to assess process and outcome of an activity (Finkler, 2005). Reflexive monitoring clearly documents what was done, how it was done, and the resources that were used. Answering "who, what, why, when, where, and how" questions is a good way to monitor professional action processes. In Chapters 11 and 12 we discuss specific methods of monitoring process. But for now, look at the example of our universal access course sequence for monitoring concepts.

Cost Analysis

In the twenty-first century, the global economy and concern for cost-effectiveness are becoming hegemonous (Finkler, 2005). While the cost of providing professional services is not always a popular topic, particularly for professionals who work in not-for-profit entities and "helping roles," it is a necessary and efficacious process. As we see the effects of untapped spending and consumption, accountability for expenditures of human and non-human resources is not only cost efficient, but we see it as ethically essential. We therefore include cost analysis in reflexive action because the cost of conducting professional activity must be considered in ethical professional processes.

Box 10.2 Course syllabus

Required Readings:
DePoy, E. and Gilson, S. (2004) *Rethinking Disability: Principles for Professional and Social Change*
Other selected readings will be assigned.

Overview
Building on previous courses, students will address the problem of unequal access to information and resources. In order to improve access, knowledge-able and skilled citizens in all domains are critically needed. Students will meet this need through examining, analyzing, and applying universal design/access theory and practices to an access problem.

The goal of this course is to provide students with the structures, processes, and materials to create social change.

Objectives

1. Demonstrate understanding of the distinction between accommodation and universal access.

---

2. Identify and discuss recent intellectual, social, economic, technological, cultural, political, and medical trends affecting accessibility.
3. Demonstrate familiarity with legislation and policies affecting accessibility.
4. Select an exemplar that limits access.
5. Through analysis, problem solving, and action, fabricate or develop a "technology" solution to advance universal access to your chosen domain.

Teaching–Learning Methods

This course will utilize a variety of teaching–learning strategies, including reading, group discussion, experiential exercises, asynchronous web conferencing, and guest speakers.

Student Responsibilities

Students are responsible for regular attendance, fulfilling all assignments, and for knowing about announcements made in class, including changes in the syllabus.

Students are expected to use respectful language in class and on all written assignments. All papers must be typed and should conform to current APA format.

Assignments

Assignment 1:

Each student will come prepared to fully participate in class activity, to discuss and share insights on readings and learning experiences, and to provide positive critical feedback to other students.   20%

Assignment 2:

For each reading, students will hand in a typed paragraph answering the following question: With what ideas that were presented in the reading did you disagree and why?
  These paragraphs will form the basis of reading analyses, and discussion and application in class.   20%

Assignment 3:

Policy Reports   20%

In small groups, select one of the following:

• The Individuals with Disabilities Education Act Amendments (IDEA) (P.L. 101–476)

- The Americans with Disabilities Act (ADA) (P.L. 101–336)
- Social Security Amendments (P.L. 84–880)
- The Rehabilitation Act of 1973 (P.L. 93–112)
- Federal-Aid Highway Act Amendments of 1973 (P.L. 93–643)
- Technology-Related Assistance for Individuals with Disabilities Act Amendments (P.L. 103–218)

Prepare and deliver a universally accessible poster presentation with the following information: please see accessible poster presentation guidelines.

1. Summary of the legislation.
2. Historical context—what intellectual, scientific, cultural, economic, political, and social factors influenced the passage of this law?
3. Who is the target of this law? Who is excluded?
4. Are the principles in line with accommodation or universal approaches?
5. How do you anticipate that this legislation will affect you in your professional activity?

Provide evidence for your claims—"How do you know?"

Assignment 4:

Universal Design: The ADA and Beyond the ADA   40%

Definition of technology
"The discipline dealing with the art or science of applying scientific knowledge to practical problems."

Everyday examples to illustrate how technology can range from the simplest device or system:

- Door knob
- Electric doors
- Ramp
- Steps
- Elevator
- Can openers
- Carrot peelers
- Jar lid openers
- Sink handles
- Cup
- Computer
- iPod (understanding, comfort, sustainability)
- Pencil or pen (understanding, ease, beauty, sustainability)
- Drinking straw (ease, safety, health)
- Key and lock (safety, strength, beauty)
- Stroller (participation, comfort, strength-caretaker, safety)

- Shopping cart (strength, ease, comfort)
- Bicycle gears (strength)
- Telescope (ease, accuracy, understanding)
- Cell phone camera (accuracy, sustainability)
- Makeup (beauty, participation)
- Handwarmers (safety, comfort, participation)

EXERCISE

Part I

Select an example of technology—a device, product (see above list for examples).

Your examples of technologies can include: a product or item, a material, a process or method, a mechanism, a means of attaching or holding, a part.

Think about all the things you see on a daily basis, describe their full range of use.

Describe how that technology might/does facilitate each of the following: understanding, participation, comfort, health, strength, ease, safety, accuracy, sustainability, beauty.

Part II

Rate that technology from 0–4 (0 = no benefit, 4 = maximum benefit) using the matrix provided with respect to the degree to which that technology might enhance any of the listed abilities or diversities.

Rate the degree to which that technology *could* enhance any of the listed abilities or conditions (0 = No potential benefit, 5 = Offers high degree of potential benefit).

Hearing	
Vision	
Mobility	
Balance	
Grasp	
Strength	
Memory	
Attention	
Safety	
Comfort	

Give a descriptive rationale for your ratings (based on the literature).

Based on your matrix ratings: What is your general assessment of the degree to which that technology might enhance or contribute to full or universal access? What is the basis for your assessment/conclusions (how do you know?)? (Base your assessment on scholarly literature.)

So what?
Select one type of technology that offers a high degree of potential benefit (score of 5, but a low score of benefit, 2 or less) and redesign that technology. Now that you have selected and described that technology, and have assessed its "accessibility," how would you redesign the technology? Create a model, drawing, or mock-up of your redesign. This must be presented in universally accessible format. Your redesign must incorporate principle, theory, and research from the literature. This literature must be presented in APA format. Base your design suggestions (drawings, mock-ups, detailed narrative) on the scholarly literature.

(Assignment adapted from Donnelly, 2002–4)

Class Schedule

Session 1 Welcome
• Course introduction and overview
• Universal access and accommodation
• In-class activity: Bad design: http://www.baddesigns.com/

Session 2 Revisiting environment and access

Session 3 Review of access—physical, sensory, geographic, language, virtual, cognitive
• In-class exercise: Misunderstood minds (use response form)
• Read handout: Definition of Cognitive Accessibility at www.necfoundation.org/impact/impact_show.htm?doc_id=275178
• Read handout: History of Universal Design
• American Access

Session 4 Legitimacy
• Sign up for policy report
• Read: Chapters 7 and 8, DePoy and Gilson

Session 5 Two legitimate policy perspectives: Accommodation (including assistance/adaptation) and universal design/access
• Read: Chapter 9, DePoy and Gilson
• Read handout: Creating Justice, Sustaining Life
• Read Handout: A Perspective on Universal Design

Session 6 Access to the virtual environment
- Read handout: The Network Society
- Read handout: User interfaces for all: New perspectives into human–computer interaction

Session 7 Policy assignment 4: Policy posters presented in class

Session 8 In-class board game exercise
- Read handout: Norman—Three Levels of Design: Visceral, Behavioural, and Reflective

Session 9 Presentation of assignment 5: Two person team simulation/access presentation
- Read handout: Norman—People, Places, and Things

Session 10 Cognitive access
- Read handout: Norman—We are all Designers
- In-class exercise—recipe creation

Session 11 Social access—SociBaFaBaFa in class

Session 12 Assignment 6: Preliminary product design presentations

Sessions 13–14 Assignment 6: Final product design presentations; Graduation celebration

Analysis of External Influences on the Intervention Process and Outcome

There are numerous influences on professions, including, but not limited to, political, economic, social, cultural, population-based, geographic, virtual, expressive, intellectual, fiscal, scientific, and technological factors (DePoy and Gilson, 2007; Finkler, 2005; Freidson, 2001). However, as part of the reflexive action process, it is essential that we be as expansive and analytic as possible in examining all the factors we can find that could impact both the outcome of our activity and the way in which we conceptualize and engage in our professional responsibilities.

Remember that we promised to answer the question of why our class failed to meet its mark? We did not do a comprehensive examination of influences. The first factor that we did not consider was the location of our courses in a disability studies unit. Students who enrolled were expecting to understand access from a medicalized diagnostic perspective. For example, special education students were hoping to learn how to teach to youth with cognitive and language impairments. Thus, their expectations and interests were not met, as we did not consider how to market our courses so that their content and processes would be clear to perspective students. Second, the college structure of our university does not facilitate interdisciplinary study outside of certain units, such as the Innovation Center. For that reason, along with the common intellectual foundations of our work, we therefore developed this important collaboration. And, finally, we did not consider the limited intellectual development in universal access theory. Because it originated from the disability community (Ostroff *et al.*, 2002), it has only recently been linked to social justice (DePoy and Gilson, 2004, 2005/6, 2006).

Main Points

1. Reflexive action refers to the systematic process of scrutinizing one's activity including its cost and the multiple influences that shape how professionals function.
2. Selection of professional action is a systematic process in which the decisions are based on the steps of problem identification, needs assessment, and establishment of goals and objectives.
3. Actualizing goals and objectives is a systematic process in which multiple factors and evidence must be considered to make decisions.
4. Once the activity is specified, reflexive action should be a consistent practice.
5. Reflexive action comprises process assessment, cost analysis, and analysis of the external influences on intervention process and outcome.

Exercises

1. Examine the processes that a professional entity to which you have access uses in order to monitor its activity, cost, and influences that affect its operation and outcome.
2. Assess the extent to which systematic data are used/generated to elaborate the professional activity that takes place within the entity. Are these processes sufficiently detailed so that you have a good picture of the action processes? Can you answer who, what, where, when, and how about activity? If so, what are the processes? If not, what is missing?
3. What cost analysis systems are in place? Who conducts these analyses?
4. How does the entity account for external influences on the process and outcome of its action?

REFLEXIVE
ACTION—
IMPLEMENTATION

CHAPTER **11**

Thinking Processes of Reflexive Intervention

In this chapter, we explore the thinking processes of reflexive action. We have posited three elements of reflection in evaluation practice: monitoring process, cost analysis, and examination of external influences on the process and outcome of intervention. In this chapter, we examine the conceptual activity in each element in detail.

Monitoring

There are five basic questions to guide your thinking in monitoring process:

1. What happened during the intervention to accomplish the intervention goals and objectives?
2. How, where, and when did it happen?
3. Who participated? Who did not?
4. What were the strengths and limitations of the approach?
5. What processes need to be changed?

Before discussing the thinking processes of each question in more detail, we advance a conceptual understanding of monitoring and how it fits with evaluation practice.

Definitions of Monitoring Processes

Professional activity denotes the set of actions that occur in order to meet specified goals and objectives. Processes fall into the five categories in Box 11.1.

Box 11.1 Monitoring processes

- *Administration*: policies, procedures, and activities that provide the structure through which to manage the internal and interactive functions of an entity or professional activity

- *Direct activity*: processes to deliver interventions to the target population(s) identified in the problem statement and need

- *Indirect activity*: processes that impact the target population but do not engage them in active participation

- *Staff development*: educational processes to advance the knowledge and skill of staff

- *Systemic interaction*: processes through which an agency, intervention structure, group, or individual articulate with systems that affect planning, development, implementation, and outcome

---

Let us look at examples from the HRTW project to clarify each of the processes in Box 11.1.

Because HRTW is a national entity, there were multiple levels of administrative structures and processes involved, beginning with Congress which authorized the funding and policies through which the Maternal and Child Health Bureau (MCHB) could fund and guide this entity. Project officers at MCHB provided the national direction and fiscal accountability for the national program and articulated with Congress for reporting.

At the project level, the HRTW initiative was a state collaborative and thus involved a complex administrative structure. However, the university, functioning both as the applicant and the lead agency in the project, was ultimately the primary administrative structure. Thus the policies and fiscal practices of the university were dominant in providing the administrative scaffold for this entity. Included in policies were:

1. the necessity to have approval from the Human Subject Review Board for all research and data collection involving humans;
2. academic, research, and informed service integrity;
3. personnel policies governing employee activity and salaries; and others.

Direct activity in the HRTW project involved the inclusive needs assessment and planning activity in which the youth who were targets of the entity participated. Indirect activity involved others such as educators, policy makers, providers, teachers, and parents in data collection and planning for youth. In the HRTW project, we were fortunate to be able to provide stipends for graduate student staff. They were the primary recipients of staff development. We also trained staff in needs assessment and planning processes to assure rigor, but, indirectly, so that training could also be considered as staff development. Systemic interaction in the HRTW initiative can be seen in the conduct of training as a collaborative entity. Policies generated by both the university and collaborative agencies were negotiated and a state–university cooperative agreement contract formed the administrative document that guided all interactive activity.

Given the multiple domains of process, an important job of all professionals within the framework of evaluation practice is to decide on the scope and detail with which the reflexive action of monitoring process will be implemented. Monitoring or process assessment (we use these terms interchangeably) is, therefore, a set of thinking and action processes to ascertain, characterize, and document the relationship between articulated objectives and what occurs during a set of activities or entity, what factors impact the action, who is involved, and what resources are used.

In the HRTW entity, the process objectives for year one were:

1. recruit a participatory action team (PAT) to conduct the needs assessment;
2. train the PAT in needs assessment methods;
3. recruit participants for focus groups, key informants for life history interview, and a sample to respond to the survey.

Each of these objectives is a process objective that guides the nature and sequence of action processes.

In many professional domains process assessment focuses on the examination of the extent to which interventions were conducted, who conducted them, and who participated (Rossi *et al.*, 2004). Look at this definition of monitoring from the United Nations Development Programme Evaluation Office (2002):

> A continuing function that aims primarily to provide managers and main stakeholders with regular feedback and early indications of progress or lack thereof in the achievement of intended results. Monitoring tracks the actual performance or situation against what was planned or expected according to pre-determined standards.

It is not unusual to see reports that assess process through counting the number of hours that the staff devoted to each project activity, the number of target participants, the number of entities created for distribution, income, and the extent to which these data met the expectations stated in the initial project. This information may provide utilization knowledge, but "how" the staff functioned, how each activity was enacted, where activities occurred, and the context of the processes are critical pieces of knowledge that might not typically be captured if monitoring is conceptualized too narrowly.

Monitoring in evaluation practice is much broader in scope and involves the application of rigorous systematic inquiry to an examination of how an intervention was enacted within cost, professional domain, policy, and community contexts. Recognition of the context in which monitoring occurs eliminates the perfunctory nature of "counting" that so frequently occurs in many professional domains. Unlike typical approaches to process assessment (Fitzpatrick *et al.*, 2004; Stufflebeam and Shinkfield, 2007), the necessity to understand the context of evaluation practice expands the scope of inquiry, the methods that are acceptable, and the utility of the knowledge derived from monitoring.

A comprehensive reflexive approach to monitoring also serves to inform others who are not directly involved in the professional activity or entity about its performance. Moreover, sound monitoring, when linked with outcome assessment, can provide exponentially greater analysis and detail regarding how and why outcomes occurred, what differences in processes produced differential outcomes, and what future changes need to be made to optimize goal attainment.

Consider Grant-maker for example. As it has proceeded with monitoring, not only did its grant-making processes change, but their emphasis significantly shifted away from requests for proposals to create new health care entities for underserved populations to a totally different approach. Its new priorities focus on integrating health care services as the basis for maximizing and expanding the reach of existing but limited human and non-human resources in its rural state.

Process assessment, therefore, has numerous purposes and domains, highlighting the importance of delimiting the scope to useful information for intended audiences and to resource-imposed boundaries.

Ideally, all monitoring is formative. This statement might seem redundant given that we have defined monitoring as process evaluation. However, to clarify our point, let us consider this issue in greater detail. Historically, evaluation has been divided into formative and summative elements (Stufflebeam and Shinkfield, 2007). Formative evaluation, whether in the field of education (Tessmer, 2005), human services (Thyer, 2001), business (Boulmetis and Dutwin, 2005), public policy (Nagel, 2001), or public health (Steckler and Linnan, 2002) ostensibly is intended to provide systematically derived input about process for the explicit purpose of improvement. And while a mere count of hours, products, participants, and so forth might provide some information about need for revision of professional activity, these limited data might not reveal what specific activities need to change, how the change might occur, and who should participate in revision. Moreover, a cursory process evaluation cannot specify how one will know if the changes have occurred. There might be significant resource and time limitations on monitoring, given the focus of funding sources on outcomes, but we urge professionals to consider how systematic, detailed process findings can save resources that might be spent on attempting to improve outcomes through uninformed revision or maintenance of the status quo. Moreover, once you get used to deliberate reflexive action, these thinking and action processes can be easily integrated into your day without much fanfare.

The following list presents the essential elements of monitoring, no matter what the scope of the inquiry:

1. Monitoring is purposive.
2. Monitoring uses systematic inquiry.
3. Monitoring has multiple audiences, some of whom might have different and possibly competing purposes for the use of the information.
4. Monitoring describes an activity or entity.

Monitoring is Purposive

Purpose not only underpins the scope of the professional action processes to be explored, but shapes how process assessment information is to be known. Thus, monitoring design as well as reporting is guided by purpose. We not only suggest that all monitoring be formative but define it as such. Thus, in the evaluation practice model, the main purpose of improving professional effort is always common to all process assessment. This important tenet of monitoring in evaluation practice is a critical link between practice, research, and knowledge. Conceptualizing monitoring as a method to improve professional activity clearly locates evaluation practice within the domain of knowledge generation. However, there are many other purposes for monitoring. These include, but are not limited to, examining efficiency, assessing input, determining resource use, determining utilization, describing similarities and differences in professional action processes, and examining contextual factors that should be considered.

As we discussed earlier in the example of our course sequence on universal access, careful and detailed monitoring, with particular attention to the university context, was critical in illuminating the changes that were needed to improve student outcome.

Monitoring Uses Systematic Inquiry

This statement might sound obvious but it is not uncommon for evaluation efforts that are considered to be formative in nature to be inferior in their rigor to outcome assessment. Perhaps this laissez-faire approach to monitoring occurs because monitoring and description are not considered as important as understanding outcome. However, any compromise of systematic rigor weakens the evaluation practice aim to contribute to advancement of professional knowledge.

As we noted in our example from our classes, had we not conceptualized a comprehensive and systematic monitoring process, we might have attributed poor student outcomes to the students, not to the courses and the university context.

In the HRTW example, one of the goals was to improve attitudes of the teachers and employers toward youth with special health care needs. The objectives delineated a set of processes through which youth trained in public speaking would present their strengths, experiences, and needs to teachers and employers. Monitoring how youth prepare and deliver presentations would be critical in any understanding of attitudinal change.

Monitoring Has Multiple Audiences

Take another look at the HRTW example. The audiences were diverse, and each had an agenda that differed in part or in total from the others. For the youth, being able to talk about their experiences and strengths could have been liberating and confidence building. However, the teachers, for example, might have been concerned if youth presented their school experiences as limiting. That same information might help employers understand why youth with special health care needs seem to lack skills possessed by youth without these conditions. Monitoring the content and process of presentations could be extremely valuable in providing feedback for formative purposes and illuminating differential outcomes for diverse audiences.

Box 11.2 lists audiences who are frequently involved in monitoring, and typical questions that each might want to have answered in a process assessment.

Looking back to the HRTW example, you can see how teachers and youth might have answered these questions differently. In the implementation phase of the project, the youth developed video presentations about themselves and selected youth used these videos in speaking engagements. To the youth who participated in public speaking, the professional-assisted

Box 11.2 Typical audiences and their questions for process assessment

Professional service or entity end-user

- What parts of the service or entity were satisfactory? Why?
- What parts of the service or entity were unsatisfactory? Why?
- What parts were easy to access or use? Which parts were difficult?
- How was I treated by the professional, service-providing salesperson?
- Did the service or entity include all that I needed?
- What else might I need?
- What changes should be made to improve access, participation, and process?
- Were the facilities and/or resources satisfactory to me?

Professionals involved in direct activity

- How much service or how many entities did I provide?
- What did I do that I would continue? Why?
- What did I do that I would not continue? Why?
- How satisfactory were the context and resources for me? For recipients of my services or entities?
- What activities helped me learn?
- What parts helped me advance my career?
- Did I feel valued? By whom?
- Were recording requirements reasonable?
- Was the workload acceptable?

Administrators

- Were my staff productive?
- Were the professional processes efficient in goal attainment?
- Were the costs and resource inputs reasonable? Sufficient?
- Were meetings productive?
- What are the policies that affect professional activity, and do they need to be changed?
- Was the flow of the activities or distribution of entities efficient relative to goals and objectives?
- Was marketing, public relations adequate/in need of change?

Funders

- How was the money used? Was resource use efficient?
- Who was intended to benefit from the activity or entity? Was the scope adequate, too broad, too narrow?

- What funding processes should be changed to improve professional activity?

Policy makers
- What policy governs the professional domain and how?
- Does the policy need to be changed and how?
- Did the professional activity comply with current policy?

Community members
- What are the goals and objectives of professional activity?
- For whom is this activity planned?
- Whom does the activity or entity serve?
- Whom should it serve?
- Is the environmental context desirable?
- Is the activity accessible to all who can benefit?
- Do I want to support this professional involvement in my community?

process and video entities were sound, but for so many who did not, these non-participants did not necessarily perceive a benefit in this narrow scope of participation. As a result of this monitoring finding, youth participation was expanded in subsequent years.

Monitoring Describes Action

This principle might seem evident but is often violated in monitoring. How many times have evaluations focused on program usage without describing what activities occurred, how, when, and where they occurred, the context in which each occurred, and factors that influenced intervention processes? We assert that any process evaluation beyond a perfunctory, compliant one must provide a multidimensional vision of how professional actions are formulated, publicized, and delivered. Moreover, it is critical to know the context of the action if monitoring is to serve a useful formative purpose.

For a recent evaluation of a national resource center that was funded to disseminate knowledge through presentations, materials, and technical assistance, we have developed a short survey for project staff to complete after they conduct each major effort. The survey assesses process and outcome for each major activity or entity generated in the project. The process items ask professionals to describe their activity, its marketing, its purpose, activity, its audience, context, venue, and sources of knowledge. See Box 11.3 below for sample process items on this survey.

Given the definitions for monitoring that have been discussed, we also highlight, in the list below, what monitoring is not.

- It is not punitive or final.
- It is not designed to be summative.
- It is not designed primarily to test the efficacy of theory.
- It is not designed to overlook unintended or unplanned results of an intervention.

Since monitoring is intended to provide information about professional action and its related contextual influences, the findings are not used to make final decisions about resources, performance, and worth. Rather, process evidence is intended to obtain detailed systematic knowledge of the elements of professional activity and entities, their sequence, and their variation. Moreover, process assessment is not a means to verify or falsify the operationalization of theory. It is primarily designed to contribute to theory development and refinement by providing feedback that can be used for revision. As we noted above, one element of evaluation practice that differs from many other evaluation approaches is that all monitoring must be formative and should be used to improve the manner in which goals are attained and objectives are accomplished, and to contribute to the advancement and improvement of professional theory and methods.

Now we turn to the second important element of reflexive action, cost analysis.

Cost Analysis

Looking at cost is increasingly important in the current climate in which professionals practice. Cost analysis is, therefore, a complex but essential part of evaluation practice. This text addresses two important approaches to examining cost: measuring the cost of process and measuring the cost of expected and unexpected outcomes. Unlike many texts and models of evaluation that discuss cost analysis as a discrete part of evaluation, we present a conceptual approach because any analysis of costs must occur as a monitoring process of inputs. We return to cost analysis in each of the remaining chapters as it applies to each subsequent area of evaluation practice being addressed.

Conceptual Approach to Examining Cost

Some of the many names for various approaches to assessing cost are cost-benefit analysis, cost efficiency, cost utility, return on investment, and cost-

---

Box 11.3 Sample process items on the evaluation survey

Thank you for providing information on your project activity. Please complete a survey for each activity. If you conducted a complex project activity that involved more than one type of activity, please complete a survey for each activity type.

1. Please check the type of activity for which you are completing this report (check only one response):

   ☐ Technical assistance

   ☐ Dissemination of materials

   ☐ Presentation

2. Please provide a brief description of the activity, including its marketing and advertising.

3. Date the activity was initiated: _____

4. Date the activity was completed: _____

5. What was the reason that you conducted this activity?
   (Please check all that apply):

   ☐ It was requested (please specify by whom and for what purpose)

   _____

   ☐ It was initiated by one or more members of the professional team

   ☐ Other (please specify by whom and for what purpose)

   _____

6. Through what venue did you conduct this activity? (Please check all that apply):

   ☐ On-site (e.g., conferences, meetings)

   ☐ E-mail

   ☐ Snail mail

☐ Video (e.g., conferencing, recording)

☐ Audio (e.g., conferencing, recording other than on the telephone)

☐ Phone

☐ Listserv

☐ Web

☐ Other (please specify) _____

_____

_____

7. Who were the recipients, participants, or audience for the activity? (Please check all that apply):

☐ Federal funders

☐ State funders

☐ Interagency

☐ Funded guarantees

☐ Family organizations

☐ Educators

☐ Federal agencies other than the funding agency (please specify)

_____

☐ Other (please specify) _____

_____

_____

8. What sources of knowledge did you use as the basis for this activity? (Please check all that apply):

☐ Formal theory (please provide references to literature)

_____

☐ Previous practice success (please provide references)

_____

☐ A body of evidence-based practice (please provide references)

_____

☐ Practical wisdom supports this

☐ Other (please specify) _____

_____

effectiveness (Finkler, 2005). What all have in common is that they address resource allocation (cost) and worth (value of attainment of goals, objectives, and consequences) (Finkler; Yates, 1996).

The following list presents the questions that you would answer in order to guide the thinking process of analyzing cost:

1. What resources will be considered as costs?
2. What worth factors will be addressed?
3. How will resources be associated with worth?

Question 1 is answered in the step of reflexive action. Questions 2 and 3 are a critical part of outcome assessment and will be addressed later in the text.

The question of what resources will be considered as costs might seem simple but, of course, it is not.

Think, for example, of Grant-maker. Although the primary costs of doing business might include funding given to individual projects, and the direct costs of running the agency such as personnel salaries and benefits, office expenses, information and communication technology, and travel, what else might be considered? Grant-maker provides bidders conferences online and on-site for its potential applicants. So the preparation and conduct of this activity is an expense that is not directly involved in the daily operation and functions of Grant-maker. What about public relations, efforts to keep employee morale high, in-service sessions, keeping the sidewalk clear of debris, and so forth?

Finally, what costs are considered to be part of the action? At this juncture, careful monitoring of resources expended is critical if questions about worth will be answered. This point will be addressed later in the discussion of outcomes. As part of reflexive action, we are concerned with the costs of providing a service, offering a program, developing and implementing a policy, or creating an entity. What should be considered as costs? Certainly the cost of providing technical assistance in the grant development process would be specified by Grant-maker. Would administrative expenses such as completing paperwork be considered as part of the cost? What about the cost of gasoline and electricity? There are many decisions to be made about what expenses should be included in cost.

There are no easy answers on what to include in costs. However, assessing costs must be consistent, rigorous, and purposive if this element of reflexive action is to be formative or useful in ascertaining the association between cost and worth.

External Influences on Intervention

As we have indicated, one of the strengths of monitoring is that the context is basic to the inquiry. How far to expand your look at context is an important thinking process. Many approaches to monitoring examine the immediate action processes without examining the factors that influence activity or entity. For example, we often see utilization statistics without any further information about recruitment, environmental, payment, or policy contexts.

Consider this example. In the HRTW program, two youth public speaking engagements to inform employers about youth strengths and accessibility costs were established in different parts of the same state. Each was based on a clear support for the need of such an activity, and both were identical in their action processes. One program had high attendance, and one did not. The disparity in attendance was a concern that could not be informed without a further examination of the context. Was it possible that the environments differed in transportation accessibility, job availability, and so forth? What if the location with low attendance had a high unemployment rate already?

Main Points

1. Reflection in evaluation practice is a careful examination of the professional action, its cost, and influences that are external to it.
2. Monitoring is an action process in which data about professional processes are systematically obtained and analyzed.
3. An essential element of evaluation practice is the use of monitoring for improving professional action and advancing new knowledge.
4. Cost analysis answers three questions that address relative cost.
5. Examining external influences on the professional process is a critical part of reflexive action.

Exercises

Select an organization of interest to you.

1. Look at how monitoring occurs. What data are obtained? How are they obtained and how are they used to assess process?
2. Critically analyze monitoring in the organization, and suggest how improvements can be made to ensure that the data are used for formative purposes.
3. In the organization, how are costs assessed? What is included in cost? What factors are considered in worth, and how are the two related?

REFLEXIVE
ACTION—
IMPLEMENTATION

CHAPTER 12

Action Processes of Reflexive Action

In this chapter, we examine methods by which reflexive action can be actualized. As we discovered when looking at thinking processes, the purpose, scope, and practical constraints that you encounter, as well as the audiences who will receive and work with the findings, are important determinants in the design that is selected for any part of reflexive action. Remember in Chapter 11 we discussed the three reflexive action elements: monitoring, cost analysis, and examination of external influences. As we proceed through the action processes, you might want to think about how each approach to design would be relevant to each element.

Experimental-Type Reflexive Action Designs

Although we often equate reflexive action with naturalistic inquiry, experimental-type designs are both useful and prevalent in process inquiry. Unlike outcome assessment, process assessment does not focus on cause-and-effect relationships between professional efforts and their results (Steckler and Linnan, 2002). Thus, true experimentation is rarely suggested as a viable design in reflexive action, unless it serves outcome purposes as well (Stufflebeam and Shinkfield, 2006). Rather, it is most valuable to use descriptive designs that can identify resource input and use, and contextual and internal correlates of professional process. According to Preskill and Catsambas (2006), reflexive action should build on the strengths of a professional organization, entity, and action. The designs used should be able to capture and communicate these. We agree that the model of

Box 12.1 Steps in nomothetic reflexive action inquiry

1. Specify the questions to be answered.

2. Detail the structure of the approach by identifying the variables and the nature of the description or relationship that you are examining.

3. Determine the boundaries of your inquiry. Will you use a sample? A population? What will be the units of analysis (individuals, families, communities, policies, entities, products, locations, etc.)?

4. Identify the constructs to be measured.

5. Articulate the lexical definitions (dictionary) and operational definitions (measurement) of the constructs.

6. Design the data analysis strategy to be used.

7. Specify how you will report your findings.

8. Specify how you will use the findings.

Appreciative Inquiry posited by these two authors is an ideal, but we also caution professionals to make sure that purpose is always the frame for climate as well as method.

Among these designs, non-experimental, pre-experimental, and quasi-experimental designs can numerically answer reflexive questions. Remember that we said that experimental-type designs are nomothetic, in that they illuminate group phenomena. These designs, therefore, are indicated when the professional wants to know something about groups of individuals, groups of groups, and/or groups of other units of analysis. You can refer to Chapter 7 for a refresher of experimental-type design.

For each experimental-type approach, follow the steps in Box 12.1.

As an example, look at the process evaluation that we just wrote for a grant proposal. If this project is funded, the aim of evaluation is to examine goal attainment on a substance abuse prevention and treatment project enacted in a rural location. The strategies to answer questions A and B in Box 12.5 fall under nomothetic designs. Remember that all assessment processes in evaluation practice are based on, and linked to, the foundation thinking processes. So first look at Boxes 12.2 through 12.4 to obtain an overview of the project problem, needs statements, and goals and objectives.

Look at Boxes 12.5 and 12.6 for an overview of the evaluation practice plan. As you can see, questions A, B, E, and F belong under the rubric of reflexive action and we therefore limit our discussion to those four questions in this chapter. Look at Box 12.6 to see the way in which the

Box 12.2 The problem

Rural County, New England, has one of the largest county land masses north of the Mississippi River, has significant youth substance abuse problems which are magnified by the County's rural character, poverty level, geographic size, and close proximity to Canada.

Box 12.3 The need

Guided by the micro-environmental management framework (DePoy, n.d.), the Rural Juvenile Drug Court/Prevention Initiative model is proposed. Our model innovative, local approach to resolving the serious substance abuse problems in our County is informed by a synthesis of evidence-based practice with local needs. This project will develop and test a model project that can be disseminated throughout the U.S. This project will be implemented in rural areas with low population density that experience similar disparities to prevention and treatment resources that place rural residents at disproportionately high risk for substance abuse and its harms.

Box 12.4 Goals and objectives

Goal

Reduce youth substance abuse and its consequences through implementing an innovative, culturally competent, collaborative, rural model program

Objective 1   establish a collaborative structure and set of procedures

Objective 2   enact tripartite model program

Objective 3   conduct preliminary and comprehensive national dissemination

Objective 4   decrease substance abuse

Objective 5   increase the efficacy of substance abuse treatment

Objective 6   improve prevention-supportive community practices, policies, and norms

---

Box 12.5 Evaluation questions

Using the evaluation practice model, the project evaluator will carry out a multi-method process and outcome evaluation to answer the following questions:

A) To what extent and how were project activities conducted and completed as planned? What are the costs and influences on the processes?

B) To what extent was cultural competence addressed in all project activities?

C) To what extent have outcomes been achieved for the total target and for target subgroups?

D) What are the main and interactive outcomes of each of the project elements?

E) How were evaluation data used to inform the project?

F) What collaborative structures and process were developed? What were the associated costs and influences?

G) What is the perceived efficacy of the collaborative structures and processes?

---

reflexive action questions will be approached. The use of non-experimental design allows the public health professional to quantify the completion of objectives.

Content analysis of narrative assessments, along with the numeric forms of evidence, provide the descriptive data through which the monitoring questions can be answered. Data analysis would be primarily descriptive looking at univariate (or the distribution of scores on a single variable) or bivariate distributions (the association of scores between two variables). See Appendix for a discussion of these basic statistics. The monitoring information obtained through these strategies would most likely be important to share within the project staff, and in the community among collaborators. Unexpected findings would be informed by the narrative identification of influential factors on the processes and attainment of process objectives.

Although experimental-type reflexive action answers many questions, queries about context and uniqueness of process cannot always be captured by quantification. Look at questions E and F above. We now turn to the naturalistic tradition to illustrate its use in reflexive action.

Box 12.6 Reflexive action plan

To answer question A, activity and cost monitoring data will be collected monthly and narrative data from collaborative and staff meetings will be audio recorded and transcribed. All narrative data will be coded and, along with statistical data, will be entered into an online database. The project evaluator will calculate measures of central tendencies and bivariate associations. Changes over time will be ascertained by the calculation of parametric statistics (to be determined).

Question B will be answered by two strategies: (1) content analysis of all documented project activities for inclusion of cultural competence strategies, and (2) staff assessment of cultural competence of project activities to be ascertained and scored on a scale of 0–4 (with ascending values indicating greater levels of cultural competence) in formal process assessment staff meetings twice during each project year.

To answer question E, formal group interviews to examine awareness of formative evaluation findings and their use will be held twice yearly with project staff.

To answer questions F and G, formal group interviews to examine the collaborations, identify influences and costs, and their perceived efficacy, will be conducted twice yearly with project staff and key collaborators.

Naturalistic Reflexive Action Designs

Complexity, flexibility, narrative, and induction, to a greater or lesser extent, are essential elements of naturalistic inquiry (Fetterman, 2007; DePoy and Gitlin, 2005). The naturalistic tradition is extremely valuable in formative processes, in that it provides a vehicle through which information can be garnered, even if this information has not been considered prior to the inquiry (Patton, 2001). The complexity of description in naturalistic inquiry also lends itself to specifying nuance, differential implementation, and context of professional action. Naturalistic methods are extremely valuable in process assessment both in describing the richness of the effort and in providing data about its context.

Review Chapter 8 for a complete discussion of naturalistic inquiry. We apply the nine essential elements of naturalistic design here, because inherent in these elements are the reasons that a professional uses this tradition in process assessment.

Nine Elements of Naturalistic Inquiry

1. *Range of purpose:* Since naturalistic methods span the range of purposes from gathering descriptive knowledge to revealing complex theoretical frameworks, these methods can meet the multiple purposes and audiences of reflexive action. Description can reveal the complexity of "what happened." More complex purposes for process assessment can also be accomplished, such as exploration of unintended correlates and outcomes of professional activity.

Think about the example described above. In order to identify the factors that influenced collaboration and program processes, naturalistic approaches to obtaining and analyzing information are proposed.

2. *Context specificity:* Since all naturalistic inquiry is conducted in a context, methods within this tradition are invaluable for examining action processes, both embedded within and influencing multiple system levels. Once again, consider how naturalistic inquiry is proposed in the example above to ascertain what contextual, local factors will influence the project.

3. *Complexity and pluralistic perspective of reality:* This element of the naturalistic tradition is most valuable in revealing different perspectives about action process and areas for improvement. As we see in our evaluation plan, nomothetic approaches yield averages and distributions while naturalistic approaches are proposed to identify the complex and unintended influences on professional activity.

4. *Transferability of findings:* Although naturalistic inquiry is context specific, the rich description that is often conducted allows reflexive action findings to be applied to comparable strategies within analogous contexts. Thus, we are proposing a model public health program that can be implemented in similar contexts. Naturalistic finding will help other rural locations assess their similarities to our location as the basis to determine if the model fits and how it might be tailored.

5. *Flexibility:* The flexibility of naturalistic strategies allows the professional to be responsive to incremental learning and need for method change throughout the action processes. The capacity to modify strategies and still maintain rigor is especially important in ongoing monitoring over a long period of time. As you can see, the naturalistic element of the proposed evaluation, in part, is designed to inform flexibility and change in the program in response to unexpected factors.

6. *Centrality of language:* As a result of the primacy of language and symbols in naturalistic inquiry, the meaning of what is communicated can be explored. This element is most valuable in understanding and improving communication within and among diverse groups involved in intervention action processes. Note that we are analyzing the content of narrative documents and processes for cultural competency.

7. *The importance of perspective:* The recognition of the emic (insider) or etic (outsider) perspective of the professional can enhance understanding and use of findings (Denzin and Lincoln, 2000). Given that evaluation practice is a model for professionals to assess their own activity, professionals using this model are always emic to their own professional action process. However, they might be etic to the context in which they act, as in the example above.

8. *Shift in knowing power:* The element of "partnership" rather than top-down investigation in reflexive action is a valuable tool in recruiting wide participation and use of findings. If diverse groups feel that their knowledge and perspectives are respected and important in informing change, it is likely that they will be increasingly invested in the process of assessment and revision. For that reason, naturalistic strategies are proposed in our example to assess the collaborative processes. Note that key informants beyond the professional project team are included in that element of the process assessment.

9. *Interspersion of gathering information and analysis:* The capacity to use findings as the monitoring proceeds is a benefit in that changes can be made based on initial data, inquiry can be flexible and changeable in response to findings, and process evaluation can be responsive to diverse groups who would benefit from even minor revision during the course of the inquiry. We therefore are able to plan preliminary dissemination, knowing that processes may change.

Strategies for Naturalistic Inquiry

As we noted in Chapter 8, naturalistic inquiry comprises multiple philosophical approaches and methodological strategies. Although we do not eschew any of these designs, we do suggest that some approaches are more useful than others in process assessment. Three strategies are particularly useful in evaluation practice: individual and group interview; passive observation; and inductive analysis of documents. Of course, methods are chosen purposively and thus this discussion provides guidelines rather than prescriptions. For detailed information on these approaches we refer you to the many excellent sources on naturalistic inquiry in the bibliography. Let us turn to the use of these three strategies in evaluation practice now.

Interview

Individual interview elicits information from an individual perspective that might not be shared in a group or in writing. Individual interview can uncover information that the professional might not have considered asking. As part of the HRTW project, youth who entered college and who participated in an experimental, comprehensive advising process were interviewed in a group about their advising experiences and needs. The findings did not reveal any need for change. However, in individual interview, the failure of the advising system became clearly evident after several students shared their resentment toward the invasion of the model into their personal lives. To the students, the advisors using this model asked them questions not only about their academic programs but about their personal lives. As a result of this reflexive action finding, students with special health care needs were asked to participate in a new needs assessment halfway through the project to revise a clear understanding of their advising needs and expectations.

Group interviews, in which small groups of individuals interact in interview sessions, are most useful in promoting "group think" and in expanding individual perspectives within a group context. Although group interview might silence individual contributions as was the case in the example above, group interview is designed to obtain consensus or to understand disagreement within homogeneous and/or heterogeneous groups. Members can support, stimulate, and/or silence others, allowing the professional to see a microcosm of group process. Data collection usually occurs through audio and field-note recording, with analysis being inductive. Remember back to the HRTW example. As the needs assessment on adolescent transition continued, the adolescents told us that our concern for them as individuals with atypical needs was not how they wanted to be perceived. It would not have dawned on us that the meaning of independence to adolescents was simply to be like their peers. As one youth said, "We want to be like others . . . sex, drugs, and rock and roll." We then realized that an important part of the monitoring process in systems change to support adolescent transition was consulting adolescents when we were not sure what questions to ask. Remember in the chapters on needs assessment that one area of need expressed by adolescents was having a voice and disseminating knowledge about their experiences and needs. Despite this articulated need, monitoring revealed that several public-speaking training sessions were poorly attended by youth. We, therefore, interviewed adolescents within a group format to seek an understanding of the poor attendance and to elicit their perspectives about increasing participation. Audio transcripts revealed explicit recommendations, but the most important information was derived from the *sub rosa* conversations in which the adolescents talked about their resistance to participating in any activity in which the principals of their schools were involved. The original planned action process of seeking nominations for leadership and public-speaking training from school principals was therefore changed.

Passive Observation

Passive observation is a strategy frequently used to monitor professional action without influencing it. Through observation, discourse and non-verbal interaction can be used as data to assess action process and to provide important feedback to the observed individuals or groups. Most frequently, data are recorded in video, audio, and field-note formats and inductively analyzed. Passive observation is not limited to actual spaces. As we noted, virtual and conceptual objects can be observed as well. For example, one method that we used in our course sequence to "passively observe" assignment processes was to monitor e-mail conversations on an e-mail conference for students.

Inductive Analysis of Documents

A common method of process assessment is document review and analysis. Because the data set already exists, naturalistic document review is particularly efficient and valuable (DePoy and Gitlin, 2005; Patton, 2001). What is written, by whom, and in what context can yield important information for assessment and informed revision. The professional can use many analytic strategies, including thematic analysis, content analysis, semiotic analysis, and so forth.

Look again at our example of the evaluation for the substance abuse grant project. In the reflexive action plan, we proposed to conduct a content analysis of documentation as one means to assess cultural competence.

Mixed-Method Reflexive Action Designs

As we have noted throughout the text, mixing methods, in our opinion, is most desirable in evaluation practice. Integrating approaches in reflexive action allows for pluralism in data collection and analysis necessary to obtain complex and diverse knowledge to develop formative suggestions. Moreover, mixed methods engage multiple interest groups and use of diverse strategies and epistemologies. In each of our cases and examples, we have illustrated how each tradition can be used to reveal information that can be used for multiple formative purposes.

Process Assessment Questions Posed by Diverse Groups

Now that we have looked at design traditions, we examine how reflexive action might look to diverse groups. What questions can reflexive action answer for the multiple groups who participate? Let us use the example of our universal access curriculum to illustrate, beginning with the "user" or student.

Students in the program were recipients of the whole program, its processes, and its entities or learning resources (books, articles, virtual resources, technology, and so forth).

The students would be likely to ask the following reflexive questions to inform their own education and that of future students:

- What parts of the program/project/entity were satisfactory to me? Why?
- What parts of the program/project/entity were unsatisfactory? Why?
- What parts of the program/project/entity were easy to access or use? Difficult?
- How was I treated by faculty and professionals?
- Did the program/project/entity include all that I needed to meet the learning objectives?
- What else might I need?
- What changes should be made to improve student access, participation, and termination?
- Were the facilities and resources satisfactory to me?

Questions that would be asked by the professional, in this case the faculty, might include:

- How much effort did I devote to this program, to developing entities, and to other processes? What did I do that I would continue? Why?
- What did I do that I would not continue? Why?
- How satisfactory are the context and resources for me?
- What activities helped me learn?
- What parts helped me advance my career?
- Did I feel sufficiently valued? By whom?
- Was my workload reasonable?

The administrators, who in this example would include the dean and provost, might ask:

- Were the objectives of the program accomplished in a timely manner?

- What was the cost? Was it in line with the efforts, entities, and processes?
- What resources beyond what projected costs were needed? Used?
- How cost and time efficient was the program?
- What changes should have been made in organizational structure? Why?
- How well did faculty perform?
- What external influences impacted the program? How?
- What policy and procedural changes need to be made?
- What other monitoring strategies are needed?

Ideally, process assessment will meet the needs of all interest groups involved directly or indirectly in an activity or entity. Of course, purpose and practical considerations limit the scope, and questions asked by all groups may not be answered.

Selecting a Method—Guiding Questions

To select method, given the multitude of factors that you need to consider, look at the questions in Box 12.7. The answers to these questions will help you structure your reflexive action approach.

The guiding questions in Box 12.7 can be valuable tools to help you find a viable and reasonable strategy for reflexive action. You will see that each

---

Box 12.7 Guiding questions for selecting a method for reflexive action

1. What are your evaluative questions?

2. What are the purposive considerations?

3. What are the practical constraints—time, resources, context (acute, time-limited activity, community-based activity, single entity or product, multiple efforts, etc.)?

4. Which type of design will be used—nomothetic, idiographic, or mixed-method?

5. Are there multiple interest groups or a single interest group?

6. What is the scope of the reflexive inquiry?

7. Who are the audiences, and how will they best be able to consume and use the assessment knowledge to improve the activity or entity?

question simplifies the thinking and planning processes necessary to choose cogent and useful action processes.

Main Points

1. Experimental-type and naturalistic traditions of inquiry each have unique uses in reflexive action.
2. A full range of non-experimental, pre-experimental, and quasi-experimental designs can be useful in monitoring group action processes and cost analysis.
3. Naturalistic inquiry can be used in reflexive action to examine contextual and pluralistic factors that are inherent in all action processes.
4. Mixed-method design is the most complete and versatile approach to reflexive action.
5. Diverse participants are interested in the answers to different and varied questions in the reflexive action process.
6. Selecting an approach to reflexive action is dependent on purpose, resources, audience, and expected use of the data.

Exercises

1. Select an organization of interest to you. Look at its mission and then examine the goals and objectives for one professional activity or entity. Identify the monitoring processes that are in place for that activity or entity.
2. Critically evaluate the monitoring process to determine what methods are used to monitor implementation processes, costs, and external influences.
3. What are the strengths and limitations of the monitoring approach?
4. To what extent does the approach specify criteria for the successful completion of process objectives? What is the scope of the inquiry?
5. What changes would you suggest to the reflexive implementation plan? Why?

During and After Professional Effort

Did You Resolve Your Problem,
How Do You Know, and How Did
You Share What You Know?

OUTCOMES

CHAPTER 13

Assessing Outcomes: Thinking Processes in Outcome Assessment

Outcome assessment is frequently considered the primary element in the evaluation process (Rossi *et al.*, 2004). However, as we have discussed throughout the text, even though outcome assessment is essential to ascertaining what resulted from professional activity, it cannot be comprehensive, soundly planned, and used without the thinking and action processes of problem statement, needs assessment, and formulation of goals and objectives. As we proceed through this chapter, note the strengths and limitations of outcome assessment. What can we come to know from it, and what can we not know? This chapter discusses the answers to these questions.

Definitions

An outcome is the result of being acted upon by or participating in an action process. We commonly think of outcomes as changes that occur following a planned effort, although in some cases change may or may not be the intended result of an action. Think, for example, of prevention in which the status quo of healthy populations is the desired outcome. This point provides a segue to the importance of recognizing intended and unintended outcomes. Intended outcomes are planned and elicited. Unintended outcomes occur but were not named as desired. Unintended outcomes can range from extremely positive to harmful, and are important to keep in mind throughout our discussion of outcome.

Outcome assessment is a set of thinking and action processes to ascertain and document what occurs as a result of being voluntarily or involuntarily exposed to a purposive process, and to assess the worth of professional activity. Assessment of both planned and unintended occurrences is contained within outcome assessment. Let us look at Grant-maker to illustrate the notions of expected and unexpected outcomes.

In the year that was the focus of our evaluation, the intended collective outcome of all projects was increased access to health care. However, as we noted, while this outcome was not always achieved, one desirable outcome was the collaboration that developed in many of the projects. As mentioned previously, because this outcome was so desirable, Grant-maker refocused priorities from the establishment of new programs to the support collaboration as the basis for maximizing existing resources.

In the professional world, most outcome assessment focuses on the examination of the extent to which planned changes result from activities, programs, and entities. However, in evaluation practice, we suggest a much broader definition:

> Outcome assessment is the application of research design to looking at professional efficacy and worth.

Note that this definition, unlike the typical notion of cause-and-effect assessment between effort and outcome, expands not only the scope of inquiry, but also the methods that are acceptable in outcome assessment. These methods will be addressed later in the chapter. Direct measurement of cause-and-effect relationships is difficult in experimental-type evaluation designs due to practical and ethical constraints of investigation in the field. If we limited our outcome assessment only to the investigation of cause-and-effect relationships using traditional quantitative methods, our understanding of outcomes, as well as our methods for accountability, would be significantly limited (Patton, 2001).

Consider how the evaluation plan for the prevention grant that we discussed in the last chapter would be truncated. If using only experimental-type inquiry, the richness of collaborative efforts and the cultural competence evaluation strategies would be simplified to measures of central tendency.

Essential Elements of Outcome Assessment

The following is a list of the essential elements of outcome assessment.

- systematic inquiry;
- articulation and testing of professional effort;
- value-based inquiry;

- linked to reflexive action;
- cost of interventions;
- investigation of problem resolution;
- contribution to professional knowledge base.

Let us look at each in more detail now.

Systematic Inquiry

Outcome assessment is systematic inquiry designed to examine the relationship between professional efforts and outcomes in multiple domains. In outcome assessment, the design used should lay the groundwork for investigating the link between a professional activity, program, or entity and its result, even if it is not feasible to conduct true experimentation.

Returning to Grant-maker, the outcome of improved access to health care was ascertained through mixed-method design in which we took a meta-look, so to speak, at the aggregate claims of each grantee. There was no control, random assignment, or manipulation in our evaluation or in any of the individual project evaluations.

At this point, you might be asking how any claims could have been made regarding the outcome of Grant-maker's funding appropriations. As we have discussed, we used a mixed-method design. For the quantitative part, we first identified benchmarks of health care access in the literature and then measured their presence or absence in each project's final report. We had numerous variables, but for instructive purposes, let us consider three essentials: health insurance, a family physician, and the ability to obtain medical appointments outside of the emergency room for acute conditions. Each variable was lexically and operationally defined so that its appearance in each final report could be scored. A total score (with ascending scores indicating greater access) was calculated and measures of central tendency were calculated for individual and aggregate final reports. A criterion score for acceptable attainment of health care access was established and we then statistically examined predictors of that score from variables such as the focus of the proposal (coded for category of content), the total budget, and the time frame.

Obtaining a comprehensive picture of correlates allows the professional to investigate the attribution of outcome to an activity, program, or entity through establishing a study to determine which individual or group of factors can predict outcome. Moreover, once predictors are known, we gain important information to inform future intervention. Adding a naturalistic element to the inquiry, such as key-informant interviews, provided further evidence about outcome and its causes.

Articulation and Testing of Professional Effort

In evaluation practice, measurement of results, in itself, is insufficient to depict outcome. A clear articulation of the activity and its parts, and an attempt to examine which parts of a total professional effort related to, or caused, a result are necessary. This point is critical when we consider intended and unintended outcomes. Without specification of the parts and processes, it is not possible even to begin to ferret out the part, or parts, of a professional process to which an outcome is related.

In the previous example, if we had looked only at the access outcome, we would have missed important information about the grant-making process itself. Thus, the process and influences had to be clearly described, along with the experimental condition of access, in order for us to identify a change that might be contributing to the improvement of access to health care.

Value-Based Inquiry

Outcome assessment specifies what should occur following a professional activity, what should change or stay the same, or what should be changed or not as a result of a professional effort. Thus, outcome assessment both specifies and examines the extent to which what is valued and desired occurred following, or as a result of, a planned action. The desired outcome is the reduction or elimination of a problem, and problems are defined as statements of value.

Furthermore, how these desired outcomes are measured and how success criteria are specified are action processes that are dependent on values and opinions. As we discuss action processes in the next chapter, keep in mind that purpose is a driving influence in the choice of methods.

Consider Grant-maker once again. Notice that Grant-maker identified access to health care, not improved health status, as its desirable outcome. The projects that were funded, therefore, focused on the payment for the delivery of professional services and not on the result of those services to individuals. If you compare the values in many of the exemplars that we have discussed in this text, you can see that health and wellness seem to be the commonalities but the actual value-based meaning of these terms and methods to promote them are diverse. To Grant-maker, health is conceived in terms of ability to pay for and obtain formal provider services, while in the substance abuse prevention project, health is conceptualized as the absence of undesirable behaviors. And as we have revealed, our passion defines health as informed decision making, and thus equality of access to information is the valued method to achieve that outcome.

Linked to Reflexive Action

Clarification of the professional effort and its variations are critical to understanding not only what happened but how and why the desired outcome occurred. Reflexive action, therefore, has an essential role in outcome assessment in that monitoring is a detailed and systematic analysis of what was done and how, when, and by whom it was done. When linked with outcomes, process assessment provides the detail about professional activity that allows you to look at how different parts and variations result in diverse outcomes.

We illustrated this point in our discussion of our course sequence on universal access. To further illustrate, we asked students to evaluate each assignment and reading for the degree to which each promoted their attainment of the course objectives. For most students, the final assignment was very difficult but it was the one that elicited the most significant learning. It was not, however, the assignment rated as most satisfactory, in that students did not expect that the course would focus on problem solving to improve access for all.

Cost of Interventions

Although cost analysis is an element of reflexive action, it is also a major part of outcome assessment. The focus of cost analysis in outcome assessment is an important determination of worth and, in large part, of continuation. Worth refers to the degree to which the outcome warrants the expenditure of resources. Both value and efficacy are factored into the determination of worth.

Consider Grant-maker again. The question that was most vexing for Grant-maker was the extent to which the grant-making priorities and processes were "worth" the money spent. And as you see, it was not fully satisfied with the outcome of its funding program and thus changed the priority away from funding new programs to obtaining "more bang for the existing buck," so to speak.

Investigation of Problem Resolution

In essence, all aspects of our evaluation practice model refer to the extent to which an identified problem has been resolved, in part or in total, as a result of, or following, a professional activity. Assessment of outcome allows the professional to make some judgments about problem resolution because each step of the evaluation practice process derives from the problem statement. All of our exemplars illustrate this point so we will not reiterate an illustration here.

Contribution to Professional Knowledge Base

Although outcome assessment is traditionally and primarily initiated for the purpose of ascertaining the success of an activity or effort in achieving its goals, we agree with the position that this inquiry contributes to the overall professional knowledge base, in the ways listed below:

- allows for replication and future planning of successful professional efforts based on empirical evidence;
- provides knowledge for comparison of approaches;
- provides feedback for knowledge and advancement of professional practices;
- allows for prediction of outcomes;
- contributes to empirical professional knowledge.

For evaluative as well as knowledge-building purposes, outcome assessment applies to numerous populations. Look at Box 13.1 for the broad range of populations that benefit from outcome evaluation. We illustrate the population segments from the evaluation of our course sequence in universal access.

Box 13.1 Typical targets of outcome assessment

- *Direct targets*: Students, faculty
- *Indirect targets*: Citizens to whom students apply their learning
- *The professional*: Faculty
- *The profession*: Higher education, interdisciplinary professions including, but not limited to, education, engineering, architecture, art, museum studies, disability studies, computer science, and new media
- *The global professional community*: All concerned with social justice through equality of access.
- *Administrators*: Dean, provost, upper university administration
- *Policy makers and policy*: Higher educational policy, state and national rights policies

---

Main Points

1. Outcome assessment is defined as a set of thinking and action processes to ascertain and document what occurs as a result of being voluntarily or involuntarily exposed to a purposive process, and to assess the worth of professional activity.
2. Outcome assessment involves the application of research design to inquiry about professional efficacy.
3. Outcome assessment is informed by process assessment.
4. These are the essential elements of outcome assessment:

   a. systematic inquiry;
   b. articulation and testing of professional effort;
   c. value-based inquiry;
   d. linked to reflexive action;
   e. cost of interventions;
   f. investigation of problem resolution;
   g. contribution to professional knowledge base.

Exercises

Select and analyze an outcome assessment from the literature for the following purposes:

1. Identify the problems to be reduced and/or resolved by the activity or entity.
2. State the explicit and implicit values.
3. Discuss the direct and indirect targets who are tested.
4. Identify the worth criteria if they are explicated.
5. Suggest how this inquiry can contribute to professional knowledge.

OUTCOMES

CHAPTER 14

Action Processes of Outcome Research

In this chapter, we present and analyze methods of assessing outcome. The purposive context of evaluation practice has been repeated throughout the text, but bear with us as we remind you once again to keep purpose in mind, especially as we discuss the processes that have been typically viewed as "objective."

Four Steps of Outcome Assessment

We now turn our focus to the discrete action elements of outcome assessment. Regardless of purpose or approach, all outcome assessment action processes involve the following four major steps:

1. Based on summative objectives, articulate lexical definitions (definitions expressed in words) of desired outcomes and criteria for success.
2. Delineate the exact evaluation questions.
3. Design the structure of assessment action processes with attention to field constraints.
4. Conduct the outcome assessment inquiry with attention to ethical, field, and resource constraints.

In this chapter, we apply the four action processes to experimental-type and naturalistic approaches to outcome assessment.

True Experimental Design in Outcome Assessment

As discussed in Chapter 7, experimental-type designs are not always practical for use. Of course, using true experimental design to understand cause-and-effect relationships between an action and the desired outcome would be considered as the gold standard from an experimental-type methodological standpoint. Let us look at how this design can be planned and implemented in the field.

Review the discussion in Chapter 7 on the logical foundation of true experimental design. Within that tradition your aim is to eliminate bias from your study such that you can be reasonably sure that the outcome was a direct result of the one variable that you manipulated, the professional action or entity. To eliminate bias from your study and to obtain a clear picture of the degree to which an independent variable (the professional effort) produced a change in the dependent variable (the desired outcome), the three elements of randomization, control, and manipulation must be present. In many instances evaluation practice presents ethical and practical challenges to structuring an inquiry with these three criteria. The condition of "withholding" necessary professional action for control is only one of the design elements that can pose an ethical dilemma when subjects are people who are in need of professional attention. The example that we present shows you some of the techniques typically used to circumvent field constraints such as withholding.

Consider the example of a new public health education program designed to prevent smoking among teenagers. In evaluation practice, all steps from the articulation of the problem statement to reflexive action would ideally have preceded outcome assessment. To examine outcome, based on previous steps, purpose, resource needs, constraints, and so forth, you decide that true experimental design would be most useful. However, you have some ethical considerations to address, including your own belief that all students should have the opportunity to participate in the smoking cessation and prevention program, so you are careful in how you structure the experimental and control conditions.

To obtain a control group, you decide to randomly stagger participation for control subjects rather than eliminate it altogether. Thus, the control condition would be the waiting list; and the desired outcomes—absence of smoking and acquisition of anti-smoking attitudes—could be measured at pre-test and post-test intervals for the experimental and waiting-list groups. By using a waiting list as a control, you are satisfied that the professional activity would be available for all teenagers while you are also meeting the conditions of true experimentation.

Unfortunately, the likelihood of implementing true experimentation with sufficient rigor is small in most cases. Threats to validity and reliability, such as sampling bias, experimental mortality, and so forth, would be factors that compromise the efficacy of the findings (DePoy and Gitlin, 2005). However, there are many ways to examine outcome even when attribution to the professional activity or entity is not directly observed. To read more about these threats, we refer you to the numerous research texts that we have listed in the bibliography.

Using Non-Experimental to Quasi-Experimental Approaches in Outcome Assessment

As discussed previously, all experimental-type designs are nomothetic because they focus on group, rather than individual, phenomena. Thus, experimental-type designs are used to examine group outcome rather than individual outcome. Also, although we discussed it previously, let us briefly revisit Campbell and Stanley's (1963) notation to describe design structures. X always denotes the independent variable, which in outcome assessment is the professional activity or entity. O signifies the outcome or set of desired outcomes that you are testing. To depict the nature of randomization, we use uppercase R to denote random selection of the sample and random assignment to experimental and control group. Lowercase r refers to random group assignment without random selection of the sample. If either R or r is absent, then we know that randomization has not occurred at all.

Experimental-type designs that do not meet the requirements for true experiments can still answer important questions about an intervention. They cannot specify that the professional activity or entity created the outcome, but these approaches to inquiry can provide systematically derived evidence to measure desired phenomena or changes following an activity at one or more intervals of time. We will illustrate how each design can be structured and used to generate outcome knowledge.

To do so, we return to our course sequence in universal access to illustrate. The planned action (X) was the implementation of an innovative certificate program to teach the concepts and application of universal access to university students from multiple disciplines. The outcome measure (O) was the aggregate score for all assignments for individual students and for the total group. To begin the program, students participated in a pilot program conducted in Year 1. To assess outcome, grades were examined at the end of the pilot year. Given the field constraints, two outcome assessment designs were possible, testing students who completed the curriculum in Year 1 and students who planned to take the curriculum in Year 2.

For the Year 1 class, an XO design had to be planned because no previous test scores were available for this group of students. For this cohort, the evaluation question was "What were student scores following the academic program?" As you can see, the degree to which the program was responsible for learning as reflected by the indicator of student grades cannot be answered by this design. All we can know from this approach is how well the first cohort of students scored after the pilot program. Why use this type of assessment if it cannot ascertain cause? At least this design can tell you what students learned, even though you might not know why. If you find that scores indicate limited learning, you have evidence to support a change in your program. If student grades are high, you know that they learned the material, and you might surmise that students learned as a result of your program. You can use mixed methods to ascertain cause. For example, you could ask students if the courses were responsible for their learning.

Now consider how you would use the second cohort. A more sophisticated design would be possible if you tested students on the knowledge and skill that you teach prior to their entrance in the class. An OXO design could, therefore, be implemented to answer the following question: "To what extent did scores change following the classes?" As you can see, the OXO design, although it still cannot attribute the cause of the outcome to the professional activity, provides stronger support for the efficacy of the program if there is improvement in scores on post-test, following the class.

Let us look at more specifics so you can see how to plan and implement this type of inquiry. You would test students at two intervals, at the beginning of the program and at its completion. Two types of statistical tests would be conducted, measures of central tendency to describe each group of scores (pre-test and post-test) and an inferential statistic, the t-test for dependent samples (provided that you have interval-level data, also referred to as continuous data (see the Appendix for a review of level of data)), to examine the degree to which any significant change occurred in the test scores of students in the second cohort.

On a scale of 0–100 with ascending scores indicating greater mastery, the mean score for students in cohort 2 on the pre-test of knowledge of universal access theory was 34, with a standard deviation of 12. Thus, approximately 66 percent of the scores in this cohort fall between 22 and 46. Following the courses, the mean score rose to 92, with a standard deviation of 4. Although it appears that the scores increased following our classes, we cannot know if the increase was a chance occurrence or not. We therefore chose a t-test for dependent samples to analyze the data. A significant difference was found, and thus we concluded that the students did learn the desired content following our classes.

Now let us use the example of tobacco cessation to illustrate a more sophisticated approach to outcome evaluation. The initial problem statement for this project was:

Smoking is an undesirable and harmful health behavior.

Through problem mapping, favorable youth attitudes towards smoking and lack of fear of negative health consequences were identified as causal factors to be addressed. The needs to change attitudes and caution were verified in systematic assessment. Goals and objectives were specified, with the outcome objectives set as prevention-positive attitudes and caution, as tested in self-report. To achieve these goals in a rural environment we have proposed an innovative web-based public health program in which youth from 12–16 will be involved. We have not yet conducted the program but in our proposal have specified a quasi-experimental approach to outcome assessment. To establish a control group, the tobacco cessation program will be first initiated in one junior high school (School #1) of two in a rural district to the full age range of students. At least theoretically, the two schools are equivalent in that they both serve the local county in which they are situated. School #1 will function as the experimental condition and School #2 will function as the control through being waiting-listed for the second pilot test of the public health innovation.

The outcome evaluation design is structured as OXO/OO, with O as the total score on a self-report test of attitude and caution, and X as the experimental condition. Both groups will be tested at the same two intervals with the only difference being the experimental condition.

Unlike the XO design that we used for our universal access program, the addition of the control school in the tobacco cessation program allows us to conduct an inquiry in which changes in scores following the public health program can be compared to changes in scores without it.

For instructive purposes, let us consider a hypothetical scenario. School #1 (experimental) had a mean pre-test score of 42, with a standard deviation of 11. School #2 (control) had a mean pre-test score of 39, with a standard deviation of 16. To examine whether the difference in pre-test scores was significant or a chance occurrence, the professional chose to conduct a t-test for independent samples. No significant difference was found, and thus the pre-test scores were considered to be equivalent. So although there was no random assignment, we could conclude no difference on pre-test. However, because random assignment is missing, we would not be able to ascertain that the experimental and control group were equivalent in other areas as we discuss below in a hypothetical conclusion.

To compare the post-test outcome, the professional would look at the mean change scores in both groups. To do this in a simple but rigorous manner, the pre-test scores would be subtracted from the post-test scores, yielding a change score for each group. The mean and standard deviation for the change scores could then be computed for each school and then compared with the t-test for independent samples.

For instructive purposes, consider how you might interpret the following scenario. Suppose a significant difference was noted, but not as expected. The control school improved significantly more than the experimental school. If we interpret these results as cause and effect, we may conclude that the program did not produce an improvement when compared to the control school. However, this design structure cannot answer questions about the cause of the outcome, because, as we said above, no random assignment of the experimental condition was accomplished. There was no way to know if the schools were actually equivalent. If the schools were randomly assigned to experimental and control condition, you might be able to conclude that the change in scores was attributable to the experimental program.

As you can see by the examples, many questions about professional action can be answered without true experimentation. The key to sound evaluation practice using these strategies is to make sure that when you interpret your findings, you do not exceed the capacity of what the design can tell you. If you cannot support a causal relationship between action or entity and outcome, do not make that claim.

As we noted, in many professional efforts, similar to the examples above, the likelihood is that true experimentation will not be feasible. So how can we structure nomothetic outcome assessment so that results can be attributed to an action or entity?

Alternative Strategies to Attribute Outcome to Professional Effort

Statistical manipulation and modeling are methods that can be used to examine cause-and-effect relationships in the absence of the ability to structure a true experiment mechanically, but they are often not feasible due to cost and practical constraints. In addition, it is not likely that the conduct of, or the findings from, these methods will be accessible to diverse audiences beyond those who are well versed in complex statistical methods. These are not often the purview of professionals who do not conduct research as their primary activity. Because we see evaluation practice as integral to all arenas of professional action, complex statistical modeling does not serve the majority of professionals, as it is a skill that even few researchers possess. We do not want to suggest that statistical complexity should never be used. Rather, cautious and purposive use is indicated in situations where the targets, audiences, and purposes provide the rationale, and where the resources allow. For example, statistical modeling might be indicated in a medical setting where the actual manipulation of an action could pose some danger. The capacity to use a modeling technique to create conditions statistically would avoid risk while contributing to an understanding of the extent to which an outcome could be predicted by the presence, absence, or degree of an action or entity offered.

There are some outcome assessment approaches that we have found extremely useful for examining cause and effect between professional effort and outcome when implementing true experimentation is not feasible. One strategy often overlooked is asking key participants themselves to report their opinion of the degree to which an action or entity caused an outcome. Although this approach does not allow empirical observation of change, it does address attribution through self-report. It is also reasonable to ask key participants how and when they expect the change to be observed. This type of outcome assessment is particularly valuable in workshops or educational efforts where the desirable outcome is participant learning and use of learning in a specified context. Consider the following example.

Let us revisit the HRTW project. As we discussed, one strategy that was implemented was public speaking on the part of youth with special health care needs, with the aim of improving employer attitudes towards hiring them. Given the nature of the activity, even pre-testing employers was infeasible. So we had to rely on employer self-report and youth reflection to assess the outcome and its attribution. We developed self-report questionnaires that were distributed to employer participants in the youth dissemination sessions. These included items testing employer willingness to hire these youth and then requesting that the employers rate the sessions for the degree to which the presentations provoked new learning and any change in intent to hire. Because these approaches are subject to socially desirable responses (Kline, 2005; Smith and Smith, 2005), we did test for those responses by including items specifically designed to ascertain that response pattern. However, while social desirability testing is advantageous, it is not crucial as long as you realize and take into account that self-report is often limited by this phenomenon.

A second strategy, using observers to judge the extent to which a change occurred, can be a very useful approach to outcome assessment. The professionals working with the youth observed responses and listened to impressions from the audience. Third, triangulating methods, or using multiple approaches to investigate a single phenomenon, provides more than one data source upon which to suggest attribution of change to an intervention. Finally, using multiple stakeholder or target groups to render opinions about the success of an action can be an important and compelling way to ascertain outcome.

In the HRTW project, we convened a steering committee and a participatory action team to form an integrated model partnership. These entities oversaw and participated in all actions and entities. To engage these informants in the evaluation of youth public-speaking sessions, a survey was developed and distributed to all members of both groups. Respondents were asked to rate the importance of this activity (and others that we have not discussed in this text) in two areas: the capacity of the activity to meet specific project goals and objectives, and the potential for each activity to achieve progress on performance indicators that were established by the Maternal and Child Health Bureau (the funders) for all programs in the nation funded under the same initiative. This strategy was used as an outcome assessment as many actual outcomes of the project were long-term, ideological, and not specifically aimed at meeting the performance indicators established by the federal government. The design allowed the professional project staff to ascertain the perspectives of multiple groups regarding the value of the activities in meeting state-wide needs, addressing the problem of difficult youth transition to adulthood, and linking the project activities to performance indicators (DePoy and Gilmer, 2000).

As you can see, there are many methods that can be used to examine outcome, including true experimental design and other experimental-type approaches. The following section will discuss idiographic methods that you can use to examine outcome, some of which can be mixed with experimental-type methods to strengthen and expand your knowledge of outcome.

Idiographic Designs

Unlike nomothetic approaches, which are intended to characterize what is most typical in groups, idiographic designs are those that investigate context-embedded phenomena. Usually these approaches are naturalistic in nature and do not seek to generalize findings to populations beyond the single investigation. However, these designs do not preclude informing theory and outcome assessment in similar contexts. Many texts use the terms idiographic and qualitative interchangeably. We use idiographic in this chapter specifically to depict the contextual nature of the approach and its potential to focus on the outcomes of individuals as well as outcomes in single instances of an activity or entity.

Many professionals suggest that experimental-type strategies that rely on numeric data and sampling procedures are the only methods by which

outcome can be examined. We believe that within the tradition of idiographic design, naturalistic methods, single-case approaches, and mixed-
or multi-method designs are extremely valuable. We discuss single-case
methods as part of mixed-methods. While they are often seen as distinct,
we suggest that single-case designs belong under the rubric of mixed
methods. They describe the richness of the intervention process and provide
data that can be used to examine causal relationships, particularly when
external validity is not an aim, as is the case with most outcome assessment.
We will explore each of the three design types in more detail.

Naturalistic Inquiry

Refer to Chapters 8 and 12 on needs assessment and process assessment,
respectively, for detailed discussions of naturalistic design. As we have
suggested, even though naturalistic design is not concerned with external
validity, neither do professionals, for the most part, have the task of generalizability. Thus, the typical criticism of naturalistic design, that it is context-
bound, is not relevant for evaluation practice unless a purpose of evaluation
is to broaden the results of an inquiry to a population represented by the
tested sample. The use of naturalistic inquiry can be powerful not only to
examine what has happened following an action, but to ascertain why and
to identify nuances in outcome that are related to specific characteristics
of the activity or entity. Moreover, because naturalistic inquiry is pluralistic and inductive, complexity can be characterized and depicted in both
activity and outcome. However, in order to use naturalistic strategies to
uncover cause-and-effect linkages between action and outcome, data analytic
approaches that move beyond description are indicated. Naturalistic inquiry
also provides the professional with the flexibility to change approaches as
the inquiry unfolds. It can, therefore, be an excellent strategy to examine
outcome when operational definitions of outcome criteria are vague.

Let us consider our universal access curriculum as example. Naturalistic
inquiry was particularly useful in identifying and assessing the unintended
factors that negatively influenced the nomothetic outcome (measured
as grades and student satisfaction) of the class. As we noted, observation
of the educational context and open-ended interview of students helped us
ferret out why the students did not do as well as expected. Had we limited
our outcome assessment to grades and student satisfaction, we might have
located the cause of the poor outcomes within the student body rather than
within our approach to education and the university context.

Similarly, consider the use of naturalistic strategies in our example of
Grant-maker. The strategies that yielded the richest outcome data on which
to suggest that Grant-maker change its processes were open-ended interview data with individual project applicants and key informants.

Despite the almost endless design possibilities offered by the naturalistic tradition, we suggest that professionals consider the purposive use of strategies that are within their skill, time, and resource constraints and those that can be explained to, and understood by, the evaluation audiences. Complex and infrequently used approaches to naturalistic outcome assessment, such as semiotic analysis (Lieblich, Tuval-Mashiach, and Zilber, 2003), heuristic methods (DePoy and Gilson, 2005; Moustaskas, 1990), and so forth, should be reserved for audiences who are familiar with these naturalistic traditions. For a discussion of these approaches, we refer you to the excellent texts listed in the bibliography.

We suggest that well-known strategies such as open-ended interview (face-to-face, web-based, or paper-and-pencil) with one or more respondents, unstructured, non-participant observation, and/or qualitative analysis of documents be considered when asking for description of experiences before, during, and following intervention. The examples above illustrate the use of these strategies in our outcome assessment work.

How might a professional go about this type of inquiry? Let us look at the long-term plan to assess the outcome of our universal access classes. Because the classes were instituted to improve access to resources, products and environments, we plan to conduct long-term outcome studies of each cohort of students who graduate from our program. These will focus on access changes that are directly or indirectly advanced by our graduates. While we had no plans to conduct such extensive follow-up, an important event changed our minds. In the 2005 graduating class, two students, Moreau and Bosse (2005), conducted a study of the accessibility of an international motion picture theater chain. Their work was so excellent that it was reviewed in the *Bangor Daily News* (the local paper) and was then acknowledged with a prestigious award from the American Public Health Association in December, 2006 (Sawtelle, 2005). And although no discernible change in access to the theater chain occurred immediately, a year later the recommendations that were made by these two students were implemented, although not credited by the corporation to the work of these students. Considering the major but unidentified impact that this student project had on expanding access, we have decided to conduct a long-term extensive outcome assessment of the result of the educational program in resolving limited accessibility in diverse domains in which our former students live, work, and recreate.

We have begun to craft a comprehensive mixed-method outcome evaluation plan to examine changes in awareness, attitudes, and accessibility in the work or home community environments of our graduates. The idiographic element of the outcome assessment will use four strategies: group interview, individual interview, environmental observation, and document analysis to answer the following query: What changes in access have resulted from the thinking, activity, products, or entities created by the graduates of our program?

For the group interview, key informants including community members, work and educational peers, supervisors, employers, retail establishment owners, and the students themselves will be recruited and asked to consent to audio-recorded group interview. These interviews will be scheduled in the environments in which the graduates live so that we can conduct comprehensive inquiry. An open-ended question to ascertain changes in access, awareness, and attitudes towards universal access will be posed and then probe questions to refine our knowledge and attribution of any changes to the graduates will follow.

Representatives of the same interest groups might be recruited for individual, face-to-face, or audio-recorded interviews if group interview suggests that we would get more complete and accurate information outside of the limitations of group process. We plan to aggregate data from group and individually derived data sets for analysis.

Document review will be used to examine recorded changes in community awareness and access practices. For example, we will examine the newspapers in each community for human interest stories, state government contracts and announcements relevant to access, articles on policy, and so forth. And, finally, we will observe the communities for accessibility and any media or signs that indicate changes. In order to determine the attribution of any accessibility improvements, we plan to ask graduates to report their activity and its outcome.

Look at how these naturalistic strategies can inform both curriculum outcome and future curricular modification. Coupled with immediate outcome assessment, this mixed-method approach provides a comprehensive picture not only of what happened, but why. A major consideration in the use of naturalistic outcome assessment is the perspective that one brings to the effort. Because we are emic to the education process and etic to the communities and workplaces of our graduates we must be careful to be reflexive and look at our own influence over the investigative process, findings, and use of outcome assessment knowledge.

Let us look at what can happen when an investigator does not engage in self-reflection, or what is termed reflexivity in the methodological literature (DePoy and Gitlin, 2005; Mollering, 2006).

In a recent evaluation class, two students conducted an evaluation of an anti-racism intervention by interviewing four individuals who attended the training. One of the students interpreted the results to mean that the training was not effective in increasing awareness of, and activism to eliminate, white racism. The other student saw the outcome of the training as an intersection between the beginning point of awareness, reason for entering the training, and process through which each individual journeyed. Why were the interpretations so disparate? Both students failed to reflect on their own experiential and theoretical perspectives and the way in which those lenses influenced their interpretations of an identical data set. Once the students looked at their personal lenses, they came to the consensus that participants brought different perspectives, experiences, needs, and expected outcomes to the training. One individual, for example, wanted to validate her openness to all persons of color and, in so doing, did not accept the premise of the training that everyone was racist. Another participant came to the training with the purpose of learning activist skills, since he had been a victim of oppression because of his sexual preference. In negotiating the interpretation of the data, the students were able to see the process of the training and identify numerous factors that theoretically predicted how participants might respond. They then agreed to test this theory with nomothetic methods.

Earlier in the chapter, we stated that cause and effect needs to be established by analytic techniques beyond descriptive analysis. Two of the more frequently used approaches are taxonomic analysis and grounded theory. Taxonomic analysis involves looking at the data set for relationships among themes (Dey, 2005). Because naturalistic analysis is inductive, cause and effect cannot be imposed. They must emerge from the data set. You can use a computer program such as NVIVO (Qualitative Solutions and Research, 2003–6) to assist in the analytic process.

Mixed-Method Designs

We now turn to a discussion of mixed-method designs. One mixed-method approach that has shown increasing acceptance and utility in outcome assessment is single-subject design.

Single-subject design has become increasingly used to examine the outcome of professional efforts in single units of analysis. These units might be individuals, a single group, a single organization, a large environment, a school, a product, a retail establishment, a geographic or virtual location, a legislative process, or some other single unit. Units of analysis might be whole single units or single units with multiple subparts. Let us first consider a definition of single-subject design.

According to Bloom *et al.* (1998: 5), single-case design is "a set of empirical procedures designed to observe changes in an identified target (a specified problem or objective) through the application of multiple methods of inquiry and multiple and repeated measures over time." While there are more contemporary definitions we have selected this one because it contains several important elements that are consistent with evaluation practice. First, data collection and analysis are not a one-shot approach as in the case of non-experimental survey design and thus can achieve a long-term outcome assessment purpose. Second, single-subject design is intended to measure change and therefore should be used when one's purpose in engaging in professional activity is change. Remember, earlier in the book we asserted that directly or indirectly, all professional action is aimed at changing human behavior. Case study design as defined by Bloom *et al.* has the capacity not only to ascertain change but to follow its evolution, causes, correlates, and consequences. And third, single-subject design most frequently relies on multiple methods of data collection (Bloom *et al.*, 1998; DePoy and Gitlin, 2005; Yin, 2002).

Consider the example of the long-term follow-up that we have planned for our universal access course sequence. Through case study design, we would be able to conceptualize each cohort, each student, or even each environment in which graduates interacted, as a single case. We already identified four naturalistic methods that we would use to investigate environments. If we wanted to add an assessment of student recall of universal access, knowledge, and skill, we might add a non-experimental follow-up questionnaire to administer to graduates at one-year intervals. Clearly, change would be ascertained through this multi-method approach along with a complex understanding of how, why, when, and where the change occurred. We would also be able to examine influences on the outcome with increasingly sophisticated case-study approaches. As you can see, this case-study design relies on multiple points and methods of data collection and analysis.

As single-subject design gains acceptance among the professional and evaluation practice community, it is critical to assure rigor in the conduct of this design tradition. The following questions will guide you so that your single-subject design will be based on rigorous, systematic action processes:

1. Are the study questions stated clearly and explicitly?
2. Is the type of single-system design clearly described?
3. Is there a sound rationale for the selection of the case? Design?
4. Are multiple measures used? Are measures consistent with the intended outcomes and justified by the theoretical approach to professional action?
5. Are the data analysis strategies justified?
6. Is the conclusion limited to the design capacity?

Now let us review the work of Yin (2002) to present common design structures of single-case study. Table 14.1 presents Yin's taxonomy.

Table 14.1 Yin's taxonomy

Holistic single case	Single unit of analysis is seen as one global phenomenon
Embedded single case	Single case comprising multiple elements or subparts
Holistic multiple	Multiple units of analysis each seen as one global phenomenon
Embedded multiple case study	Multiple cases comprising multiple elements or subparts

Let us revisit Grant-maker to illustrate each outcome assessment approach. You might want to revisit the problem, needs, goals and objectives, reflexive action and experimental-type outcome assessments that were used in evaluation practice with Grant-maker. In essence, Grant-maker's outcome evaluation was a complex case study design in which all four categories of Yin's (2002) taxonomy were invoked. Grant-maker was interested primarily in its own activity, with no intended purpose to inform grant-making theory or practice in similar contexts. So it made ultimate sense to structure the outcome through case study methods. An assessment of Grant-maker's grant-making processes would be an example of holistic single-case design. The unit of analysis was the organization and the indicator that was of interest was "efficacy of the grant-making processes." As is characteristic of case study, multiple methods of data collection were used to inform that indicator, including document review, interview, and staff rating scales of the efficacy of the process in attaining Grant-maker's goals and objectives.

Now consider Grant-maker as a single embedded case study. The indicator of efficacy of the grant-making process was still the single indicator but the case is reconceptualized not only as the single Grant-maker entity, but as Grant-maker and the full network of funded projects that comprised the case of one funding year. Again, consistent with case study tenets, multiple forms of data collection and analysis from embedded parts were used to assess the single indicator of efficacy of the grant-making process.

In treating Grant-maker as a holistic multiple case, we looked at multiple indicators of the single Grant-maker organization. Not only did we examine grant-making processes, but we also looked at the extent to which Grant-maker achieved the goal of increasing access to health care and its related objectives through each of its activities.

Finally, in the multiple embedded approach to Grant-maker's outcome evaluation we looked at multiple indicators in subparts of the "network of Grant-maker," its grantees and its activities. These success indicators included efficacy of the grant-making process, cost efficiency, goal and objective attainment by each of the units as they related to the overall case of the Grant-maker network and attainment of the goal of improving health access state-wide.

There are many configurations of mixed-method design. In our own evaluation practice, we attempt to mix naturalistic and experimental-type methods whenever purposive and possible. Mixing approaches is a powerful design in outcome assessment even when true experimentation can be used. Mixing methods allows for diversity of data and analytic methods and yields outcome information that captures both the linear sequence of intervention and outcome, as well as the complexity of the context that influences how the intervention is actualized. Moreover, use of diverse strategies renders it more likely that the epistemological preferences of multiple stakeholders will be met.

Main Points

1. All outcome assessment consists of four essential steps.
2. True experimental design is difficult to implement but methodologically sound for attributing outcomes to professional activity. Techniques such as staggering waiting lists and participation can be ethical and reasonable ways of creating control conditions.
3. The use of true experimentation is infrequent due to field and ethical constraints.
4. Non-experimental to quasi-experimental strategies for examining outcomes can answer important questions about description and change in desired outcomes but do not attribute change to the professional effort.
5. Alternative inquiry approaches such as self-report and triangulation can be used to explore a causal relationship between an effort and outcome when true experimentation is not possible.
6. Idiographic approaches focus on contextually embedded phenomena rather than group norms.
7. Naturalistic inquiry can be used for many purposes beyond description.
8. Mixed-method designs are the most potent for outcome assessment.

Exercises

1. Select an article that describes a professional activity or entity of interest to you. Identify its desired outcome and pose a true experimental strategy to ascertain if the desired outcome has been achieved.

Consider the design structure, the lexical and operational definition of the outcome variables, and an analytic plan.

2. Compare and contrast the use of true-experimental strategies with quasi-experimental methods and alternatives for looking at a causal relationship between your selected professional effort and outcome.

3. Find an example of a true-experimental outcome assessment in the literature. Critically analyze the ethical concerns presented. How would you address these concerns using an alternative nomothetic design?

4. List the ethical concerns that you believe can result from each of the outcome approaches we have discussed.

5. How would you methodologically address the ethical concerns that you listed in Exercise 4?

6. Obtain an outcome assessment from the literature that uses idiographic designs. Critically analyze the article for its efficacy in establishing cause-and-effect relationships between professional activity and outcome.

7. Plan an idiographic approach to outcome evaluation for a community, product, and policy activity. Begin with the problem statement, and proceed through each step of evaluation practice to justify your approach.

8. Find and analyze a mixed-method outcome assessment for its capacity to provide compelling evidence for a cause-and-effect relationship between each activity, entity, or product and outcome.

SHARING
AND USING
KNOWLEDGE

Commencement: Sharing Evaluation Practice Knowledge and On To a New Problem Statement

We have come to the part of evaluation practice that is the essence of its worth: reporting and using knowledge. There are many evaluation studies that have been completed, reported on, and then placed on a physical or virtual shelf, never to be seen again except perhaps in an academic journal article or website. We are not dismissing the critical importance of scholarly publication as one venue for dissemination. However, we assert that the process in evaluation practice has failed unless the knowledge derived from the systematic inquiry is used for the purposes for which the thinking and action processes were intended: informing the improvement and/or status of professional activities and entities.

Reporting and Using Knowledge

Evidence

Before we discuss dissemination, we begin with an experience that sets the context for our discussion. Several summers ago, we attended a seminar on qualitative inquiry related to disability and work. The seminar was designed to bring together those who were well known in the field with those who were relatively new to the topic or the methodology. Each participant was asked to prepare a short description of a current or future project on which he or she was involved, or wanted to work. The presentations and sessions in this week-long seminar were intended to inform the development of individuals' projects for implementation. Among the participants were attorneys, policy makers, philosophers, educators, and health providers. Although we learned nothing new about methodology or content relating to disability and work, that summer session was one of the most valuable learning experiences in which we have participated. We did not learn what we expected, but we did learn an important principle that we now advance to you:

> Since evidentiary standards differ so greatly across fields, communicating knowledge is a task that requires much more than clarity in the presentation of one's work.

We have emphasized that the beauty of our evaluation meta-model for practice is the set of organized, systematic, and substantiated thinking and action processes that it brings to diverse professional fields and domains. However, what we want to emphasize here is that the nature of the evidence that is sought and considered as credible within these thinking and action processes is quite diverse. Therefore, the action process of dissemination must be preceded by an understanding of what the audience will value as accessible, comprehensible, and believable. This point, as the foundation of sound dissemination practice, will be discussed in detail.

Let us first look at professionals and the different ways, even within our own fields, that we accept a claim. We have written this text to urge professionals to think and act in concert with the principles of empirical inquiry. We have asserted that any claim made by a professional should be linked to a value statement (problem) for which what is needed to resolve all or part of the problem is discovered through systematic inquiry. Each step that follows in the evaluation practice sequence, in our view, should systematically respond to the empirically supported need and show systematically obtained evidence that the action processes were sound, were well executed, and produced the desired outcome. Evidence to the contrary, therefore, highlights areas for improvement and/or change. In our model, it would be insufficient to develop a professional activity or entity without a logical, well-articulated, systematically supported reason to do so. However, this approach to professional action is not always espoused, at least on a surface examination, by all.

Let us think about other ways that professionals claim to know about their activity and its outcomes. As discussed earlier, many professionals espouse a theory or set of theories, apply these theories to problems, and then look at the action processes from beginning to termination through theoretical lenses (DePoy and Gilson, 2007). Turning points are often based on the degree to which professionals believe that the intervention has met its goal or cannot go further.

Think of the Drug Abuse Resistance Education (DARE) program for example. According to Hansen (2006), the DARE program was generated in 1983 as an intuitive approach to prevention.

In response to extensive criticism due to lack of empirical support for the program or evaluation of its outcome, DARE (1996) has changed its approach. In concert with contemporary trends DARE now emphasizes the critical role of systematic evidence in any expenditure of fiscal, human, and other resources. Look at the extract below for the current narrative that introduced the DARE website.

> The Drug Abuse Resistance Education (D.A.R.E.) program, the pioneer prevention effort founded in Los Angeles in 1983, is going high-tech, interactive, and decision-model-based. Gleaming with the latest in prevention science and teaching techniques, D.A.R.E. is reinventing itself as part of a major national research study that promises to help teachers and administrators cope with ever-evolving federal prevention program requirements and the thorny issues of school violence, budget cuts, and terrorism.
>
> (DARE, 1996)

There has been significant discussion about the critical role of intuition in professional activity and the extent to which empirical approaches interfere with one's ability to be spontaneous and intuitive. But what is intuition and is it impeded by systematic thinking and action, or is the professional using empirical evidence in intuition but not articulating it? This question will be addressed later in this chapter.

Let us consider another example. Several years ago, we were involved in a policy effort aimed at the development and passage of lemon-law legislation for assistive technology used by individuals with disabilities (wheelchairs, lifts, hearing aids, and so on). These devices were not protected by any legislation in the state of Virginia and, thus, if one's equipment malfunctioned, there was no recourse for repair or replacement. The empirical evidence collected about the frequency and consequences of malfunctioning was compelling. However, this set of evidence was not the evidentiary support directly reported to orchestrate the passage of the legislation. Rather, individual testimony and narratives about the devastation of broken equipment, alliances among agencies, and the recognition that other states had parallel laws served as the evidentiary foundation upon which arguments for the passage of the legislation were made (Gilson, 2007).

In both of these examples, if we look at what was communicated as evidence, we might not immediately see systematically derived knowledge.

However, peering below the articulated surface, we see systematic thinking and action processes that follow the principles of our model. Theory, even not articulated, by definition is grounded and testable with systematic inquiry (DePoy and Gilson, 2007). In the DARE exemplar, even Hansen identified its original theoretical base as eclectic (Hansen, 2006). In the lemon-law legislative action, the magnitude of the failure of assistive technology and the significant financial costs were clearly documented.

However, at the point of communication about knowledge use in each example, the evidence used to justify an approach to action was not articulated in the form of formal research results. Rather, the empirical evidence was translated, transformed, or used as the basis to develop forms of communicated evidence that were credible and compelling for diverse audiences. This point creates the context for our discussion of dissemination and use of knowledge. The thinking and action processes of evaluation practice are grounded in empirical evidence and systematic, logically developed inquiry. Communicating the knowledge, however, is pluralistic in format and must consider why, who, what, where, when, and how.

Why Disseminate?

This question identifies purpose and precedes any consideration of the structure, timing, format, and scope of dissemination. Let us look at the universal access web portal project. Several purposes frame the dissemination strategy. First, in order to produce this entity, funding is necessary. However, in the long term the entity is proprietary. So in order to successfully obtain funding, we identified sources with values that were in concert with our problem statement, provided compelling evidence that the portal would fill an essential unmet need, and then provided information about the product and its use. However, we did not divulge too much technical information to walk the line between privacy and adequacy of information for judgment and favorable funding response. Second, because this project is central to our own professional activity and research agendas, a second purpose of dissemination is contributing to knowledge. Third and, perhaps, most important is the purpose of improving equality of access to information for all population segments and individuals. As we see below, each purpose shaped a different dissemination strategy.

Who Communicates and Who is the Recipient of the Dissemination?

Who communicates and to whom are critical considerations in the dissemination process. The fit between audience and communicator is an important determinant in the extent to which the knowledge will be heard, comprehended, respected, and used. For the purpose of funding, we communicated in the required format to potential grant-making agencies. To accomplish our second purpose, we communicated in articles in scholarly journals (DePoy and Gilson, 2006) and through presentations at scholarly conferences (Gilson *et al.*, 2006; Gilson and DePoy, 2005). And for the third purpose, we communicated with multiple audiences, including potential users, health care providers, and literacy centers.

What Should be Shared and How?

What and how are often intertwined because what is shared is dependent on how it is phrased and presented, and vice versa. For purpose #1, as we noted above, we identified and followed grant proposal guidelines for what to include and how to prepare the dissemination. Grant proposal writing is both an art and skill that we refer to as the "art of conceptual figure ground." In other words, one must understand the values and priorities of the grant-maker and craft the dissemination of a proposal not only to disseminate a good idea, but to make it stand out from the backdrop of ideas submitted. Scholarly presentations and articles include theory, empirical support, limitations, and conclusions and thus we used those guidelines for content and method of dissemination. For the third purpose, we were careful to ascertain the preferences of our audiences and presented the level of detail in the format that was desired.

But the how question, for us, goes beyond response to individual audiences. Consistent with our research agenda, we present all of our work in universally accessible formats to the extent possible. Doing so requires that within the context in which you disseminate your work, you anticipate the diverse ways in which people need and prefer to receive information, and then aim to disseminate information in those multiple formats. As example, when we use PowerPoint to present at a conference, we do not assume that all audience members can see the slides. So we read them aloud, post our work on the web or link to it, and create handouts on CD ROM that can be translated by the user into multiple formats. Similarly, we aim to publish our work in journals that provide multiple formats for access. In broad dissemination we use diverse formats for communicating knowledge.

When?

Purpose and opportunity influence the timing. This point seems self-evident so we will not belabor it.

As you can see from the example, sharing knowledge is an important action process in and of itself in contributing to problem resolution. Careful consideration of format, timing, audience, and communicator is important if the purposes of your activity and its scrutiny are to be maximized. Most critical is to select the content and evidence that are compelling and credible and to share information in accessible and comprehensible formats. As we found, what evidence is accepted by a group may differ from the evidence that you consider to be convincing. Thus, knowing what type of evidence to present in your reporting is one of the most important points to consider in any dissemination effort.

Structures

Now let us consider typical structures used to disseminate information. As we introduced above, we support full accessibility of knowledge to all audiences, ergo the beauty of digital and electronic technology. Attention to accessibility includes the presentation of information in diverse sensory modalities (for example, closed captioning or Braille) and in language that is understandable. Sharing evaluation practice knowledge in the form of a formal report with those who do not understand the language of statistics or naturalistic analysis does not result in transmission of knowledge.

Formal Evaluation Report

There are many formal structures to report systematic evaluation practice, and all have common elements. Each report includes a statement of the problem, need, goals and objectives, intervention and assessment methods, findings, and conclusions; however, we are not prescribing how these elements should be treated. A purpose statement might be clear and identified or might be implicit in how the report is framed and applied. It is unusual to see methods, data, and conclusions omitted from a formal written report, unless the structure is metaphoric or in a form that transmits knowledge in atypical ways. We discuss these later in the chapter. Box 15.1 presents the four basic principles in evaluation practice that should be used for formal presentation, regardless of format.

Given these four principles, we now look at typical styles for formal evaluation research reporting. Note here that we do not include all dissemination in formal reporting, as illustrated in the third purpose from our example above. Although reporting can occur anywhere in the process of evaluation practice, in this chapter we address reporting all steps in the evaluation practice model from problem statement through outcome assessment. You can extrapolate the four principles to delimit your dissemination to specific parts of the model.

As a result of the systematic and evidence-based foundations of evaluation practice, formal evaluation reports are usually written to follow the conventions of the inquiry traditions that professionals employ. We address typical formats for experimental-type, naturalistic, and mixed-method reporting.

Box 15.1 Four principles for formal reporting

Clarity
One of the primary elements of all inquiry is clarity. If a report is vague, convoluted, or verbose, clarity is compromised and the knowledge cannot be understood.

Precision
Precision in this context means accuracy in reporting. No matter what venue or format, dissemination should clearly describe the thinking and action processes of the evaluation practice.

Parsimony
Although reports are often lengthy, one of the most important principles in writing is to be parsimonious. Writing too much, repeating your points, or just being too wordy are deterrents to consumers. Keep your report as brief as possible, without compromising clarity and content.

Attention to structure
Attending to the preferred or desired structure of a report is critical.

Preparing an Experimental-Type Evaluation Report

Within the experimental-type tradition, language and structure for presentation are logical, usually presented in the third person to allow the data to stand alone, and detached from unsubstantiated personal opinion. Any conclusions and interpretations must not exceed what the data analysis can tell you, and all are tied to the statistical evidence revealed in the findings section.

In the experimental-type report, there are usually six sections within the body of the report (listed below), an abstract, and a list of references used to support the inquiry. The abstract precedes the narrative report and serves as a summary of each section of the evaluation. The reference list contains full citations of all literature identified in the report. Many citation formats exist. We suggest that you consider the use of a computerized program such as Procite or Endnote to keep track of your literature and to automatically format your references in your style of choice.

Elements usually included in the body of an experimental-type report are:

- Introduction
- Problem and need

- Reflexive action
- Outcome assessment methods
- Results of both
- Discussion and conclusions

The introduction of an evaluation practice report contains a brief statement of the problem to which the action or entity is addressed, a purpose statement, and an overview of the approach and questions answered in the report.

The section on problem and need varies depending on the point at which you are reporting. As we discussed in Chapter 4, the literature review provides the conceptual foundation and evidence for the problem statement. Review Chapter 4 for suggested formats for this section of your report. The limits and comprehensiveness of the literature section will depend on your audience. For example, in a journal article, the literature is usually bounded within five years unless historical references are made; whereas in an online report, the degree of detail varies. If the need was documented by existing literature, it is useful for that part of the literature to be discussed in detail. If a needs assessment inquiry was conducted, the methods and results of the study should be overviewed and located within current literature.

Following the section on problem and need, the reflexive action within the context of goals and objectives is presented. The degree of detail is dependent on venue and purpose of the report. In professional journals, it is customary to provide extensive detail in this section so that the reader knows what action processes were conducted. Monitoring methods might be discussed in this section, but they can also be detailed in the methods section.

The assessment methods section must contain the evaluation question or questions, the boundaries of the evaluation (that is, the respondents or other units of analysis), a section on data collection and analysis, and the procedures used throughout reflexive implementation and outcome assessment. The degree of detail and specificity is, once again, determined by the purpose and audience.

In the findings or results section, the analyzed data are presented. Data can be presented in narrative, chart, graph, or table form.

The discussion and conclusions section aggregates and interprets reflexive action and outcome assessment data to address the extent to which goals and objectives were accomplished to meet needs and resolve the part of the problem that was addressed by the effort. Within this section, conclusions about the efficacy of a professional effort and changes that could improve outcome should be included.

Writing an experimental-type evaluation report involves a temporal and logical sequence detailing the steps in the evaluation practice model and drawing conclusions about the extent to which the process and outcome demonstrated problem resolution. The degree of detail and precision in each section is dependent on the purpose and audience for the report.

Preparing a Naturalistic Report

Since there are so many different types of naturalistic designs, we cannot assert a single reporting structure. However, evaluation practice rarely covers the full spectrum of naturalistic designs. Thus, a formal report often conforms to commonalities contained in experimental-type evaluation reports. See the list above for the six elements that are usually contained in the body of the report. The difference lies in the language, the nature of data, and data analysis.

Naturalistic reports typically rely heavily on narrative data. Thus, in reading the report, you might come across quotations in all sections from diverse informants. For example, Artivista uses visual representations, theater, performance, and narrative to deliver and assess an anti-racism curriculum. Regardless of the format, the four principles of clarity, precision, parsimony, and attention to structure should guide the reporting process.

Preparing a Mixed-Method Report

Review the two previous sections to guide the preparation of this type of report. Even if you are preparing a report of an activity in which single-subject methods were selected for outcome assessment, the same six sections need to be included. Data analysis is typically reported in graphic format, so that pre and post patterns can be visualized.

Other Reporting Formats

There are too many methods, structures, and venues for reporting evaluation practice knowledge to cover in this text. As we discussed above, purpose drives the choice of format. To help you structure reporting formats that do not follow the formal guidelines discussed, look at the following list of guiding questions for dissemination and reporting:

1. What is the purpose of the report?
2. Who is the audience? What role(s) do they play in the activity? What do they want to know? What do you want them to know?
3. What evidence is compelling to your audiences?
4. What format and venues will be most likely to reach these audiences?
5. What type of reporting is most likely to attract and keep the attention of the audiences?

6. What do you expect to occur from sharing your report?
7. What do you want to avoid in sharing your report?
8. What access issues do you need to address in preparing your report?
9. How many formats will you need to prepare and for whom?

If you can answer all of these questions, you can begin to delimit report structures and venues. Box 15.2 summarizes some of the more frequent ways in which evaluation practice knowledge is shared. Each has its strengths and limitations; so if possible, sharing in multiple ways is most desirable if you want to reach diverse audiences.

As you can see, even a very limited list of methods to share evaluation practice knowledge is diverse. Purposive selection to accomplish dissemination goals is the key to selection of the most efficacious dissemination methods in evaluation practice.

Box 15.2 Summary of methods of sharing evaluation practice reports

1. Publishing your work in print

   - Professional paper and online journals
   - Mailed and electronic newsletters
   - Monographs
   - Books and book chapters
   - Technical reports
   - Reporting for consumers
   - Executive summaries
   - Legislative brief
   - Blogs

2. Oral presentations

   - Presentations at scholarly conferences
   - Continuing and in-service education
   - Presentations at professional meetings
   - Presentations at community meetings
   - Presentations at legislative sessions
   - Online presentations
   - Podcasts

3. Presentation through art and literature

On to a New Problem Statement

There are multiple uses for evaluation practice knowledge. The intended use is important in shaping the format and nature of sharing of knowledge. Traditional uses fall into two categories: formative and summative. Formative uses apply evaluation knowledge to the improvement of professional activity, while summative use of knowledge is aimed at determining the value of an effort and the degree to which resources should be devoted to it.

In our model, the use of knowledge both completes and commences the sequence of steps in evaluation practice. Knowing the extent to which, and how, a professional activity or entity addressed a problem in essence redefines or reaffirms the problem. Revisit Grant-maker to illustrate this point. The evaluation both assessed the process and value of its funding program and redefined the problem and need for its subsequent activity.

Since the final step in our evaluation practice model is the first step as well, we have come full-spiral. We do not use the term "full-circle," because while we arrive back at the problem, it is revised by our previous thinking and action processes, and we therefore do not return to the same place from which we began. Each time a full round of thinking and action processes of the model is completed, the problem that was the focus of the intervention becomes redefined, reaffirmed, or perhaps at some point, eliminated. Of course, given the nature and expanse of problems and issues that professionals address, these problems are rarely resolved in total. As the problem changes in nature, a new approach to professional activity commences with clarification of the problem.

Prognosis for Evaluation in Contemporary Contexts

The age of accountability is upon us and, to us, rightfully so. The field of evaluation has grown into a profession in itself in which complex strategies are apprehended and owned by those who just "do" evaluation for a living. And while we see the necessity of this field for some, our prognosis for evaluation is one that locates it squarely within the context of daily professional activity rather than in the hands of external judges. Thus, in our model, rather than scrutiny and judgment coming from without, we see evaluation practice as part and parcel of all professional thinking and action and as a praxis model for framing everything that you do, regardless of whether you are providing services, creating policies, producing entities, or seeking to improve the health and welfare of communities.

Go For It!

We hope that you have seen that evaluation practice can range from simple to complex and can, and should, be integrated into all professional thinking and action. What all approaches have in common is the commitment to look in on ourselves, to use systematic strategies to do so, and to affirm that our activity accomplishes what we claim it does. That is the moral imperative of professional activity and the reason that we wrote this book. Hopefully, by following the praxis model in it, you will be the one who assesses your own thinking and action.

Go for it!

Main Points

1. Different forms of evidence are credible for different professional and other stakeholder interest groups.
2. Answering why, who, what, where, when, and how questions helps you select a reporting format and strategy.
3. The four principles for formal reporting are clarity, precision, parsimony, and attention to structure.
4. Both formal and informal reporting should be considered.
5. The guiding questions are a valuable resource to help you select methods for purposively sharing evaluation practice knowledge.
6. Evaluation practice knowledge both completes and restarts the sequence of steps in the evaluation practice model.
7. Our prognosis for evaluation practice is that it should, and will increasingly, land within the daily practices of all professionals.

Exercises

1. In the evaluation literature, identify and critically analyze an experimental-type report, a naturalistic report, and a mixed-method report. Compare and contrast the credibility of the evidence in supporting the claims of the authors.
2. Consider the multiple stakeholders in each report. How might you format and present the evaluation practice knowledge in each report to convince each stakeholder group to support the claims made by the author?
3. Find evaluation practice reports in unusual formats (art or literature, for example), and critically analyze them for their credibility.
4. Analyze the accessibility of each of the reports that you have found in Exercises 1 and 3 for diverse audiences.

5. Select a report, and use the knowledge presented in it to redefine or affirm the problem statement.
6. Suggest how the problem statement is informed and redefined by the evaluation findings.
7. Go for it!

Appendix: Data Analysis

Introduction

This appendix presents information to refresh your memory of data analytic concepts and techniques. Basic methods of experimental-type analysis (statistics) and naturalistic analysis (interpretive techniques) are included.

Statistical Analysis

Statistical analysis is a set of procedures, techniques, and rules that organizes and interprets data. The term *data* refers to numerical representation of concepts and/or observed phenomena obtained through systematic inquiry.

The selection of a statistical procedure is determined by five factors:

1. specific research question(s) to be answered by analysis of the data set;
2. level of measurement;
3. quality of the information collected;
4. sampling procedures used;
5. sample size obtained.

Statistical analysis can be categorized into three levels:

1. descriptive—observations reduced and stated in numerical form;
2. inferential—drawing conclusions about population parameters based on findings from a sample selected from the population;
3. associational—identifies relationships between multiple variables and determines the nature of those relationships.

Level 1: Descriptive Statistics

Basic descriptive statistics describe the characteristics of a set of data. The following is a list of the techniques addressed in this appendix:

- frequencies;
- central tendencies (mean, mode, and median);
- variances;
- contingency tables;
- correlational analyses.

Frequency Distribution

DEFINITION

Frequency distribution refers to the range of values occurring for a given variable and the number of times each value occurs.

HOW TO COMPUTE

Frequency distributions are computed by listing all measured values and counting the number of times each occurs.

HOW TO REPORT

Numeric charts, histograms, or bar graphs and polygons (dots connected by lines) are the usual reporting formats. Frequencies can be converted into percentages of the occurrence of each value relative to the total number of observations.

WHEN TO USE

When you need to know the most frequently occurring class of scores and any pattern in the distribution of those scores. Use at the beginning of each data analysis session as a way to clean data.

Measures of Central Tendency

DEFINITION

Central tendency is the most typical or representative score in a distribution.

- Mode—most frequently occurring value in a distribution of scores.
- Median—midpoint of a distribution; 50 percent of the scores fall above and 50 percent fall below value.
- Mean—average value.

How to Compute

- Mode—simple count.
- Median—rank order from lowest to highest score and identify the score below and above which 50 percent of all scores fall. In an odd number of values, the median is one of the values in the distribution. When an even number of values occur in a distribution, the median might or might not be one of the actual values because there is no middle number. Calculate as an average of the scores surrounding it.
- Mean—sum all raw scores and divide by the number of scores.

How to Report

- Mode—report as single most frequently occurring number(s).
- Median—single score, or in the case of a frequency distribution based on grouped data, report as that interval in which the cumulative frequency equals 50 percent (or as a midpoint of that interval).
- Mean—actual computed value.

When to Use

- Mode—when you need to know the most frequently occurring score(s).
- Median—when you have an uneven distribution and you want a test that is insensitive to extreme scores.
- Mean—when your data set is interval or ratio, when you want to know most representative score, and as the basis for subsequent statistics. The major advantage of the mean over the mode and median is that all observations are used in the calculation.

Measures of Variability

Definition

Variability is the degree of dispersion among a set of scores.

- Range—difference between the highest and lowest observed value in a collection of data.
- Standard deviation—average deviation of scores around the mean.

How to Compute

- Range—subtract lowest score from the highest.
- Standard deviation—square each deviation and then calculate the average sum of the squared deviations (variance). To find the standard deviation, calculate the square root of the variance.

How to Report

- Range—as lowest to highest values.
- Standard deviation—single computed value.

When to Use

- Range—to present the simplest measure of variation.
- Standard deviation—to indicate how much scores deviate on the average from the mean.

Contingency Tables

Definition

Contingency tables are also referred to as cross-tabulation, a two-dimensional frequency distribution that is used primarily with categorical data.

How to Compute

Identify vertical and horizontal variable values and compute frequencies for each separate group.

How to Report

As a two-dimensional table.

When to Use

To examine frequencies in subgroups.

Correlational Analysis

Definition

Correlation analysis is a calculated index of the magnitude and direction of association between two variables. There are many correlational statistics. Selection is dependent primarily on level of measurement and sample size. Three types of directional relationships can exist among variables: positive correlation in which variable values move in the same direction; negative correlation in which variable values move in opposite directions; and no correlation, termed zero correlation.

How to Compute

Simple formulae can be found in any basic statistics text.

How to Report

To indicate magnitude or strength of a relationship, the value that is calculated in both Pearson r and Spearman rho ranges from -1 to $+1$, where

−1 indicates a perfect negative correlation, and +1 signifies a perfect positive correlation. A value of 0 indicates no correlation.

WHEN TO USE

To examine how two sets of scores are related to one another. Pearson r is calculated on interval-level data; Spearman rho is used with ordinal data.

Level 2: Drawing Inferences

These procedures examine the extent to which observations of the sample represent the population from which the sample was selected. Inferential statistics include statistical techniques for evaluating differences between sets of data. These techniques are used to evaluate the degree of precision and confidence of one's measurements.

Conduct the following steps for all inferential statistics:

- Action 1: State the hypothesis.
- Action 2: Select a significance level.
- Action 3: Compute a calculated value.
- Action 4: Obtain a critical value.
- Action 5: Reject or fail to reject the null hypothesis.

Parametric statistics are mathematical formulas that test hypotheses based on three assumptions:

1. The samples come from populations that are normally distributed.
2. There is homogeneity of variance.
3. The data are interval level.

Nonparametric statistical formulas are used when:

- normality of variance in the population is not assumed;
- homogeneity of variance is not assumed;
- the data generated from measures are ordinal or nominal;
- sample sizes may be small.

Basic Parametric Statistical Procedures

Two basic techniques are used to compare two or more groups to see whether the differences between group means are large enough to assume that the corresponding population means are different: t-tests and analysis of variance.

t-Test

DEFINITION

A t-test is a statistical procedure used to compare two sample means. A t-test for independent samples is used when the two data sets to be compared are measured in two separate groups. A t-test for dependent samples is used when the two sets of data are generated by two measures of the same group.

HOW TO COMPUTE

$$t = \frac{\text{difference between group means}}{\text{variability of groups}}$$

HOW TO REPORT

Report t as a calculated value. Degrees of freedom and probability are reported with the calculated value of t. Degrees of freedom refer to the "number of values, which are free to vary" in a data set.

WHEN TO USE

When examining the difference between means of two groups of interval-level scores.

One-Way Analysis of Variance (ANOVA)

DEFINITION

One-way ANOVA is a statistic used to compare two or more sample group means to determine if a significant difference can be inferred in the population.

HOW TO COMPUTE

$$F = \frac{\text{variance between groups}}{\text{variance within groups}}$$

HOW TO REPORT

One-way ANOVA yields an F value that may be reported as $F(a, b) = x$, $p = 0.05$, where x equals computed F value, a equals group degrees of freedom, b equals sample degrees of freedom, and p equals level of significance.

WHEN TO USE

To compare differences among two or more groups of interval-level data. There are many variations of ANOVA, some of which test relationships when variables have multiple levels and some of which examine complex relationships among multiple levels of variables. When a one-way ANOVA is used to compare three or more groups, a significant F value means that the sample data indicate that the researcher should reject the null hypothesis. However, the F value in itself does not tell you which of the group means are significantly different. The selection of one of several procedures referred to as multiple comparison or post-hoc comparison is necessary to determine which group is greater than the others. These procedures are computed if a significant F value is found.

Each of the tests mentioned thus far has a nonparametric analogue. See Bibliography for excellent texts that detail these procedures.

Level 3: Associations and Relationships

Due to the complexity of these procedures, we mention only a few. The techniques in this group identify the nature of the relationships among variables. Included among these statistical tests are factor analyses, discriminant function analysis, multiple regression, and modeling. All seek to predict one or more outcomes from multiple variables.

- *Multiple regression* is used to predict the effect that multiple independent (predictor) variables have on one dependent (outcome or criterion) variable. This approach is used only with interval-level data.
- *Discriminant function analysis* is used with categorical or nominal data.

Other techniques, such as modeling, are frequently used to understand complex relationships.

Naturalistic Data Analysis

Naturalistic analysis is an inductive, dynamic set of processes. The techniques vary depending on one's approach to the inquiry.

Basic techniques involve four thinking and action processes: thinking inductively, developing categories, developing taxonomies, and discovering meaning and underlying themes. Unlike statistical analysis, there is a large and diverse range of naturalistic techniques, as well as numerous forms of data such as narrative, image, and so forth. We cannot cover all techniques here and so we provide a brief reminder of the three processes that you will be most likely to use in evaluation practice: thematic analysis, taxonomic analysis, and grounded theory.

- *Thematic analysis* involves examining data for emergent patterns and themes. This is an iterative process in which the investigator critically and inductively reviews the data set. Emergent themes are identified and labeled and exemplars of each are used as illustrative.

- *Taxonomic analysis* builds on thematic analysis, in which relationships among themes are sought. Using a process similar to that of thematic analysis, the investigator looks for patterns of relationships and depicts them in multiple ways, including narrative and visual presentations.
- *Grounded theory*, also called constant comparative method, compares and contrasts each datum to previous information and impressions. Examination of data reveals patterns that are coded. As new data are examined, they are coded and categorized. If data do not fit into previous categories, new or revised categories emerge.

References

Agar, M. (1996). *The professional stranger* (2nd edn). New York: Academic Press.

Aikenhead, G. S. (2005). *Science education for everyday life: Evidence-based practice* (Ways of Knowing in Science and Mathematics). New York: Teachers College Press.

Albion, M. (2006). *True to yourself: Leading a values-based business*. San Francisco, CA: Berrett-Koehler.

Alkin, M. E. (1990). *Debates on evaluation*. Newbury Park, CA: Sage.

Alpert, S. and Gruenberg, K. (2000). Concept mapping with multimedia on the web. *Journal of Educational Multimedia and Hypermedia*, 9, 313.

Alter, K. and Even, W. (1990). *Evaluating your practice: A guide to self-assessment*. New York: Springer.

American Psychiatric Association (1968). *Diagnostic and statistical manual of mental disorders* (7th Printing, 1974). Washington, DC: Author.

Anastas, J. and MacDonald, M. L. (2000). *Research design in social work and the human services* (2nd edn). New York: Columbia University Press.

Andreasen, A. (2006). *Social marketing in the 21st century*. Thousand Oaks, CA: Sage.

Atkinson, P., Coffey, A., and Delamont, S. (eds). (2001). *Handbook of ethnography*. Thousand Oaks, CA: Sage.

Babbie, E. (2006). *The practice of social research* (10th edn). Belmont, CA: Wadsworth.

—— (2007). *The basics of social research* (3rd edn). Belmont, CA: Wadsworth.

Bamberger, M., Rugh, J., and Marbry, L. (2006). *Real world evaluation*. Thousand Oaks, CA: Sage.

Bardi, A. and Schwartz, S. H. (2003). Values and behavior: Strength and structure of relations. *Personality and Psychology Bulletin*, 10, 207–220.

Barney, D. (2004). *The networked society*. Malden, MA: Polity.

Bens, C. (1994). Effective citizen involvement: How to make it happen. *National Civic Review*, 83, 32–38.

Berkowitz, A. D. (2003). Applications of social norms theory to other l ealth and social justice issues. In H. W. Perkins (ed.), *The social norms approach to prevent`ng school and college age substance abuse*. San Francisco, CA: Jossey-Bass.

Berlin, S. B. and Marsh, J. C. (1993). *Informing practice decision*. New York: Macmillan.

Biglan, A., Smolowski, K., and Cody, C. (2007). *The impact on tobacco use of branded youth anti-tobacco activities and family communications about tobacco*. Paper presented at the 15th Annual Meeting of the Society for Prevention Research, May 30, 2007. Washington, DC.

Bloom, M., Fischer, J., and Orme, J. (1998). *Evaluating practice: Guidelines for the accountable professional*. Boston, MA: Allyn & Bacon.

Boden, M. and Hong, H. D. (2003). *R&D programme evaluation: Theory and practice*. Burlington, VT: Ashgate.

Bodhanya, S. (2002). *Diversity: Multiple ways of knowing & multiple worldviews.* Paper presented at the 8th Annual Qualitative Methods Conference: "Something for Nothing" 1 May to 30 September 2002. Retrieved June 3, 2007 from http://criticalmethods.org/p95.mv.

Bourdieu, P. (1992). *Invitation to a reflexive sociology.* Chicago, IL: University of Chicago Press.

Bourque, L. B. and Fielder, E. (1995). *How to conduct self-administered and mail surveys.* Thousand Oaks, CA: Sage.

Brace, I. (2004). *Questionnaire design: How to plan, structure and write survey material for effective market research.* London: Kogan Page.

Brager, G. and Holloway, S. (1992). Assessing prospects for organizational change: The uses of force field analysis. *Administration in Social Work*, 16(3–4), 15–29.

Buckingham, A. and Saunders, P. (2004). *The survey methods workbook: From design to analysis.* Malden, MA: Polity Press.

Buss, D. (2007). *Evolutionary psychology: The new science of the mind* (3rd edn). Boston, MA: Allyn & Bacon.

Campbell, D. and Stanley, J. (1963). *Experimental and quasi-experimental designs for research.* Chicago, IL: Rand McNally.

Carpenito-Moyet, L. (2005). *Understanding the nursing process: Concept mapping and care planning for students.* Philadelphia, PA: Lippincott, Williams and Wilkins.

Caughey, J. (2006). *Negotiating cultures and identities: Life history issues, methods, and readings.* Lincoln, NE: University of Nebraska Press.

Centers for Disease Control and Prevention. Alcohol and Public Health (2006, June 9). Excessive Alcohol Use. Retrieved June 15, 2007 from www.cdc.gov/alcohol/faqs.htm#10.

Charlton, J. I. (1998). *Nothing about us without us: Disability oppression and empowerment.* Berkeley, CA: University of California Press.

Chelimsky, E. and Shadish, W. (1997). *Evaluation for the 21st century: A handbook.* Thousand Oaks, CA: Sage.

Chen, H. T. S. (1994). *Theory-driven evaluations* (New edn). Thousand Oaks, CA: Sage.

—— (2005). *Practical program evaluation.* Thousand Oaks, CA: Sage.

Chronbach, L. J. (1982). *Designing evaluations of educational and social programs.* San Francisco, CA: Jossey-Bass.

Cohen, M. (1994). Overcoming obstacles to forming empowerment groups: A consumer advisory board for homeless clients. *Social Work*, 39, 742–748.

Coley, S. M. and Scheinberg, C. A. (2000). *Proposal writing.* Thousand Oaks, CA: Sage.

Commission on Accreditation (2002). *Educational policy and accreditation standards.* Old Town, VA: Council on Social Work Education.

Common Sense for Drug Policy (2000–2005). *Drug war facts.* Retrieved June 4, 2007 from www.drugwarfacts.org/medicalm.htm.

Connors, G. J. and Maisto, S. A. (1994). Alcohol beliefs scale (ABS). In J. Fischer and K. Corcoran, *Measures for clinical practice: A sourcebook* (2nd edn) (pp. 30–34). New York: Free Press.

Cooper D. and Schindler, P. (2005). *Business research methods with CD* (9th edn). New York: McGraw-Hill/Irwin.

Cottone, R. R. and Tarvydas, V. M. (2006). *Counseling ethics and decision making* (3rd edn). Upper Saddle River, NJ: Prentice Hall.

Cournoyer, D. E. and Klein, W. C. (2000). *Research methods for social workers.* Boston, MA: Allyn & Bacon.

Coutinho, M. J. and Repp, A. C. (1999). *Inclusion: The integration of students with disabilities.* Belmont, CA: Wadsworth.

Cozby, P. C. (2006). *Methods in behavioral research with PowerWeb.* New York: McGraw-Hill.

Creswell, J. (2006). *Qualitative inquiry and research design: Choosing among five approaches* (2nd edn). Thousand Oaks, CA: Sage.

Creswell, J. W. and Plano-Clark, V. L. (2006). *Designing and conducting mixed methods research.* Thousand Oaks, CA: Sage.

D.A.R.E. (1996). *The new D.A.R.E. program.* Retrieved June 15, 2007 from www.dare.com/home/newdareprogram.asp.

Denzin, N. K. and Lincoln, Y. S. (2000). *Handbook of qualitative research.* Thousand Oaks, CA: Sage.

—— and —— (2003). *Strategies of qualitative inquiry.* Thousand Oaks, CA: Sage.

De Panfilis, D. (1996). Implementing child mistreatment risk assessment systems: Lessons from theory. *Administration in Social Work*, 20(2), 41–60.

DePoy, E. (2004). Universal health literacy: An idea whose time should have come? *Psychosocial Process*, 17, 49–50.

—— and Gilson, S. (2006). Universal web access: An intelligent web interface. *International Journal of Technology, Knowledge and Society*, 1, 128–131.

—— and —— (2007). *The human experience: Description, explanation, and judgment*. Lanham, MD: Rowman & Littlefield.

—— and Gitlin, L. (2005). *Introduction to research* (3rd edn). St Louis, MO: Mosby.

—— and MacDuffie, H. (2004). Force field analysis: A model for promoting adolescent involvement in their own health care. *Journal of Health Promotion Practice*, 5, 306–313.

——, Gilmer, D., and Haslett, D. (2000). Adolescents with disabilities and chronic illness in transition: a community action needs assessment. *Disability Studies Quarterly*, 20, 41–60.

DiMaggio, P. and Hargittai, E. (2001). *From the 'digital divide' to 'digital inequality': Studying internet use as penetration increases*. Working Paper #15. Princeton, NJ: Center for Arts and Cultural Policy Studies, Princeton University. Retrieved June 4, 2007 from www.princeton.edu/~artspol/workpap15.html.

Donaldson, L. J. (2001). Professional accountability in a changing world. *Postgraduate Medical Journal*, 77, 65–67.

Donnelly, B. (2002–2004). Universal design education on line. Universal design – Reaching the mainstream. Module 3 Universal Design—Searching for Innovation. Center for Universal Design, N.C. State University; IDEA Center, University at Buffalo; Global Universal Design Educator's Network, Retrieved August 15, 2006 from www.udeducation.org/teach/course_outlines/courses_focus/donnelly.asp.

Dorn, J. M., Hovey, K., Williams, B. A., Freudenheim, J. L., Russell, M., Nochajski, T. H., and Trevisan, M. (2007). Alcohol drinking pattern and non-fatal myocardial infarction in women. *Addiction*, 102(5), 730–739; Retrieved June 4, 2007 from www.ingentaconnect.com/content/bsc/add/2007/00000102/00000005/art00011.

Dottin, E. S. (2001). *The development of a conceptual framework*. Lanham, MD: University Press of America.

ED.Gov. U.S. Department of Education (n.d.). *No Child left behind*. Retrieved June 1, 2007 from www.ed.gov/nclb/landing.jhtml.

ESRI (2007, April 4). *What is GIS?* Retrieved June 1, 2007 from www.gis.com/whatisgis/index.html.

Etzioni, A. (1969). Preface. In A. Etzioni (ed.). *The semi-professions and their organization: Teachers, nurses, social workers* (pp. v–xvii). New York: The Free Press.

Evans, C., Whitworth, A., Davenport, A., and Griffin, R. (2007, May 31). *An evaluation of the how to cope program: Empowering families and friends dealing with substance abuse*. Paper presented at the 15th Annual Meeting of The Society for Prevention Research, May 30–June 1, 2007, Washington, DC.

Fetterman, S. M. (2007). *Ethnography: Step-by-step* (2nd edn). Thousand Oaks, CA: Sage.

Field, A. (2005). *Discovering statistics using SPSS (Introducing statistical methods series)*. Thousand Oaks, CA: Sage.

Fink, A. (1995a). *How to ask survey questions*. Thousand Oaks, CA: Sage.

—— (1995b). *How to design surveys*. Thousand Oaks, CA: Sage.

—— (1995c). *How to report on surveys*. Thousand Oaks, CA: Sage.

—— (1995d). *The survey handbook*. Thousand Oaks, CA: Sage.

Finkler, S. (2005). *Financial management for public, health and not-for-profit organizations* (2nd edn). Upper Saddle River, NJ: Pearson/Prentice Hall.

Fischer, J. (1973). Is casework effective? A review. *Social Work*, 18, 5–20.

—— and Corcoran, K. (2000). *Resources for clinical practice: A sourcebook* (3rd edn). New York: Free Press.

Fitzpatrick, J. L., Sanders, J. R., and Worthen, B. R. (2004). *Program evaluation: Alternative approaches and practical guidelines*. Boston, MA: Pearson.

Flegal, K. M., Williamson, D. F., Pamuk, E. R., and Rosenberg, H. M. (2004). Estimating deaths attributable to obesity in the United States. *American Journal of Public Health*, 94, 1486–1489.

Ford, E. S., Mokdad, A. H., Giles, W. H., Galuska, D. A., and Serdula, M. K. (2005). Geographic variation in the prevalence of obesity, diabetes, and obesity-related behaviors. *Obesity Research*, 13, 118–122.

Fournier, V. (2000). Boundary work and the (un)making of the professions. In N. Malin (ed.), *Professionalism, boundaries and the workplace* (pp. 67–86). London: Routledge.

Frechtling, J. (2007). *Logic modeling methods in program evaluation.* Hoboken, NJ: Jossey-Bass.

Freidson, E. (2001). *Professionalism, the third logic: On the practice of knowledge.* Chicago, IL: University of Chicago Press.

Friedson, E. (ed.) (1973). *The professions and their prospects.* Beverly Hills, CA: Sage.

Friis, R. H. and Sellers, T. A. (2003). *Epidemiology for public health practice* (2nd edn). New York, NY: Aspen.

Gambrill, E. (2001). *Authority-based profession: Research on social work practice,* 11(2), 166–175.

Gilson, S. and DePoy, E. (2005/2006). Reinventing atypical bodies in art, literature and technology. *International Journal of Technology, Knowledge and Society,* 3, 7, www.Technology-Journal.com.

—— and —— (2007). Geographic analysis for the social sciences: Illustration through prevention science research. *The International Journal of Interdisciplinary Social Sciences,* 1, 89–96.

Gould, S. (1996). *Mismeasure of man.* New York: Norton.

Graig, E. (2006). *Usable logic models.* Retrieved June 4, 2007 from www.usablellc.net/Logic%20Model%20(Online)/Presentation_Files/index.html?gclid=CLD04amIjowCFSBESgodMWZc8w.

Grinnell, R. and Unrau, Y. A. (eds) (2004). *Social work research and evaluation* (7th edn). New York: Oxford University Press.

Gubrium, J. and Holstein, J. (2001). *Handbook of interview research: Context & method.* Thousand Oaks, CA: Sage.

Hall, I. and Hall, D. (2004). *Evaluation and social research: Introducing small-scale practice.* New York: Palgrave Macmillan.

Hardy, M. A. and Bryman, A. (2004). *Handbook of data analysis.* Thousand Oaks, CA: Sage.

Hartman, A. (1990). Many ways of knowing. *Social Work,* 35, 3–4.

——, DePoy, E., Francis, C., and Gilmer, D. (2000). Adolescents with special health care needs in transition: Three life histories. *Social Work & Health Care,* 31(4), 3–58.

Hernstein, R. J. and Murray, C. (1996). *Bell curve: Intelligence and class structure in American life.* New York: Free Press.

Hess, P. M. and Mullen, E. J. (1995). *Practitioner-researcher partnerships: Building knowledge from, in, and for practice.* Washington, DC: NASW Press.

Hickey, D. T. and Zuiker, S. J. (2003). A new perspective for evaluating innovative science programs. *Science Education,* 87, 539–556.

HiSoftware. (2003–2007). *HiSoftware® Cynthia Says Portal.* Retrieved June 4, 2007 from www.cynthiasays.com/.

Hogan, J., Gabrielsen, K., Lunda, N., and Grothaus, D. (2002). *Substance abuse prevention: The intersection of science and practice.* Upper Saddle River, NJ: Allyn & Bacon.

Holstein, J. and Gubrium, J. F. (2003). *Inside interviewing.* Thousand Oaks, CA: Sage.

House, E. R. (2005). The role of the evaluator in a political world. *The Canadian Journal of Program Evaluation,* 19, 1–16.

—— and Howe, K. R. (1999). *Values in evaluation and social research.* Thousand Oaks, CA: Sage.

Hustedde, R. and Score, M. (1995). *Force-field analysis: Incorporating critical thinking in goal setting* (4, EDRS, ED384712, microfiche). Milwaukee, WI: Community Development Society.

Institute for Child Health Policy (n.d.). *Healthy and ready to work.* Retrieved June 4, 2007 from www.mchbhrtw.org/.

Ippoliti, C., Peppy, B., and DePoy, E. (1994). Promoting self-determination for persons with developmental disabilities. *Disability and Society,* 9(4), 453–460.

Joint Committee on Standards for Educational Evaluation (2003). *The student evaluation standards.* Thousand Oaks, CA: Corwin Press.

Juicy Studio (2000–2007). *Readability tests. Flesh Kincaid Readability Tests.* Retrieved on June 4, 2007 from http://juicystudio.com/services/readability.php.

Kane, M. and Trochim, W. (2006). *Concept mapping for planning and evaluation.* Thousand Oaks, CA: Sage.

Kirst-Ashman, K. K. and Hull, G. H. (1999). *Understanding generalist practice* (2nd edn). Chicago, IL: Nelson Hall.

Krandall, T., Klied, N. A., and Soderston, C. (1996). Empirical evaluation of concept mapping: A job performance aid for writers. *Technical Communication*, 43(2), 157–164.

Krueger, R. A. and Casey, M. A. (2005). *Focus groups: A practical guide for applied research*. Thousand Oaks, CA: Sage.

Kukathas, C. (2003). *The liberal archipelago: A theory of diversity and freedom*. New York: Oxford University Press.

Leeuw, F. L. (2003). Reconstructing program theories: Methods available and problems to be solved. *American Journal of Evaluation*, 24(1), 5–20.

Leon-Guerro, A. (2005). *Social problems, community, policy and social action*. Thousand Oaks, CA: Pine Forge Press.

Lewin, K. (1951). *Field theory in social science*. New York: Harper & Row.

——, Lippitt, R., and White, R. K. (1939) Patterns of aggressive behavior in experimentally created "social climates." *The Journal of Social Psychology*, 10, 271–299.

Lewis-Beck, M., Bryman, A. E., and Liao, T. F. (2004). *The Sage encyclopedia of social science research methods*. Thousand Oaks, CA: Sage.

Lockee, B., Moore, M., and Burton, J. (2001). Old concerns with new distance education research. *Education Quarterly*, 2, 60–63.

Macdonald, K. (1995). *Sociology of the professions*. Thousand Oaks, CA: Sage.

MacQueen, K. M. and Buehler, J. W. (2004). Ethics, practice, and research in public health. *American Journal of Public Health*, 94, 928–931.

Margulies, N. and Maal, N. (2001). *Mapping inner space: Learning and teaching visual mapping*. New York: Oxford University Press.

McCracken, G. (1988). *Long interview*. Thousand Oaks, CA: Sage.

McDavid, J. C. and Hawthorn, L. R. (2006). *Program evaluation and performance measurement: An introduction to practice*. Thousand Oaks, CA: Sage.

McDonald, H. P. (2004). *Radical axiology: A first philosophy of values*. Amsterdam, NE: Rodopi Press.

McMillan, J. and Shumaker, S. (2005). *Research in education: Evidence based inquiry* (6th edn). Boston, MA: Allyn & Bacon.

Mertens, D. (2005). *Research and evaluation in education and psychology: Integrating diversity with quantitative, qualitative and mixed methods*. Thousand Oaks, CA: Sage.

Miles, M. B. and Huberman, A. M. (1994). *Qualitative data analysis: An expanded sourcebook*. Thousand Oaks, CA: Sage.

Miller, K. (2005). *Communication theories*. New York: McGraw Hill.

Mind Tools (1995–2007) *Force field analysis: Understanding the pressures for and against change*. Retrieved June 4, 2007 from www.mindtools.com/pages/article/newTED_06.htm.

Mollering, G. (2006). *Trust: Reason, routine, reflexivity*. St Louis, MO: Elsevier Science.

Murray, C. A. and Hernstein, R. J. (1994). *The bell curve: Intelligence and class structure in American life*. New York: Free Press.

Nast, J. (2006). *Idea mapping: How to access your hidden brain power, learn faster, remember more, and achieve success in business*. Hoboken, NJ: Wiley.

Novak, J. D. and Gowin, D. B. (1996). *Learning how to learn*. New York: Cambridge University Press.

Office of Disability Employment Policy, U.S. Department of Labor (2007, January 22). Job Accommodation Network. Tax incentives. Retrieved June 20, 2007 from www.jan.wvu.edu/media/tax.html.

Ostroff, E., Limont, L., and Hunter, D. G. (2002). *Building a world fit for people: Designers with disabilities at work*. Retrieved June 4, 2007 from www.adaptiveenvironments.org/adp/profiles/1_mace.php.

Owen, J. M. (2006). *Program evaluation: Forms and approaches* (3rd edn). New York: Guilford Press.

Patton, M. Q. (1987). *Creative evaluation*. Newbury Park, CA: Sage.

—— (1997). *Utilization-focused evaluation*. Newbury Park, CA: Sage.

—— (2001). *Qualitative research & evaluation methods* (3rd edn). Newbury Park, CA: Sage.

Peirce, C. S. (Au.) J. Buchler (ed.) (1955). *The fixation of belief*. New York: Dover.

Preskill, H. S. and Catsambas, T. T. (2006). *Reframing evaluation through appreciative inquiry*. Thousand Oaks, CA: Sage.

Qualitative Solutions and Research PTY (2000). *QSR NUD*IST 4: Software for qualitative analysis.* Thousand Oaks, CA: Scholari.

Reamer, F. G. (2006). *Social work values and ethics* (3rd edn). New York: Columbia University Press.

Reed, C., Spicer, D., Harris, D., and Haslett, T. (2006). Australian government health evaluation: Who are the evaluators? *Australian Evaluation Society.* Darwin, Australia. 2006 International Conference. September 4–7, 2006. Final Papers. Retrieved June 1, 2007 from www.aes.asn.au/conferences/2006/papers/113%20Cheryl%20Reed.pdf.

Reike, R. D., Sillars, M. O., and Peterson, T. R. (2004). *Argumentation and critical decision making* (6th edn). Upper Saddle River, NJ: Allyn & Bacon.

Robertson, P. (1999). *Authority and control in modern industry: Theoretical and empirical perspectives (Routledge Studies in Business Organization and Networks, 10).* London and New York: Routledge.

Rokeach, M. (1973). *The nature of human values.* New York: Free Press.

Rossi, P. H., Lipsey, M. H., and Freeman, H. E. (2004). *Evaluation: A systematic approach* (7th edn). Thousand Oaks, CA; Sage.

Royse, D., Thyer, B., Padgett, D. K., and Logan, T. K. (2005). *Program evaluation: An introduction* (4th edn). Belmont, CA: Wadsworth.

Rubin, A. and Babbie, E. (2007). *Research methods for social work* (6th edn). Belmont, CA: Wadsworth.

Sapsford, R. (2006). *Survey research* (2nd edn). Thousand Oaks, CA: Sage.

Scriven, M. (1991). *The evaluation thesaurus.* Newbury Park, CA: Sage.

Shadish, W. (1998). Some evaluation questions. *Practical Assessment, Research & Evaluation,* 6(3). Retrieved August 13, 2006 from http://PAREonline.net/getvn.asp?v=6&n=3.

——, Cook, T. D., and Leviton, L. C. (1991). *Foundations of program evaluation.* Newbury Park, CA: Sage.

SkyMark (2006). *Force field analysis.* Accessed on August 31, 2006 at www.skymark.com/resources/tools/force_field_diagram.asp?gclid=CKXoo7DGiocCFQoSHgodGhee6Q.

Sloboda, Z. and Bukoski, W. J. (2006). *Handbook of drug abuse prevention (Handbooks of sociology and social research).* New York: Springer.

Smith, R. D. (2005). *Strategic planning for public relations* (2nd edn). Mahwah, NJ: Lawrence Erlbaum.

Steier, F. (1991). *Research and reflexivity.* London: Sage.

Stein, M. (2006). *Distributive justice and disability.* New Haven, CT: Yale University Press.

Steinberg, S. J. and Steinberg, S. L. (2005). *Geographic information systems for the social sciences: Investigating space and place.* Thousand Oaks, CA: Sage.

Stephanidis, C. (ed.) (2000). *User interfaces for all: Concepts, methods and tools.* Mahwah, NJ: Lawrence Erlbaum.

Stone, D. (2001). *The policy paradox: the art of political decision making* (Rev. edn). New York: Norton.

Stufflebeam, D. L. and Shinkfield, A. J. (2007). *Evaluation theory, models, and applications.* Hoboken, NJ: Jossey-Bass.

Substance Abuse and Mental Health Administration, Center for Substance Abuse Prevention (n.d). *Applying health communications and social marketing to alcohol, tobacco, and other drug problem prevention.* Retrieved on June 3, 2007 from http://preventiontraining.samhsa.gov/comm2/comm2ttl.htm.

Sullivan, T. (2001). *Methods of social research.* Fort Worth, TX: Harcourt College.

Sundin, O. (2003). Towards an understanding of symbolic aspects of professional information: An analysis of the nursing knowledge domain. *Knowledge Organization,* 30, 170–181.

Tashakkori, A. and Teddlie, C. B. (2002). *Handbook of mixed methods social and behavioral research.* Thousand Oaks, CA: Sage.

The National Organization of Nurse Practitioner Faculties (NONPF) www.nonpf.com in partnership with The American Association of Colleges of Nursing (AACN) www.aacn.nche.edu. (2002, April). Nurse Practitioner Primary Care Competencies in Specialty Areas: Adult, Family, Gerontological, Pediatric, and Women's Health. Prepared for: Department of Health and Human Services Health Resources and Services Administration Bureau of Health Professions Division of Nursing. Rockville, MD. Retrieved June 4, 2007 from www.nonpf.com/.

The University of Maine. Web Office (n.d.). *Free 508-compliant redesign for university-related web sites.* Retrieved June 4, 2007 from www.umaine.edu/weboffice/redesign.htm.

The U.S. Equal Employment Opportunity Commission (1997, January 15). *Facts About Disability-Related Tax Provisions. TARGETED JOBS TAX CREDIT (Title 26, Internal Revenue Code, section 51).* Retrieved June 4, 2007 from www.eeoc.gov/facts/fs-disab.html.

Thyer, B. (2001). *The handbook of social work research methods.* Thousand Oaks, CA: Sage.

Tripodi, T. (2000). *A primer on single-subject design for clinical social workers.* Washington, DC: NASW.

Trochim, W. and Linton, R. (1986). Conceptualization for evaluation and planning. *Evaluation and Program Planning,* 9, 289–308.

Underage Drinking Prevention and Social Marketing Project. West Virginia Prevention Resource Center (n.d.). *Frequently asked questions.* Retrieved June 15, 2007 from www.prevnet.org/ru21/links.asp.

Unrau, Y. A., Gabor, P. A., and Grinnell, R. M. (2001). *Evaluation in the human services.* Itasca, IL: Peacock.

——, ——, and —— (2006). *Evaluation in social work: The art and science of practice.* New York: Oxford University Press.

U.S. Department of Commerce (2007). *U.S. Census Bureau.* Retrieved June 4, 2007 from www.census.gov/.

Walton, D. (2005). *Abductive reasoning.* Tuscaloosa, AL: University of Alabama Press.

Weinbach, R. W. (2005). *Evaluating social work services and programs.* Upper Saddle River, NJ: Allyn & Bacon.

Weiss, C. (1997). *Evaluation* (2nd edn). Englewood Cliffs, NJ: Prentice Hall.

Wilson, J. (2006). *Thinking with concepts.* New York: Cambridge University Press.

World Health Organization (2007, April 5). *Evidence-based strategies and interventions to reduce alcohol-related harm. Report by the Secretariat.* Sixtieth World Health Assembly A60/14. Provisional agenda item 12.7. 5 April 2007. Retrieved June 4, 2007 from www.add-resources.org/index.php?id=452470.

Yates, B. T. (1996). *Analyzing costs, procedures, processes, and outcomes in human services.* Thousand Oaks, CA: Sage.

Yegidis, B. L., Weinbach, R. W., and Morrison-Rodrigues, B. (1999). *Research methods for social workers* (3rd edn). Boston, MA: Allyn & Bacon.

Yin, R. (1994). *Case study research: Design and methods.* Thousand Oaks, CA: Sage.

Glossary/Index